MW01002427

Truth and Reconciliation in South Africa

Truth and Reconciliation in South Africa

Miracle or Model?

Lyn S. Graybill

BOULDER
LONDON

Published in the United States of America in 2002 by
Lynne Rienner Publishers, Inc.
1800 30th Street, Boulder, Colorado 80301
www.rienner.com

and in the United Kingdom by
Lynne Rienner Publishers, Inc.
3 Henrietta Street, Covent Garden, London WC2E 8LU

Library of Congress Cataloging-in-Publication Data
Graybill, Lyn S.
Truth and reconciliation in South Africa : miracle or model? / Lyn Graybill
p. cm.
Includes bibliographical references and index.
ISBN 1-58826-081-X (alk. paper) — ISBN 1-58826-057-7 (pbk. : alk. paper)
1. South Africa. Truth and Reconciliation Commission. 2. Reconciliation—Political aspects—South Africa. 3. Amnesty—South Africa. 4. Apartheid—South Africa. 5. South Africa—Race relations. I. Title.

DT1974.2.G73 2002
968.06—dc21

2001048642

British Cataloguing in Publication Data
A Cataloguing in Publication record for this book
is available from the British Library.

Printed and bound in the United States of America

∞ The paper used in this publication meets the requirements of the American National Standard for Permanence of Paper for Printed Library Materials Z39.48-1984.

5 4 3 2 1

To Jamie, Pia, and Britt

Contents

Preface

This project began in the summer of 1995 when I traveled to South Africa as a delegate with the World Affairs Council of Washington, D.C. Our group met with a variety of government, business, and civic leaders in an attempt to assess the success of the recent transition to democracy. We were struck by the goodwill, compassion, and magnanimity of black South Africans toward their former enemies. No one we met spoke of bitterness, vengeance, or hatred; expressions of a desire to move on, to forgive, and to build a united "rainbow nation" were typically heard.

Talk of a truth commission was just beginning to surface publicly. Although the concept of a truth commission was first articulated by Kader Asmal in his inaugural speech as the new chair of human rights law at the University of the Western Cape in 1992, it was not until 1994 that the debates began to surface in Parliament, nongovernmental organizations, and the media. The Institute for Democracy in South Africa (IDASA) held two major conferences that year that brought public attention to the need for a commission. The organizers of that conference (including Alex Boraine, who would go on to become the cochair of the Truth and Reconciliation Commission [TRC]) hoped to learn from other countries' experiences and adapt them to suit the particular circumstances of South Africa. As our World Affairs Council group was returning to the United States, the bill that would become the Promotion of National Unity and Reconciliation Act was being debated in Parliament. It was signed into law on July 19, 1995.

I came home excited about the novel experiment of reconciliation that South Africans were fashioning. When hearings began in earnest in the spring of 1996, I was fortunate to be selected for a National Endowment for the Humanities summer seminar in South Africa led by Bernth Lindfors and David Attwell. Based at the University of Natal at Pietermaritzburg, I attended the local hearings on human rights violations scheduled in that area. The Trust Feed massacre of 1988, in which a white constable, Brian Mitchell, authorized the killing of African National Congress (ANC) supporters in KwaZulu, was the subject of one especially riveting hearing.

I cannot begin to describe the pathos of those hearings. Such palpable pain! I found myself weeping along with the victims. I watched black South Africans in the audience nodding in assent to the wrenching testimony. The omnipresent praying and hymn singing during the procedures were clearly comforting to the witnesses. Although my own research on South Africa had persuaded me that religion was an important influence on South Africans,[1] I nevertheless was startled by the number of references to God and the Bible in witnesses' testimony. I was also (perhaps naively) surprised at how few whites attended the hearings at the large town hall. Even greater was my astonishment that the commissioners praised the "large white contingent" for their turnout (present were no more than a dozen whites, half of whom were U.S. educators).

I returned to the University of Virginia determined to share with my students my insights into this "miracle" of reconciliation (as it seemed to me) that was taking place in South Africa. However, when Antjie Krog's wonderful book *Country of My Skull* was published in 1998, I had only limited success using it with undergraduates. They were confused by the mixture of fact and fiction—journalistic reporting interwoven with a fantasy tale of a woman's illicit love affair. This tool may have had literary merit, but my students, mainly political science majors, wanted the hard facts.

In late 1997, I was back in South Africa talking to TRC staff and researching this book. I was there during the "Mandela United Football Club" hearings, which were broadcast live for nine days to a spellbound audience. Accusations against an icon of the resistance were heard by millions. What the hearings revealed—often neglected by the U.S. media—were deep divisions in the country. Black South Africans were almost unanimously critical of the commission's harsh treatment of Winnie Madikizela-Mandela, whom they revered as "Mother of the Nation," contrasting it with the kid-glove treatment former president P. W. Botha had received from Desmond Tutu. Whites, on the other hand, felt Madikizela-Mandela was a cold-blooded killer who had been "coddled" by the commissioners. It reminded me of the racial divisions unmasked in the United States by the O. J. Simpson verdict. I left South Africa less optimistic than

I had been in 1996 about the ability of the Truth and Reconciliation Commission to reconcile a society with such deep racial fault lines.

This book is an attempt to provide not only the "facts" that my students had craved, but also the broader context in which the TRC operated. Although my seminar at the University of Virginia was on South African politics, students in disciplines as diverse as theology, human rights, psychology, ethics, even conflict resolution, will find here useful material in a case study of the most important, ambitious truth commission on record. I wanted to produce a work that avoided the noncritical approach of many recent books (mainly the "insider accounts" by the commissioners); I equally wanted to avoid the conceptual approach of "experts" (mainly philosophers and international lawyers) who in numerous edited volumes theorize about truth commissions, but whose reflections seem to me overly abstract, not situated in this particular truth commission, in this particular country with a unique history, culture, and set of leaders.

In following the TRC, I have learned an enormous amount from theology and psychology as well as from my own field, politics. To understand the issues with which the TRC grappled, one has to be willing to engage intellectually across many disciplines. In researching the TRC, I read widely in many fields and tried to summarize the best thinking and writing on the subject while articulating my own perspective. My hope is that the thorough literature review and the extensive bibliography will be useful to the many scholars who will follow me. Interest in South Africa's truth commission is high, and the TRC undoubtedly will be studied and analyzed for years as scholars pore over the archived transcripts.

My goal in these pages is to provide a framework for assessing South Africa's attempt—some would say bold experiment—at reconciliation. Did the TRC process lead to reconciliation and healing? What events led to South Africa's choice to "pardon" rather than "punish"? Did politics alone necessitate this "evil compromise," as one analyst has put it? Or were ethical values at play, given the importance of religion in South Africa and the prophetic message of Christianity that prevailed even during the darkest days of apartheid? Can the TRC serve as a model for other countries in the aftermath of serious human rights abuses? Or was the TRC a "miracle" of the sort that occurs but rarely in the life of nations, dependent solely on the compelling personalities of extraordinary leaders? This book attempts to begin answering these questions.

Chapter 1 discusses the precedents of earlier truth commissions, the novel features of South Africa's truth commission, and the organizational structures of the TRC. Chapters 2 and 3 focus on two personalities who were essential to the success of the TRC, President Nelson Mandela and Archbishop Desmond Tutu—two of the world's most respected leaders. If moral leadership of this caliber is a prerequisite for a successful truth commission, will reconciliation be a nonstarter in most of the world's conflict spots?

Chapter 4 deals with the theory and practice of forgiveness. Tutu's expectation that perpetrators would "confess" and victims "forgive" did not universally occur. This chapter highlights some concrete examples of both forgiveness and nonforgiveness. Amnesty, the most controversial aspect of the TRC, is the topic of Chapter 5. Following a review of the academic debate on amnesty versus prosecutions, I present several examples of how the amnesty principles were applied and discuss the problematic application of both the "proportionality" and the "political motivation" criteria.

Chapter 6, "Storytelling," examines the psychological value of speaking out, again from both the theoretical perspective and the practical perspective. What do psychologists say about the value of testifying publicly? Do victims themselves view testifying as psychologically beneficial? Chapter 7 examines how gender issues were handled by the TRC. Relying on women's testimony at the three all-women hearings, I analyze women's distinct experiences of repression.

Chapter 8 raises the issues of bystander beneficiaries—those who enjoyed the fruits of apartheid but who were not themselves directly involved in human rights violations. The TRC held a series of institutional hearings into various professions—the media, business, law, and others—in order to bring these beneficiaries into the process. The medical and business professions are highlighted in this chapter. Two other sectors—media and faith communities—deserve special attention, because, as noted by the commissioners, they influenced the "ideas and morals of generations of South Africans."[2] They are the subjects of Chapters 9 and 10.

In Chapter 11, I look at the rest of the story—the findings made by the commissioners in their final report, the delayed reparations to victims, and the post-TRC initiatives by independent groups who were challenged by then president Nelson Mandela to be "seized with the matters that the TRC brought to the fore."[3] Finally, Chapter 12 raises the question of the appropriateness of the TRC model for other countries in the aftermath of massive human rights violations. The choice by Rwandans to punish is contrasted with the decision by South Africans to pardon.

Wherever possible I have chosen to let victims, oppressors, and beneficiaries speak for themselves, relying on testimony from the transcripts of hearings. (Scholars owe an enormous debt to Steve Crawford, who managed the TRC's website—www.truth.org.za—and made the documents accessible to thousands of scholars worldwide.) From the thicket of theories about punishment versus pardon, and reconciliation versus justice, it is important not to lose sight of the victims and their disposition—the distinct ways South Africans suffered under apartheid, what they now hope for, and how they express their vision for the future. This book is hopefully a start in that direction.

A word about the subtitle—*Miracle or Model?*—is in order. When Nelson Mandela was inaugurated president in May 1994, Desmond Tutu proclaimed, "What we have achieved is nothing less than a miracle."[4] The words "a miracle" were heard on many lips with the realization that this was an unprecedented case of a ruling group relinquishing its monopoly of power without imminent military threat to its continued rule. On the heels of an exceptional transition of power, South Africa embarked on an equally unprecedented process of national reconciliation in the Truth and Reconciliation Commission. As the TRC began its work, chairman Desmond Tutu remarked: "South Africans have seen a miracle unfold. We have lived through the institutionalized racism of apartheid; and we have won a spectacular victory over injustice, oppression and evil. It is an achievement that has inspired the admiration of the world. The miracle must endure."[5]

And yet there are those who viewed the TRC not as a "miracle" but as an "evil compromise" between the African National Congress and National Party.[6] Where was justice for the victims? the critics asked. Was too much conceded in the interests of peace? These are twin but opposite dangers: rejecting the TRC as an evil exercise, born of a political expediency that abandoned justice in favor of peace, or seeing it as a miracle somehow unique to South Africa. To say that what happened in South Africa is a miracle is to suggest that it was not the result of dedicated individuals committed to making the process work, but rather a fluke of history that ultimately cannot be replicated. As surely as South Africa benefited from other countries' experiences of dealing with the past, so too nations moving through democratic transitions may find a workable model in South Africa's pragmatic but ethical experiment in designing a truth commission.

* * *

I wish to thank the National Endowment for the Humanities, the Virginia Foundation for the Humanities, the Carter G. Woodson Institute for Afro-

American and African Studies, and the Center for the Study of Professional Military Ethics at the U.S. Naval Academy for their support. I am especially indebted to Kenneth W. Thompson, former director of the White Burkett Miller Center of Public Affairs, Michael Joseph Smith, professor of social and political thought at the University of Virginia, and Vamik Volkan, director of the Center for the Study of Mind and Human Interaction, for their personal interest in this project. In South Africa, a special thanks goes to Brandon Hamber, associate of the Center for the Study of Violence and Reconciliation (CSVR) in Johannesburg. I am appreciative to *Ethics & International Affairs, Africa Today, Iris, Current History, Women's Studies International Forum,* and *Human Rights Review* for publishing my earlier work on the TRC.

Notes

1. See Graybill, *Religion and Resistance Politics in South Africa.*
2. *Truth and Reconciliation Commission of South Africa Report,* vol. 5, chap. 6, "Findings and Conclusions," p. 249.
3. Parliamentary debate on the TRC, February 25, 1999.
4. Desmond Tutu, "We Are Going to Make It," *Los Angeles Times* (March 30, 1994).
5. Desmond Tutu, foreword to *Dealing with the Past,* p. vii.
6. SAPA, "South Africans Find Truth a Tall Order" (August 25, 1997).

1

Setting Up the TRC

The Precedents

Abundant examples of how other countries have chosen to deal with human rights abuses committed by former regimes can be found in the aftermath of the fall of the Nazi regime in the 1940s, and in the transition periods accompanying the waves of democratization in the 1970s (mainly Latin America) and in the late 1980s and early 1990s (mainly Eastern Europe). Besides the Nuremberg and Tokyo tribunals of the early post–World War II era, there were no fewer than fifteen truth commissions as of 1994.[1] But these precedents offered warnings more than guidance for South Africa.[2] Nuremberg, for instance, dispensed harsh retribution to the top echelon of Nazis but permitted ordinary Germans to live in a state of denial. In Chile and Argentina, the army and police made general confessions in exchange for blanket amnesties that allowed individual assassins and torturers to evade personal responsibility.[3] All of these cases ignored the victims and made it possible for the truth about past atrocities to remain largely hidden.

Kader Asmal, minister for water affairs at the time the South African truth commission was being set up, played an influential role in the early thinking about the Truth and Reconciliation Commission (TRC): "There is no prototype that can be automatically used in South Africa. We will be guided, to a greater or lesser extent, by experiences elsewhere, notably in those countries that managed to handle this highly sensitive—even dangerous—process with success. But at the end of the day, what is most important is the nature of our particular settlement and how best we can consolidate the transition in South Africa."[4]

From the beginning, South Africans sought to learn from past mistakes and develop a different kind of truth commission. At two major conferences held in Cape Town in 1994,[5] sponsored by the Institute for Democracy in South Africa (IDASA) and its Justice in Transition Project, delegates from Chile, Argentina, and eastern and central Europe shared their countries' struggles over the question of how to treat former enemies and oppressors with delegates from South Africa.[6] The reports that came out of these conferences were widely discussed, and workshops and meetings were held around the country to debate the issues that had been raised. This democratic approach to the formation of the TRC distinguished it sharply from the truth commissions of other countries, which had been shaped by executive decrees rather than by representative parliaments.[7] South Africa's was the very first example of a process officially encouraging public debate and input on the goals, makeup, and procedures of a truth commission.[8] The whole notion of amnesty in the TRC, for example, was largely the outcome of various compromises that had been hammered out between the African National Congress (ANC) and the National Party (NP) in the transition period leading to the adoption of an interim constitution in 1993, with input from twenty-six political parties.[9]

Minister of Justice Dullah Omar introduced legislation to Parliament in May 1994 that ultimately became the Promotion of National Unity and Reconciliation Act, the law that empowered the Truth and Reconciliation Commission. The parliamentary Standing Committee on Justice, composed of members from all the major political parties, held public hearings asking individuals, groups, and parties to make recommendations about what to include in the draft legislation. Under the chairship of Johnny de Lange, the committee listened to more than twenty hours of submissions and discussed, compiled, and drafted various clauses of the bill, taking into consideration the suggestions that had been submitted. Nongovernmental organizations (NGOs), for instance, recommended against conducting amnesty hearings in private, arguing that this would be contrary to the Bill of Rights. (To the National Party's bitter disappointment, the Justice Committee overturned the cabinet's decision on secrecy.)

Journalist Antjie Krog has described the red eyes and disheveled appearance of the many civil servants who often worked through the night to prepare new discussion documents for the committee. The committee met daily during March 1995 to debate the submissions and draft the legislation, a process that took some 127 hours, and eventually tabled it to the National Assembly. The bill was passed by Parliament on May 17, 1995, nearly a year after it was first presented. Concluding the debate in Parliament, de Lange argued: "What makes this piece of legislation so unique is that it really is a patchwork of all the viewpoints of the country."[10] Enacted by a show of hands when the electronic voting equipment failed, the legislation passed resoundingly. The yea votes from the ANC, NP, and Pan-Africanist Congress (PAC) members trumped the nay votes of the Freedom Front (FF); the Inkatha Freedom Party (IFP) members abstained. The bill was regarded as "the most sensitive, technically complex, controversial and important legislation" ever to be passed in Parliament.[11] It was also the most time consuming; more time was spent on this bill than on any other legislation this first postapartheid Parliament considered.[12]

The legislation was next sent to the Senate, where certain points were debated—blanket amnesty, most importantly, and other issues such as the advisability of having two non–South Africans on the commission. Although amnesty had been agreed to in the interim constitution, the procedures had been left open. The later requirement for individual application and disclosure (unique among truth commissions) left many in National Party circles feeling betrayed, although there was a precedent: the temporary indemnities granted to ANC members during the negotiations in the early 1990s had been based on full disclosure by individuals.[13] The National Party therefore found it difficult to oppose such a provision when it came to amnesty for its own members.

Finally the bill found its way to the Department of Justice, and the Promotion of National Unity and Reconciliation Act was signed into law on July 19, 1995, by President Nelson Mandela. This was the first example anywhere of a truth commission that was established not by a presidential decree but by Parliament as representative of the people. But, as Ian Liebenberg and Abebe Zegeye point out, "The process reflects to a certain degree party political compromises and not so much 'the will of the people.'"[14]

The next step was the search for commissioners. The legislation required the selection of seventeen commissioners, men and women of character who were highly regarded in the community. There were three options available for selection: the president could come up with his own list and discuss it with the cabinet; the president and cabinet could compile a list together; or nominees could be suggested by NGOs, churches, and parties and interviewed in public by a selection panel with the president and cabinet choosing from a short list. The third option was chosen, no doubt in the interest of promoting democracy and transparency. Krog notes that the advantage of this approach was in keeping politics at bay and also in rekindling public interest in the TRC, which had waned after the debates.[15]

A multiracial selection panel that included a representative from every major political party, two ecumenical church leaders, a trade unionist, and two human rights lawyers then picked 45 individuals out of some 299 nominees for public interviews.[16] A short list of 25 individuals was sent to President Mandela, and the public was invited to submit questions to the short-listed nominees, further winning credibility for the process. Each prospective commissioner was asked how he or she envisioned the role of a commissioner, which of the three committees most suited his or her experiences and interests, and what obstacles there might be to his or her becoming a commissioner.[17] On November 29, 1995, President Mandela, in consultation with his bipartisan cabinet, made the final selection, people he considered to be of high moral integrity, impartial, and committed to human rights. They could not be high-profile members of political parties,[18] nor could they be people who intended to apply for amnesty. Behind the scenes, it was said that the cream of the crop with strong human rights backgrounds had already been taken into the ranks of government and its various commissions, such as those on gender, youth, and human rights.[19] Mandela later revealed that he had not personally approved of all the commissioners but had appointed them in the interest of national unity.[20]

The original commissioners included seven blacks: Chair Desmond Tutu, Dumisa Ntsebeza, Bongani Finca, Mapule Ramashala, Hlengiwe Mkhize, Sisi Khampepe, and Khoza Mgojo; two Coloureds (people of mixed race): Denzil Potgieter and Glenda Wildschut; two Indians: Fazel Randera and Yasmin Sooka; and six whites: Afrikaners Wynand Malan and Chris de Jager, and English-speakers Alex Boraine, Mary Burton, Wendy Orr, and Richard Lyster. (Khoza Mgojo and Denzil Potgieter had not been nominated, interviewed, or short-listed but were appointed by the president and the cabinet to make the TRC more representative of the general population—representing KwaZulu-Natal and Coloureds, respectively—"in violation of an otherwise transparent and accountable process.")[21] The majority of commissioners (seven) were from the legal profession, while four (including Tutu) were ordained ministers who had been the national heads of their respective denominations. The remaining commissioners were from the medical, mental health, and NGO communities.

Politically, the commissioners spanned the political spectrum, from a PAC member on the left to an FF member on the right. However, there was no one aligned with the IFP, and relations with this party were rocky from the beginning. On balance the appointees were "reasonably representative of the broad, political, ethnic and cultural spectrum in South Africa."[22] The original goal had been to have as commissioners people without a high political profile, but just the opposite occurred. Many had been activists in the struggle against apartheid and were political leaders in their communities. When Archbishop Tutu suggested at an early meeting that it might be a worthwhile gesture for all to resign any membership in a political party or organization, it was pointed out to him that people had been nominated for TRC membership precisely because of their political affiliations and that for those who were members of political parties to resign and to pretend that they were apolitical would be to engage in a misleading charade.[23]

Another feature distinguishing this truth commission from past ones was the speed with which it was set up. The Promotion of National Unity and Reconciliation Act was promulgated just fifteen months after the first all-race elections in April 1994—a time frame that must have seemed an eternity to many people at the time, but given its ambitious mandate was a relatively short one. Just a few months after the bill was passed, the commissioners had been selected, regional offices established, and a staff hired. The TRC held its first meeting only a day after the appointments of the commissioners were officially announced in the *Government Gazette* on December 15, 1995, appropriately on the public holiday called the Day of Reconciliation.[24] By January 1996 the TRC had conducted a retreat for its commissioners and was ready for business, having opened offices in Durban, East London, Johannesburg, and Cape Town (which also served as the national headquarters) and having hired a staff of nearly 350, the largest truth commission to date.

The swiftness with which the TRC got on its feet was envied by South Africa's other commissions and government bodies, notes Krog.[25] This was all the more remarkable given the strong objections from the NP, which argued the process would only amount to a "witchhunt," from the IFP, which believed it would be "biased" in favor of the ANC, and from sectors of the ANC, which felt that too much had been conceded in terms of the amnesty provision. Both the swiftness of its setup and the limited time span of its operation were positive indicators for the TRC.[26] As deputy commissioner Alex Boraine has said, it was seen as important to quickly deal with the past so as not to dwell on it.[27]

The Work of the TRC

Headed by Nobel laureate Desmond Tutu, the commission was mandated to hold hearings over two years about allegations of human rights abuses committed from March 1, 1960, through May 10, 1994, the date of Nelson Mandela's inauguration.[28] The original cutoff date had been December 6, 1993, the date of the adoption of the interim constitution, but Parliament extended the cutoff date to May 10, 1994, at the TRC's request to enable victims and perpetrators of human rights abuses committed after December 1993 to approach the commission. This enabled those parties responsible for the killings at the Heidelberg Tavern and St. James Church (the PAC) and for election-day bombings—the Afrikaner Weerstandsbeweging (AWB; Afrikaner Resistance Movement)—to be eligible for amnesty.

The goals of the TRC as set out in the Promotion of National Unity and Reconciliation Act were to develop a complete picture of the gross violations of human rights that took place in and came through the conflicts of the past; to restore to victims their human and civil dignity by letting them tell their stories and recommending how they could be assisted; and to consider granting amnesty to those perpetrators who carried out their abuses for political reasons and who gave full accountings of their actions to the commission. To achieve these goals, the TRC worked through three committees: the Committee on Human Rights Violations (HRV), the Committee on Amnesty, and the Committee on Reparation and Rehabilitation. Fifteen of the seventeen commissioners were split between the HRV Committee and the Reparation and Rehabilitation Committee, and two commissioners served on the Amnesty Committee, along with three judges.

The HRV Committee was entrusted to hear victims' stories in order to establish whether gross violations of human rights had occurred. A gross human rights violation was defined as the "violation of human rights through the killing, abduction, torture, or severe ill treatment of any person . . . which emanated from conflicts of the past . . . and the commission of which was advised, planned, directed, commanded or ordered by any person acting with a political motive."[29] Although it was conceived that the three committees simultaneously would hold hearings around the country during the two years of operation, the HRV Committee took center stage in 1996. Thousands of victims queued up to tell their horrifying stories of apartheid-era abuses, and approximately 22,000 victim statements were processed. Over two years, hearings were held in town halls, hospitals, and churches all around the country. Some high-profile cases were heard, as well as stories from "ordinary" South Africans.

The Committee on Amnesty, working independently of the rest of the TRC, was appointed on January 24, 1996, without any transparent process. Originally made up of five members (three judges and two commissioners from the legal community),[30] and enlarged first to thirteen and later to nineteen in order to deal with the heavy workload, this committee took applications from those seeking amnesty for "acts associated with political objectives." It decided which applicants met the "political objective" qualification. To be political, an act had to have been committed by a member or supporter of a "publicly known political organization or liberation movement" or by an employee of the state, acting either "in furtherance of a political struggle (including both acts by or against the state and acts by one political organization or liberation movement against another) or with the object of countering or otherwise resisting the said struggle." The act must have been committed "in the course and scope of his or her duties and within the scope of his or her express or implied authority."[31] (The requirement to be acting under orders was a break with the Nuremberg/Tokyo tribunal's precedent that had established that obedience to superior orders did not exculpate a criminal act if there had been an option to act otherwise.) The legislation allowed the possibility of including high-ranking intellectual authors of atrocities, as it referred to "any attempt, conspiracy, incitement, instigation, command or procurement to commit an act." Writes Richard Wilson, "This was the widest mandate of any truth commission to date."[32]

By the latter part of 1996, the TRC began shifting the focus of attention away from the victims to the perpetrators as the Amnesty Committee's work began in earnest. Some of the high-profile amnesty cases heard during 1997 included the 1981 killing of human rights lawyer Griffiths Mxenge by former security policeman Dirk Coetzee; the April 1993 assassination of communist leader Chris Hani by two Conservative Party (CP) followers; and the 1977 death of Black Consciousness (BC) leader Steve Biko by five former security policemen. Of particular interest to Americans were the amnesty hearings of the four young men charged with the brutal killing of American Fulbright scholar Amy Biehl in 1993.

The TRC's third committee, the Committee on Reparation and Rehabilitation, was responsible for deciding how each victim should be compensated, and for making recommendations to the president "in an endeavour to restore the human and civil dignity of such victim."[33] The committee held regional hearings across the country in 1996 and 1997 in an attempt to find out what victims were seeking in terms of redress, after which it finalized its recommendations on reparations and submitted them to the government.

By the time its term was over, having been extended by government decree, two of the commissioners had resigned. Dr. Mapule Ramashala left to take over the position of vice chancellor of the University of Durban–Westville, and Chris de Jager felt so at odds with the direction of the commission that he resigned but stayed on as a member of the Amnesty Committee. The lone remaining Afrikaner commissioner so disagreed with the findings and recommendations of the commission that he issued a minority statement as part of the TRC's final report.

It was an exhaustive process in terms of money, time, and energy: 140 hearings took place in sixty-one towns; 22,000 victim statements were taken covering 37,000 violations; over 7,000 perpetrators applied for amnesty; and eighteen months became six years[34]—all to the tune of 200 million rand (the most expensive truth commission in history). There were numerous twists and turns on the road to reconciliation: the National Party sued Bishop Tutu and Alex Boraine over allegedly not being evenhanded; amnesty decisions given to thirty-four ANC activists without a public hearing came under fire and the Amnesty Committee was directed to review them; Steve Biko's family unsuccessfully challenged the amnesty provision of the TRC; a former president was hauled into court for failing to comply with a subpoena to testify; and in the end, even the ANC rejected the findings of the body it had established.[35] And yet, by most accounts, it was a remarkable, unparalleled, and unprecedented process, holding out the possibility of a workable model for other countries moving through democratic transitions and away from divided pasts. What made the process possible, if not entirely successful, will be explored in succeeding chapters.

Notes

1. See Hayner, "Fifteen Truth Commissions—1974 to 1994" and *Unspeakable Truths.* The South African TRC brought the number up to twenty-one by 2000.

2. Storey, "A Different Kind of Justice," p. 788.

3. President Patricio Aylwin established the National Commission on Truth and Reconciliation in Chile, which documented 957 disappearances and other abuses. No attempt was made to prosecute individuals, and the commissioners refused to name names of the perpetrators. The military had granted itself amnesty in any event.

In Argentina, justice was limited. President Raul Alfonsin appointed a commission to investigate the disappearances during the "Dirty War." This Sabato commission submitted more than 1,800 cases for prosecution. Nine members of the previous military juntas that had ruled Argentina were prosecuted, and five were convicted. With restive armed forces, Alfonsin pushed through a Punto Final (Full Stop) law, setting a deadline for new criminal complaints, and adopted a Due Obedience law, which exonerated officers below the rank of colonel for most crimes if they were following orders. When Alfonsin was succeeded as president by Carlos Saul Menem in 1989, he pardoned the officers awaiting trial and later the five junta members who had already been convicted. Despite these limitations, in the Latin America context Argentina is considered a relatively successful instance of accountability for crimes against humanity.

4. Boraine and Levy, eds., *The Healing of a Nation?* p. 27.

5. "Justice in Transition: Dealing with the Past" was held in February 1994. "The South African Conference on Truth and Reconciliation" was held in July 1994.

6. Books on the proceedings were subsequently published. See Boraine and Levy, eds., *The Healing of a Nation?* and Boraine, Levy, and Scheffer, eds., *Dealing with the Past.*

7. Stremlau, *A House No Longer Divided,* p. 21.

8. Hayner, "Fifteen Truth Commissions—1974 to 1994," footnote 102, p. 639.

9. The final constitution was adopted by the Constitutional Assembly in 1996.

10. Cited in Krog, *Country of My Skull,* p. 10.

11. Krog, *Country of My Skull,* p. 9.

12. Van der Merwe, Dewhirst, and Hamber, "Non-Governmental Organisations and the Truth and Reconciliation Commission," p. 58.

13. See Andre du Toit, cited in Steiner, ed., *Truth Commissions,* p. 47. See also van der Merwe, Dewhirst, and Hamber, "Non-Governmental Organisations and the Truth and Reconciliation Commission," pp. 56–57.

14. Liebenberg and Zegeye, "Pathway to Democracy?" p. 551.

15. Krog, *Country of My Skull,* p. 16.

16. Chaired by Mandela's legal adviser, Fink Haysom, the panel included Jody Kollapen (Lawyers for Human Rights attorney), Jayendra Naidoo (National Economic Development and Labor Council [NEDLAC] head), Baleka Kgositsile (ANC member of Parliament [MP]), Harriet Ngubane (IFP MP), Rossier de Ville (FF senator), Bishop Peter Storey (Methodist bishop), Ray Radue (NP senator), and Brigalia Bam (South African Council of Churches [SACC] general secretary).

17. Frost, *Struggling to Forgive,* p. 143.

18. Two, however, were former MPs.

19. Krog, *Country of My Skull,* p. 20.

20. Shea, "Are Truth Commissions Just a Fad?" p. 13.

21. Sarkin, "The Development of a Human Rights Culture in South Africa," footnote 199, p. 665.

22. Cochrane, de Gruchy, and Martin, eds., *Facing the Truth,* p. 2.

23. Desmond Tutu, *No Future Without Forgiveness,* p. 77.

24. The pubic holiday had originally been called Dingaan's Day in celebration of the Afrikaner victory at Blood River over the Zulus, and later had been called the Day of the Covenant to emphasize the Afrikaner belief that it was God who had given the Afrikaners the victory.

25. Krog, *Country of My Skull,* p. 21.

26. Beginning with an explicit time limit written into the mandate bodes well for the success of a commission even if it is extended. See Hayner, *Unspeakable Truths,* pp. 221–222.

27. Boraine and Levy, eds., *The Healing of a Nation?* p. 139.

28. The TRC was mandated to complete its work within twenty-four months, but the term was extended by additional legislation to July 1998. It submitted its five-volume final report to then president Nelson Mandela in October 1998. The Amnesty Committee, however, continued its work until it was dissolved on May 31, 2001, by President Thabo Mbeki. A subcommittee convened by commissioner Denzil Potgieter will prepare two additional volumes, which will contain summaries of each victim and an update on amnesty decisions and reparations.

29. Promotion of National Unity and Reconciliation Act (no. 34 of 1995).

30. Original Amnesty Committee members were Judges Hassan Mall (the chair), Andrew Wilson (the deputy chair), and Bernard Ngoepe; also present were two commissioner lawyers, Chris de Jager and Sisi Khampepe.

31. Promotion of National Unity and Reconciliation Act (no. 34 of 1995).

32. Wilson, "Reconciliation and Revenge in Post-Apartheid South Africa" (paper presented at the "TRC: Commissioning the Past" conference), p. 10.

33. Promotion of National Unity and Reconciliation Act (no. 34 of 1995).

34. President Thabo Mbeki issued a proclamation dissolving the TRC effective on December 31, 2001.

35. The TRC was the first truth commission to have its powers and decisions challenged in court. See Hayner, *Unspeakable Truths,* p. 44.

2

Nelson Mandela: Pragmatic Reconciler

The establishment of South Africa's Truth and Reconciliation Commission (TRC) was but one manifestation of the move toward reconciliation that motivated the country after Nelson Mandela's election in 1994. Indeed, more than any other individual, Mandela set the example of the great reconciler, amazing the world with his lack of rancor or bitterness against his former oppressors despite a twenty-seven-year imprisonment. When asked how it was possible for him to be so magnanimous toward his oppressors, Mandela simply said, "I could not wish what happened to me and my people on anyone."[1]

How was this man able to endure nearly three decades of prison without becoming rancorous, without demonizing the enemy? This is an important question for divided nations to ponder, for if the answer is that Mandela is a unique individual, a veritable saint as some suggest, and if his example of leadership cannot be replicated, then war-torn countries and those stricken by ethnic conflicts will need to look elsewhere for solutions. If, on the other hand, the conditions that produced a Mandela are not unique, there is value at looking at his life and the way his experiences shaped his thinking. Some reflections from his autobiography, *Long Walk to Freedom* (a national bestseller in South Africa translated into dozens of languages), indicate how his philosophy of nonracialism, forgiveness, and reconciliation developed.

Mandela had little contact with whites as a young boy in the tiny village of Qunu in the Transkei, but when his father died, he became part of the household of his uncle, the acting paramount chief of Thembuland, in the Great Palace at Mqhekezweni. Mandela adopted his uncle's benign attitude toward whites with no thought of their role in displacing Africans. Like his uncle, he saw the white man as a benefactor to the African, especially for providing education in missionary schools. However, at Clarkebury Institute, Healdtown, and Fort Hare—missionary institutions for Africans—he came in contact with African teachers and fellow students who served as role models. Some of his new acquaintances refused to behave in a servile manner around the white man and did not accept uncritically their assigned place in society.[2]

Life as an Activist

Mandela left Fort Hare in 1941 for Johannesburg, a magnet for Africans from the countryside seeking work. He soon found work in the law office of Witkin, Sidelsky, & Eidelman. A Jewish law firm, it was more liberal than most, allowing, for example, African clients to sit down, something other firms would not permit.[3] But an incident occurred on his first day of work that exposed the hypocrisy of even so-called liberals. A young white secretary emphatically denied there was a "color bar" at the firm, but indicated that in honor of Mandela's arrival they had purchased two new tea cups for him and the other African employee, Gaur Radebe. Mandela writes: "I knew that the 'two new cups' she was so careful to mention were evidence of the color bar that she said did not exist. The secretaries might share tea with two Africans, but not the cups with which to drink it."[4] Radebe ignored the two new cups and selected instead one of the old ones. Mandela, not wanting to offend the secretaries or alienate his new colleague, declined tea altogether and from then on took his tea in solitude. He explains: "I saw the middle path as the best and most reasonable one."[5]

A white articled clerk at the firm, Nat Bregman, was to become Mandela's first white friend and would make a profound impression on him. Bregman introduced him to the Communist Party of South Africa (CPSA). Mandela writes: "I discovered a lively and gregarious group of people who did not seem to pay attention to color at all."[6] Nevertheless, he was unconvinced that class analysis was relevant in South Africa, believing instead that the conflict was purely racial. At this time, he was also exposed to the African National Congress (ANC), a group formed in 1912 to advocate for African political rights. In August 1943 he marched in support of the Alexandra bus boycott against rising fares.

Mandela enrolled at the University of Witwatersrand (Wits) for a bachelor of law degree; he was the only African student in the law faculty. While he had had occasional contacts with whites at Fort Hare from nearby Rhodes University in Grahamstown, and regular contact with whites at the law firm, this was the first time that Mandela had regular contact with whites his own age. He discovered that most of the whites at Wits were neither liberal nor color-blind. In his autobiography, Mandela recounts the story of a time he was late to a lecture, when, after taking a seat next to a fellow student (who was later to become a member of Parliament for the United Party), the student moved to a seat far away from Mandela. "This type of behavior was the rule rather than the exception. No one uttered the word *kaffir;* their hostility was more muted, but I felt it just the same."[7]

Nevertheless, he found a core of sympathetic whites who became friends and later fellow comrades in the struggle. These included Joe Slovo, Slovo's future wife, Ruth First, George Bizos, Bram Fischer (an Afrikaner from a prominent political family), and Harold Wolpe. He befriended a number of Indians as well, including Ismail Meer and J. N. Singh.[8]

Influenced by the young ANC Africanists Anton Lembede and A. P. Mda, who preached that Africa was a black man's continent and that the inferiority complex among Africans who were aspiring to be like whites was the greatest barrier to liberation, Mandela along with others like Walter Sisulu and Oliver Tambo formed a Youth League within the ANC to push the organization in a new, militant direction. These young men were highly suspicious of communism, calling it a foreign ideology unsuited to the African situation. They also felt that the Communist Party was dominated by whites, and that by working in cohort with white communists, Africans' self-confidence and self-reliance would be undermined. At the time the Youth League was formed, Mandela was firmly opposed to allowing either communists or whites to join forces with African resisters, as well as to conducting joint campaigns with either them or Indians, whom he feared would dominate the movement. "While I was not prepared to hurl the white man into the sea, I would have been perfectly happy if he had climbed aboard his steamships and left the continent of his own volition," Mandela says of his thinking at the time.[9] The Youth League drafted a Program of Action calling for peaceful but nevertheless illegal boycotts, strikes, stay-at-home, and demonstrations to replace the polite and fruitless deputations and petitions the ANC typically employed.

By 1950, Mandela was finding it more difficult to justify his prejudice against the CPSA. Not only were there communists whom he admired, like Joe Slovo and Moses Kotane, but also his reading of Marx, Engels, and Lenin convinced him that a classless society was remarkably similar to traditional African culture, where the needs of all were answered. The call to revolutionary action also appealed to the young activist, who amended his view of communists and accepted the ANC position of welcoming them into its ranks.[10]

It took a while longer for Mandela to amend his view on Indians; many African supporters viewed them as a merchant class of exploiters of black labor. When the ANC decided in 1952 to embark on its Defiance Campaign in protest of unjust laws, Mandela was against allowing the Indians to join, but was voted down by the other members of the ANC executive. Mandela's biographer, Martin Meredith, says that he underwent a personal transformation as a result of the Defiance Campaign:

> For practical reasons, Mandela had come to accept that a multiracial strategy was necessary in dealing with the government, abandoning the Africanist notions that he had held for so long. In time, his support for a multiracial strategy developed into a unshakable conviction about the importance of a multiracial approach in striving for non-racial democracy which never wavered, even under the greatest pressure the government could inflict.[11]

Discussion ensued regarding whether the campaign should follow the Gandhian principle of nonviolence, which was popular with the Indians and also the hallmark of the ANC to this point. Mahatma's son, Manilal, insisted that the campaign be run along the lines of his father's campaign in India. For Gandhi, nonviolence was an inviolable ethical principle to be followed whether it worked or not, but Mandela would concede only that it was a tactic to be used as the situation demanded, and only for as long as it was successful. In addition to being the national volunteer-in-chief of the Defiance Campaign, Mandela was also president of the Youth League, and shortly after became president of the Transvaal ANC, and later one of four deputy presidents of the ANC.

When in 1953 the ANC began discussing how to combat the removals of blacks from Sophiatown, which the government had decided should be reserved for whites, Mandela was at odds with the ANC's strict policy of nonviolence. He writes: "Nonviolent passive resistance is effective as long as your opposition adheres to the same rules as you do. But if peaceful protest is met with violence, its efficacy is at an end. For me, nonviolence was not a moral principle but a strategy; there is no moral goodness in using an ineffective weapon."[12]

The ANC, together with other groups, met for a Congress of the People in 1955 to adopt its Freedom Charter, which stated: "South Africa belongs to all who live in it, black and white, and . . . no government can justly claim authority unless it is based on the will of the people." Subsequently, Mandela found himself among 156 defendants under indictment in the Treason Trial of 1956, which covered the period from the Defiance Campaign through the 1955 Congress of the People. The prosecution's position was that the goals envisioned by the Freedom Charter were impossible without the violent overthrow of the state, so unwilling would whites be to share political power. Although Mandela had come personally to accept the necessity for violence in the struggle for African rights, this was not the official position of the ANC, and all defendants in time were acquitted. "In the case of the Treason Trial, the three judges rose above their prejudices, their education, and their background. There is a streak of goodness in men that can be buried or hidden and then emerge unexpectedly," writes Mandela.[13]

A group of young Africanists broke away from the ANC in 1959 to form the Pan-Africanist Congress (PAC). These militants objected to the Freedom Charter's inclusiveness. "Africa for Africans" became their credo, and they objected to the participation of whites and Indians in the Congress Alliance. In his autobiography, Mandela admits that while he too had felt this way at an earlier stage in his life, his thinking had evolved. "While I sympathized with the views of the Africanists and once shared many of them, I believed that the freedom struggle required one to make compromises and accept the kind of discipline that one resisted as a younger, more impulsive man."[14] It was this breakaway organization that called for the March 1960 identity-pass campaign that led to the Sharpeville massacre, when police fired on unarmed protesters turning in their passes in that township. The PAC and ANC were declared illegal organizations the following month. Shortly afterward the ANC, along with the South African Communist Party (SACP),[15] set up Umkhonto We Sizwe (Spear of the Nation; MK), a military organization with Mandela as commander in chief, to fight the government with acts of sabotage against government installations. Mandela's explanation to Albert Lutuli, then head of the ANC, was that violence would begin whether the ANC initiated it or not.[16] Mandela justified the strategy on practical grounds: "Because it did not involve the loss of life it offered the best hope for reconciliation among the races afterward."[17] (Ironically, the day after Lutuli returned from Oslo with the Nobel Peace Prize, MK exploded its first bombs at electric power stations and government offices in Johannesburg.)

Lessons from Prison

In the ninth month of a five-year prison sentence for inciting people to strike and for leaving the country without a passport, Mandela and every member of MK's High Command were together charged with sabotage when documents highlighting MK's underground activities were found at the underground's farm at Rivonia. The court's verdict: life imprisonment. At the time of sentencing, Mandela had evolved from a young lad who thought whites were almost gods, to a man who saw that whites were not in fact superior beings. If not selfless benefactors (as he had once believed), neither were they inevitable foes. He came to view whites as necessary allies in the struggle.

In the crucible of prison, Mandela continued his evolution. It was during his twenty-seven years in prison that Mandela's commitment to nonracialism would be sorely tested. Some of the warders were cruel and vindictive. He saw his jail time as an opportunity to convert to the cause not only the nonpolitical African inmates but also the white warders: "I always tried to be decent to the warders in my section; hostility was self-defeating. There was no point in having a permanent enemy among the warders. It was ANC policy to educate all people, even our enemies; we believed that all men, even prison service warders, were capable of change, and we did our utmost to try to sway them."[18]

When one particularly unpleasant warder, Piet Badenhorst, was to be transferred to another prison, Mandela was called to his office and was told, "I just want to wish you people good luck." Mandela wished the warder luck as well, and in his autobiography recollected:

> I thought about this moment for a long time afterward. Badenhorst had perhaps been the most callous and barbaric commanding officer we had had on Robben Island. But that day in the office he had revealed that there was another side to his nature, a side that had been obscured but that still existed. It was a useful reminder that all men, even the most seemingly cold-blooded, have a core of decency, and that if their heart is touched, they are capable of changing. Ultimately, Badenhorst was not evil; his inhumanity had been foisted upon him by an inhuman system. He behaved like a brute because he was rewarded for brutish behavior.[19]

During his time at Robben Island, Mandela developed an appreciation for the importance of compromise. For instance, when informed that his wife, Winnie, could only visit him if she carried an identity pass (clearly, an attempt to humiliate both her and Mandela, since the ANC had been protesting passes for years), he advised her to consent. "I thought it was more important that we see each other than to resist the petty machinations of the authorities."[20] Mandela demonstrated that he knew when to compromise and when not. In 1976, Jimmy Kruger, the minister of police, offered Mandela a reduced sentence if he would recognize the legitimacy of the Transkei government, which the South African government had set up as an independent "nation" for Xhosas to demonstrate to the international community that black South Africans had political rights in their own "homelands" (these homelands were, of course, unrecognized by any other government). The decision was simple: "It was an offer only a turncoat could accept."[21] Periodically, offers of release would come from the government in exchange for his renouncing violence as a political instrument. Mandela refused to disavow the armed struggle, which was ANC policy. However, he was open to negotiations with the government. Africans had been engaged in armed struggle for over two decades with little success. "We had right on our side, but not yet might. It was clear to me that a military victory was a distant if not impossible dream. It simply did not make sense for both sides to lose thousands if not millions of lives in a conflict that was unnecessary. . . . It was time to talk."[22]

Along with other political prisoners, Mandela continued his education in prison, working on degrees through correspondence courses and running political seminars for the inmates. Mandela even learned Afrikaans in prison and encouraged others to do the same. To those who argued that it was the language of the oppressors, Mandela replied that it was a means of understanding the oppressor's mind. "It was long-term possibilities that Mandela always managed to keep in sight," writes Meredith.[23] This is perhaps the key to Mandela's strength of character: he was willing to compromise, to forgive, to be magnanimous, because one day he would rule, and he would need the goodwill of whites to support the new democracy.

Robben Island (aptly called "The University") was the perfect training ground for leadership. Mandela's positive experiences with some white warders enabled him later to see National Party leader F. W. de Klerk as a person capable of change. He learned well the importance of compromise. So, while he would not renounce violence as a condition of his release, once free he was willing to temporarily suspend the armed struggle to help de Klerk with his constituency as long as the government was negotiating in good faith. Upon his release, Mandela called his former enemy de Klerk "a man of integrity," words that went far in placating white fears (though he was to later regret them).[24] Relations between the two were often strained, and Mandela later publicly criticized de Klerk for not stopping the violence in Natal in the early 1990s. But when asked how he could accept the Nobel Peace Prize jointly with de Klerk in 1993, Mandela insisted that de Klerk had made a genuine and indispensable contribution to the peace process. Ever the pragmatist, Mandela explained: "To make peace with an enemy one must work with the enemy, and that enemy becomes one's partner."[25] During negotiations with the National Party, the ANC was willing to make concessions by accepting amnesty for security officials, honoring contracts of civil servants for five years, and agreeing to power sharing for five years as determined by percentages parties received of the national vote. On the ANC alliance with the SACP, Mandela would not compromise: "Which man of honour will desert a lifelong friend at the insistence of a common opponent and still retain a measure of credibility with the people?"[26]

Postapartheid Reconciliation

When the ANC won the first democratic election, Mandela said he saw his mission as "one of preaching reconciliation, of binding the wounds of the country, of engendering trust and confidence."[27] Meredith notes that Mandela had attained such stature during the four years since his release from prison in 1990 for his lack of bitterness, insistence on reconciliation, and willingness to compromise that while the white community would not vote for him, they would accept a government under his presidency.[28] When criticized for overly placating whites, Mandela argued that reassuring whites involved no cost. Without their confidence, the transition to democracy would have been endangered by the possibility of civil war. "Courageous people do not fear forgiving, for the sake of peace," he once said.[29] A saint, or a politician of great subtlety?

For mainly pragmatic reasons, reconciliation was the very hallmark of Mandela's presidency. People marveled at his lack of bitterness. He simply had none. "In prison, my anger toward whites decreased, but my hatred for the system grew. I wanted South Africa to see that I loved even my enemies while I hated the system that turned us against one another."[30] He cited the example of jailer James Gregory, who had always treated him with respect, who had done much to "wipe out any bitterness which a man could have" about losing twenty-seven years of his life. Mac Maharaj has observed: "In his political life in the early years he gave vent to the anger he felt. In prison he got his anger almost totally under control. That control has come about through a deliberate effort by Mandela, for political reasons as well as personal."[31] Mandela explains his transformation in prison this way: "It was during those long and lonely years that my hunger for the freedom of my own people became a hunger for the freedom of all people, white and black. I knew as I knew anything that the oppressor must be liberated just as surely as the oppressed, for all had been robbed of humanity. When I walked out of prison, that was my mission, to liberate the oppressed and the oppressor both."[32]

Analysts look in vain for the key to this personality trait, expecting to find its source in some religious conviction. Mandela has admitted that he is "not particularly religious or spiritual,"[33] although he admires what the faith community did to oppose apartheid, and is especially grateful to individual clerics like Father Trevor Huddleston (an activist Anglican priest) and Beyers Naudé (an Afrikaner clergyman who was defrocked by his church) who fought the system so valiantly. He recognizes the contribution of the churches to the struggle: "When others inside the country were gagged and could not speak and could not travel and others were thrown in jail, it was the Church that kept the fire burning and kept the ideas for which they were suffering alive."[34]

It was not religion but rather the strength of his commitment to a nonracial democracy that sustained him. The key is that Mandela never doubted that one day he would be a free man and eventually president.[35] He simply did not have the luxury of succumbing to hate and revenge. Overcoming white fears of a nonracial democracy was crucial, and earning the trust and confidence of whites made the political settlement possible. He was aware of the larger-than-life expectations thrust upon him to exemplify moral leadership. When asked how he had changed during his time in prison, Mandela's simple reply was: "I came out mature."[36]

Or perhaps, more pragmatic. In typologies of leadership, it is often the pragmatist who makes peace processes possible.[37] Mandela's metamorphosis from protagonist to pragmatist was completed during his prison years. In an interview in 1996, he explained: "We have got to learn to live together, to transcend our prejudices, to resolve our differences amicably, to respect one another and together to reach towards co-operation and attainable common goals. Those are some of the things that I learned in prison."[38]

Several anecdotes about Mandela highlight the generosity of spirit that he developed during his years in prison. Who would have expected him to invite former adversaries to his inauguration as president? Yet three of his former warders were in fact invited to sit in the VIP section at his inauguration on May 10, 1994, including Gregory, the jailer who had been assigned to him for most of his imprisonment on Robben Island and who wrote a bestseller about his relationship with Mandela.[39] Gregory was among the many whites rallied by Mandela's inaugural address, in which he set the tone for the incoming government: "Let us stretch out our hands to those who have beaten us and say to them that we are all South Africans. Now is the time to heal the old wounds and to build a new South Africa."[40] His address was filled with the message of conciliation, forgiveness, and hope.

A second anecdote involves a luncheon Mandela held for the wives of former South African prime ministers, presidents, and leaders of liberation movements. Once again, he played the role of reconciler. Along with the expected invitations to Albertina Sisulu and Adelaide Tambo—wives of ANC luminaries Walter Sisulu and Oliver Tambo—Mandela included Tiene Vorster and Elize Botha, wives of former prime ministers John Vorster and P. W. Botha. Mandela said he brought the wives together as a "practical way of forgetting."[41] Adelaide Tambo commented that Mandela set an example for reconciliation: "We cannot forget the past, but we can endeavour to forgive."[42] And when Betsie Verwoerd, widow of prime minister Hendrik Verwoerd, the so-called architect of apartheid, politely declined to join the spouses of the other heads of state at the luncheon, South Africa's first black president quickly responded to her pro forma invitation to "drop in for tea when you're ever in the area" by traveling to the white enclave of Orania in the isolated Karoo region to pay his respects to the ninety-four-year-old grande dame, whom he proceeded to disarm with his charm.

Even more remarkable was his invitation to Percy Yutar to join him for lunch. Yutar was the prosecutor in the Rivonia Trial who had argued unsuccessfully for the death sentence for Mandela, and he had expressed regret when Mandela received a life sentence instead. Yutar was struck at this gesture: "I wonder in what other country in the world you would have the head of government inviting someone to lunch who prosecuted him thirty years ago."[43]

Another example of Mandela's willingness to reconcile with former enemies was his handling of the 1995 Rugby World Cup games, the first significant international event that took place in South Africa after the end of apartheid. Rugby in South Africa had been considered a white man's sport and a "symbol of white Afrikaner unity and pride dating back to the Boer War."[44] Like most black South Africans, Mandela had always supported any team opposing the South African Sprinkboks. Yet when in his capacity as president he presented the South African and New Zealand teams, who had made it to the finals, he did so wearing the Number 6 rugby jersey of the once despised Springboks, referring to them as "my sons." The mostly white crowd went wild at this magnanimous (and politically astute) gesture on the part of their new president. Africans too accepted this reidentification of the team, and when the Springboks beat the All Blacks in overtime, the *Sowetan*, a popular black newspaper, ran the headline "Amabokoboko"—Zulu for "Our Springboks"—the following day.[45] By example, Mandela was able "to teach a new way of thinking and behaving to his people, especially to black South Africans."[46] It was as if the game, which once typified white domination, "had magically drawn all sectors towards the centre and opened a new path, shown a new direction," according to the *Mail & Guardian*.[47] It was a simple act of "almost salvific power," writes Robin Petersen, senior lecturer in Christian studies at the University of the Western Cape.[48] Through such gestures, Mandela was modeling forgiveness to his people.

Could this remarkable president persuade South Africans to reconcile? In a letter to the TRC soon after it had begun its work, Mandela wrote: "[P]ersonal bitterness is irrelevant. It is a luxury that we, as individuals and as a country, simply cannot afford."[49] The TRC thoroughly embodied the notion of reconciliation: mainly white perpetrators were offered forgiveness through amnesty in exchange for disclosure of past offenses against mainly black victims, who were encouraged to turn the other cheek. If this man—whom Desmond Tutu called "an icon of forgiveness"—could endure his lengthy captivity without clamoring for revenge, how could those who suffered less do otherwise?

Inspired perhaps by their president's example, black South Africans appeared extraordinary in their willingness to forgive whites in an effort at national reconciliation. In that spirit, Africans were eager to embrace the TRC, which would uncover the truth about the past, and offer amnesty to those who admitted to having committed gross human rights abuses. Yet early polls indicated that whites were not in favor of a truth commission to explore the past, even though its end goal was the pardon, not the punishment, of mainly white perpetrators. A poll taken by the Institute for Democracy in South Africa (IDASA) shortly after the 1994 elections revealed that 65 percent of Africans supported "a Commission to investigate crimes that occurred under the previous government."[50] But only 39 percent of whites were in favor of a truth commission, and 40 percent were opposed. Another poll conducted by the Human Sciences Research Council (HSRC) in May 1995 as the Promotion of National Unity and Reconciliation Act was being discussed in Parliament indicated 53 percent of white South Africans rejected it; rejection was higher among Afrikaners (59 percent) compared to English-speaking whites (48 percent).[51] A Market Research Africa poll taken in May 1996 showed that most whites were ready to close the book about the past: 57 percent of whites said the TRC "should not be allowed to continue for as long as necessary," while two out of three black respondents held the opposite view.[52]

The popular view, in the United States at least, of South Africa's "rainbow nation" miraculously embracing in a spirit of reconciliation is inaccurate. Unfortunately for the country's future, this spirit seems one-sided. Blacks have demonstrated an amazing grace and capacity to embrace former enemies,[53] following the lead of their president, while whites for the most part have remained aloof and unresponsive, surprised and grateful perhaps by the lack of bitterness and acts of vengeance toward them by blacks, but still unwilling to be transformed by the grace offered to them in such great measure.

Notes

1. Nelson Mandela, cited in Gutmann and Thompson, "The Moral Foundations of Truth Commissions," p. 42.
2. Mandela, *Long Walk to Freedom,* pp. 42–46.
3. Meredith, *Nelson Mandela,* p. 34.
4. Mandela, *Long Walk to Freedom,* p. 63.
5. Ibid.
6. Ibid., p. 65.
7. Ibid., p. 78.
8. Ibid., p. 80.
9. Meredith, *Nelson Mandela,* pp. 66–67.
10. Mandela, *Long Walk to Freedom,* p. 105.
11. Meredith, *Nelson Mandela,* p. 98.
12. Mandela, *Long Walk to Freedom,* p. 137.
13. Ibid., p. 226.
14. Ibid., p. 199.
15. The CPSA was banned in 1950 and reorganized itself in 1953 as the SACP.
16. Mandela, *Long Walk to Freedom,* p. 239.
17. Ibid., p. 246.
18. Ibid., p. 365.
19. Ibid., pp. 402–403.
20. Ibid., p. 370.
21. Ibid., p. 420.
22. Ibid., p. 457.
23. Meredith, *Nelson Mandela,* p. 297.

24. Mandela, *Long Walk to Freedom,* p. 494.
25. Ibid., p. 533.
26. Ibid., p. 476.
27. Ibid., p. 540.
28. Meredith, *Nelson Mandela*, p. 498.
29. Cited in Gerloff, "Truth, a New Society, and Reconciliation," p. 37.
30. Mandela, *Long Walk to Freedom,* p. 495.
31. Cited in Frost, *Struggling to Forgive*, p. 4.
32. Ibid., p. 6.
33. Cited in Villa-Vicencio, *The Spirit of Freedom*, p. 148.
34. Nelson Mandela, press statement (March 14, 1993), cited in Frost, *Struggling to Forgive*, p. 123.
35. Mandela, *Long Walk to Freedom*, p. 437.
36. Meredith, *Nelson Mandela*, p. 407.
37. INCORE, "From Protagonist to Pragmatist" (February 2001).
38. Cited in Villa-Vicencio, *The Spirit of Freedom*, p. 150.
39. See Gregory, *Goodbye Bafana*.
40. Nelson Mandela, election-day speech, May 10, 1994.
41. Cited in Frost, *Struggling to Forgive*, p. 12.
42. Ibid.
43. Cited in Meredith, *Nelson Mandela,* p. 529.
44. E. M. Swift, "Bok to the Future," *Sports Illustrated* (July 3, 1995), p. 32.
45. Ibid.
46. Volkan, "The Power to Heal or Poison," p. 4.
47. "How Rugby Scored a Try for the New South Africa," *Mail & Guardian* (June 23, 1995).
48. Petersen, "The Politics of Grace and the Truth and Reconciliation Commission," p. 60.
49. Nelson Mandela, foreword to *Reconciliation Through Truth,* p. viii.
50. Cited in Theissen, "Between Acknowledgment and Ignorance," p. 55.
51. Ibid., p. 57.
52. Ibid., p. 73.
53. Support for granting amnesty to perpetrators of politically motivated crimes was mostly supported by blacks, according to the Market Research Africa poll.

3

Tutu's Theology of Reconciliation

Religion and Society

It is hardly surprising that religious notions informed the working of South Africa's Truth and Reconciliation Commission (TRC). South Africa is a country that is "Christian" in a sense that would be unrecognizable to citizens of most countries. The vast majority of South Africans are church members for whom Christianity is the most important ideological frame of reference. Biblical language and Christian discourse resonate powerfully, and theological discourse on political matters is taken seriously.[1]

Christianity was used by the National Party (NP) to rationalize apartheid, and was also employed by the resistance leaders to justify the struggle against it. The NP argued that Christianity taught that Afrikaners were God's elect in southern Africa and that separate development was God's will and plan.[2] For resistance leaders from the African National Congress (ANC), Pan-Africanist Congress (PAC), and Black Consciousness Movement (BCM), Christianity served as an ethical critique of apartheid, a source of righteous anger that inspired action, and a wellspring of confidence in eventual victory.[3] Given the importance of Christianity in South Africa, the framework under which the TRC operated was heavily influenced by Christian thought and tradition.

The Christian Church from its beginning has been concerned with truth, reconciliation, confession, guilt, and forgiveness—issues with which the TRC grappled.[4] Notions of reconciliation come squarely from Christian theology and have been central to theological debate in South Africa for years. The publication by the South African Council of Churches (SACC) (and the Christian Institute [CI]) of *The Message to the*

People of South Africa in 1968 began the debate. The Study Project on Christianity in Apartheid Society (SPROCAS) was launched, and later the Special Program for Christian Action in Society (SPROCAS II) was organized to relate the message of reconciliation to the realities of South Africa. The most critical expression of reconciliation was expressed in the *Kairos Document* in 1985, which called on the churches to confess their guilt for apartheid and to work for reconciliation on the basis of justice. Five years later at the Rustenburg conference, church leaders repented and pledged their support to work for reconciliation.

Against the common view of the TRC as a Christian-inspired effort (for it was the church's vocabulary of forgiveness, repentance, and reconciliation that guided the hearings), Carl Niehaus argues instead that the church was irrelevant to its establishment. During the transitional phase of negotiations, the church in South Africa "except for a vague call for peace and reconciliation" contributed very little theologically. Niehaus writes that when the issue of amnesty threatened to shipwreck the whole process, he was "ashamed to have to admit, as a believer, that during that time, no significant contribution was made from the religious angle with regard to matters that address so clearly the essential question of confession, reconciliation, and forgiveness. The church was confused and silent."[5] This interpretation of the TRC as a compromise thrashed out by political negotiators is at odds with the widely held view that it was the church that first came up with the idea of offering amnesty (forgiveness) in exchange for truth (confession). But once amnesty had been hammered out by the political leadership, the church's teachings were readily available to support the process.

That theology would so thoroughly inform the working of the TRC mainly has to do with the personal role of Desmond Tutu as its chair. As the new government began to explore in 1994 the possibility of establishing a truth commission, Tutu called on the faith community for support, reminding them that "Reconciliation is . . . the central message of faith."[6] Tutu recalls that as soon as he was appointed to the TRC, he asked the secretariat of the worldwide Anglican Communion to alert its nuns and monks "to our desperate need for regular intercession during the life of the commission."[7] For Tutu, "what we were being asked to undertake was profoundly religious and spiritual, and consequently spiritual resources were appropriately brought to bear on our task."[8]

Recognizing the centrality of reconciliation to all religious traditions, Bishop Tutu called on all faith communities to contribute to the TRC process.[9] He encouraged churches to make available their resources to provide counseling to people before, during, and after the hearings and asked churches, mosques, synagogues, and temples to provide liturgies for corporate confessions and absolution.[10] In response to his call, an interfaith service at St. George's Cathedral in Cape Town was held as a prelude to the work of the TRC. Commissioners each received a candle and an olive branch, symbols of the quest for truth and peace, and were blessed by Jewish, Christian, Buddhist, Muslim, and traditional African religious leaders as they stood in a semicircle with their lighted candles.[11]

On the first day of hearings, Tutu appealed to the different communities of faith to uphold the TRC "in fervent prayer and intercession" and acknowledged that a great deal would depend on the spirituality of the commissioners.[12] Tutu had emphasized the need to reach deep into the "spiritual wells of our different religious traditions" in order to address the challenge of healing and nation building. He added, however, that those who stand in the Christian tradition have "a special responsibility" because of the way that Christian theological resources in the past promoted apartheid.[13]

Secular critics have attacked not only the emphasis on reconciliation (as opposed to justice) but also the excessively religious atmosphere and discourse of the proceedings. Certainly, church leaders and members were among those instrumental in prompting the government to establish a truth commission, and a good number of the seventeen commissioners come from the faith community.[14] The TRC's chair and deputy chair, Desmond Tutu and Alex Boraine, came squarely from the church. Tutu was a former archbishop in the Anglican Church and Boraine was previously a president in the Methodist Church of Southern Africa.[15] Bishop Tutu clearly operated as a religious figure during the proceedings, garbing himself in a purple cassock and reverently lighting the candles as if he were officiating at a sacred service. Such demeanor prompted one observer to comment on the "liturgical character" of the hearings,[16] and some critics found Bishop Tutu an inappropriate figure to have led the hearings, faulting him for his outbursts of tears and deriding the TRC as the "Kleenex Commission."

Others, however, viewed Bishop Tutu as the perfect person to have led South Africa in the process of national healing and reconciliation, given his Christian compassion and moral stature as an activist bishop. Bishop Peter Storey has written: "He has wept with the victims and marked every moment of repentance and forgiveness with awe. Where a jurist would have been logical, he has not hesitated to be theological. He has sensed when to lead an audience in a hymn to help a victim recover composure, and when to call them all to prayer."[17] According to Tutu,

"Very few people objected to the heavy spiritual and indeed Christian emphasis of the commission. When I was challenged on it by journalists, I told them I was a religious leader and had been chosen as who I was. I could not pretend I was someone else. . . . It meant that theological and religious insights and perspectives would inform much of what we did and how we did it."[18]

But even within the TRC there were some commissioners and staff who felt that the hearings proceeded altogether too religiously. When the TRC was to begin hearings in Johannesburg in May 1996, Fazel Randera, the head of the Johannesburg office, argued that prayers and hymns did not belong in a judicial hearing. Tutu agreed to a moment of silence at the beginning. But when the first witness was brought to the stand, Tutu, visibly uncomfortable, said: "No, this won't work! We really cannot start like this. People, close your eyes so that we can pray!" Piet Meiring notes that Randera and his supporters good-naturedly acquiesced, and prayers continued to be offered at TRC hearings, as well as hymns when the bishop felt they were necessary to give a distraught witness time to recover him- or herself.[19]

Life and Career

Since Tutu was central in setting the tone for the TRC, emphasizing the sacred nature of the work of the commission, and articulating the theological underpinnings of the TRC's work, it is important to examine Tutu's theology. The development of Tutu's theology of reconciliation developed over many years. In his early ministry, he preached a dual theology based on man's creation in the image of God, and the reality of the reconciling work of Christ on the cross. In later years, he has taken these thoughts forward in developing a theology based on traditional African notions of *ubuntu* (discussed below).

Born in 1931 in the North West Province (formerly the Transvaal) to Methodist parents, Tutu was educated at St. Anagar, a Swedish mission boarding school, and Madibane, an Anglican institution, and obtained a teacher's diploma at Pretoria Bantu Normal College and a bachelor of arts degree through the University of South Africa. He taught school in Krugersdorp for four years, but resigned over the 1953 Bantu Education Act, which took control of schools away from churches. After leaving the teaching profession, he received ordination training at St. Peter's Theological College in Johannesburg and became a priest in 1961.

As a young man, Tutu was not active in political protest. The Defiance Campaign of 1952, in which Africans protested a host of discriminatory laws, had little impact on him. As well, the 1960 Sharpeville massacre, a peaceful identity-pass protest that ended in the killing of sixty-nine PAC members, although it did shock Tutu's sensibilities, did not draw him into politics, as he was busy finishing requirements for ordination in the Anglican Church.[20] However, his early acquaintance with Father Trevor Huddleston, a white activist preacher involved in the Defiance Campaign and in the later protest against the destruction of the African township Sophiatown, had a lasting impact on Tutu.[21]

Travel abroad also gave Tutu a chance to meet other white individuals. He won a scholarship to study from 1962 to 1966 at King's College in England, where he received his bachelor of divinity and master's degree in theology. He credits his time in England with forestalling bitterness against whites, for he discovered his fellow students at King's College and his parishioners at St. Alban's to be ordinary human beings, some good and some bad.[22]

Although Tutu believed whites were enslaved by their sinfulness, he did not consider them irredeemable devils, as the Good News of the gospel for the white sinner was forgiveness. Tutu prayed for them—for the president, for jailers, for the police—"because they are God's children too," he explained.[23] He sympathized with whites, realizing it would be difficult to give up so much privilege, admitting he too would need "a lot of grace" to do it if he were in their position.[24]

Tutu returned from England to take a position at his alma mater, St. Peter's, which in the intervening years had become part of the Federal Theological Seminary (FEDSEM).[25] He arrived on campus as black theology was gaining ground, and during this time was also the chaplain at the government-controlled black university, Fort Hare, where Black Consciousness was surfacing. By the time of the Black Consciousness–inspired Soweto uprising in 1976, a brutally put down protest of school children against the requirement that courses be taught in Afrikaans, he was thrust into politics as dean of the cathedral in Johannesburg, comforting the parents in Soweto whose children had been killed.

Following his tenure as dean of the cathedral from 1975 to 1976, Tutu held the positions of bishop of Lesotho, bishop of Johannesburg, and archbishop of Cape Town, heading the Anglican Church of the Province of Southern Africa. But it is for his work from 1978 to 1984 with the South African Council of Churches,[26] the umbrella group of churches critical of the government's race policies, that Tutu became especially renowned and for which he received the Nobel Peace Prize. Under Tutu's tenure as its general secretary, the once moderate SACC became both more Africanized, with Africans taking over positions of responsibility, and more radicalized, often sustaining accusations of being a black power base.

Tutu's Twin Doctrines

Underpinning the efforts of the SACC was a theology of opposition to apartheid articulated by Tutu. His disavowal of apartheid rests on twin doctrines: man as the image of God, and reconciliation through Christ's redemption. Tutu regards man's creation in the image of God as his most important attribute; the Bible makes no reference to racial, ethnic, or biological characteristics.[27] But apartheid holds that some are more like God than others. "Skin colour and race become salvation principles, since in many cases they determine which people can participate in which church services—which are believed to be of saving significance." In short, apartheid "can make a child of God doubt that he is a child of God."[28]

Apartheid also denies the central act of reconciliation that the New Testament declares was achieved by God in His Son, Jesus Christ. For Tutu, the heart of the Christian message is that Christ's work on the cross has restored human brotherhood, which sin had destroyed. Whereas the Bible declares that God's intention for humankind is harmony, peace, justice, wholeness, and fellowship, "apartheid says that human beings fundamentally are created for separation, disunity, and alienation."[29] Apartheid holds that Christ has *not* in fact broken down the dividing wall of partition that used to divide Jew from Gentile, rich from poor, slave from free. Apartheid denies the unity of the family of God. But for Tutu, there is neither black, white, Indian, nor Coloured, but a brother, a sister—one family, God's family, the "rainbow people of God."

Tutu saw parallels between South Africa's oppressed blacks and the Israelite slaves in the Exodus story whom God favored.[30] God later confirmed His preferential option for the oppressed by sending Hebrew prophets to denounce injustices perpetuated by the powerful against the powerless—the widows and orphans.[31] God again showed His alliance with the poor when He decided to come to earth as one of the oppressed. Tutu placed great store in the fact that in becoming human in Christ, God was not born into sumptuous surroundings but into a stable.[32] He wrote that God is on the side of the oppressed not because they are better or more deserving than their oppressors, but simply because they are oppressed.[33]

As SACC's leader, Tutu advocated nonviolent methods. "Because our cause is just," he writes, "we cannot afford to use methods of which we will be ashamed when we look back."[34] Tutu's leadership in the international campaign for sanctions against South Africa reflects his deep belief in nonviolent protest, and his choice of boycott rather than bloodshed won him the Nobel Peace Prize in 1984.[35]

In 1983, Tutu became a patron of the United Democratic Front (UDF), which was initiated to fight President P. W. Botha's new constitutional bill that extended the franchise to Indians and Coloureds in separate chambers from whites but denied the vote to Africans.[36] Tutu was vociferous in his rejection of the proposal. He saw it as a refinement rather than a refutation of apartheid. Tutu criticized the so-called reform of co-opting a segment of the oppressed as junior partners in order to add their numbers to the white oppressors.

Tutu was convinced that the gospel could change the hearts of white Christians, and that black South Africans must continually try to persuade (rather than fight) whites. Shirley du Boulay explains that Tutu's instincts were to negotiate rather than to confront, to reconcile rather than to attack. Although aware that militant blacks would see him as politically naive, Tutu persisted in this view and attempted to meet with President Botha time and time again.[37] Tutu explained, "Whether I like it or not, Mr. P. W. Botha and I are brothers, members of the same family. I cannot write him off. I cannot give up on him because God, our common Father, does not give up on anyone."[38] Of Botha's successor, F. W. de Klerk, Tutu said in 1990 he had witnessed a change of heart: "Give him credit, man. Do give him credit. I do."[39]

Tutu's Ubuntu Theology

During the apartheid era, Tutu emphasized the equal worth of blacks with whites, which is understandable given the inferiority complex that 300 years of colonial control and 40 years of apartheid domination had wrought on the psyches of blacks. The sermons and writings from this period were aimed at convincing whites that blacks were their equals, since they were all children of God, and to accept them as full citizens. Tutu stressed not only that reconciliation was possible, but that it had already occurred through Christ's work on the cross.

A side theme of Tutu's was that white supremacists were themselves victims in need of liberation and God's grace. But when Tutu retired as archbishop and took up the chairship of the TRC, he refocused his effort toward encouraging blacks to accept whites back into the fold. He came to stress the bondage of the white oppressor, that the white man was not an irredeemable devil but a fellow brother in the family of God who needed to be restored back into the community. Tutu has since changed his message from telling whites that blacks are their brothers to trying to convince blacks that whites are their equals: "We will grow in the knowledge that they [whites] too are God's children, even though they may be our oppressors, even though they may be our enemies. . . . Therefore, they belong together with us in the family of God, and their humanity is caught up in our humanity, as ours is caught up in theirs."[40]

If Tutu at one time had articulated God's preferential option for the oppressed, recently he has preached something akin to a preferential option of the former oppressor, for Tutu now views the former oppressor as a victim in need of healing. In Tutu's recent writings, he takes up God's "bias for sinners."[41] He notes: "However diabolical the act, it did not turn the perpetrator into a demon. We had to distinguish between the sinner and the sin, to hate and condemn the sin while being filled with compassion for the sinner."[42] Ultimately, no one is irredeemable. Tutu's theology "seeks to restore the oppressor's humanity by releasing and enabling the oppressed to see their oppressors as peers under God."[43] Forgiveness is at the heart of what God expects of his children. In the South African context, this means mainly black victims are urged to "turn the other cheek" to mainly white perpetrators.

Ubuntu and African Tradition

Tutu's expectation that former enemies can be reintegrated into the community is based not only on his expectation that black Christians would forgive as their religion teaches them, but also on his understanding of the African philosophy of *ubuntu.* There is no precise definition for *ubuntu,* but it connotes humaneness, caring, and community. *Ubuntu* derives from the Xhosa expression *"Umuntu ngumuntu ngabanye bantu"* (People are people through other people). It conveys the view that an environment of right relationships is one in which people are able to recognize that their humanity is inextricably bound up in others' humanity. For Tutu, a person who lives in *ubuntu* is "more willing to make excuses for others."[44]

To what extent does *ubuntu* exist in African traditional culture? Or rather, is it a construct of Tutu's alone? Certainly, finding justification for the process in indigenous African thought gives legitimacy to the TRC process, which otherwise has been accused of being both too "Christian" and too "Western." If real, *ubuntu* would provide an African source for making racial reconciliation intelligible.

Tom Lodge in *South African Politics Since 1994* discusses the validity of *ubuntu* in precolonial African societies. According to Lodge, *ubuntu* was first given systematic written exposition in the novels of Jordan Ngubane, a founder of the ANC Youth League, member of the Liberal Party, and president of Howard University.[45] For Ngubane, *ubuntu* was the common foundation of all African cultures and involved "a consciousness of belonging together."[46]

John Pobee writes, "It is often said that where Descartes said, 'I think, therefore I am,' the African would say, 'I am related, therefore we are.'"[47] This aspect of African culture underscores a concern for the well-being of others. Muendanyi Mahamba describes someone with *ubuntu* as someone who cares about the deepest needs of people and who adheres to all social obligations of the community.[48] The importance of community is something shared by all Africans, writes scholar of African religions John Mbiti: "Whatever happens to the individual happens to the whole group, and whatever happens to the whole group happens to the individual. The individual can only say: 'I am because we are, and since we are, therefore I am.' This is a cardinal point in the understanding of the African view of man."[49] Emphasizing the communal over the individual, *ubuntu* emphasizes the importance of reintegrating the individual into the group.

In African traditional thought, the emphasis is on restoring evildoers back into the community rather than punishing them. *Ubuntu* emphasizes the priority of "restorative" as opposed to "retributive" justice.[50] Tutu's own description of *ubuntu* is enlightening: "*Ubuntu* says I am human only because you are human. If I undermine your humanity, I dehumanise myself. You must do what you can to maintain this great harmony, which is perpetually undermined by resentment, anger, desire for vengeance. That's why African jurisprudence is restorative rather than retributive."[51]

For Mfuniselwa John Bhengu, *ubuntu* reflects tolerance, compassion, and forgiveness and means that "the person cannot be thrown away like trash."[52] *Ubuntu*'s understanding of the indivisibility of humanity creates a capacity for forgiveness. Njongonkulu Winston Ndungane writes, "Once an African detects that a person means well, and that there is a readiness to move away from the wrong of the past, there is a willingness to move forward to a future that seeks to enhance the well-being of humanity."[53] (One could argue, however, that very few perpetrators or beneficiaries of apartheid are truly willing to move forward; in short, it seems true contrition is a precondition for the offering of *ubuntu*).

Ubuntu also figures in the final clause of the interim constitution, titled "On National Unity and Reconciliation," which laid the guidelines for a truth commission. It states: "there is a need for understanding but not for revenge, a need for reparation but not for retaliation, a need for *ubuntu* but not for victimisation." Interestingly, the call for amnesty originally came not from the churches at all, which really had little input in the direct negotiations that led to the adoption of the interim constitution. It was political negotiators rather than church leaders who hammered out the unique concept of a truth commission in which truth would be traded for punishment. Thus the idea of offering amnesty was mainly a political necessity to bring the National Party on board, and secondly a social necessity indebted more to the notion of *ubuntu* embedded in African tradition than to the Christian ideas on repentance and forgiveness. As Carl Niehaus remarks, "There was very little, if indeed any, theological input."[54]

Constitutional court judge Yvonne Mokgoro argues that *ubuntu* principles such as collectivity, unity, and group solidarity could promote harmony between society's members rather than the desire for retribution, embodied in the adversarial approach in litigation. In a society founded on *ubuntu* principles, duty trumps individual rights. In such an order, then, group interests should prevail over individual rights.[55]

While there is nothing outwardly wrong with *ubuntu*—Lodge points out that the concept expresses a compassionate social etiquette that, if everybody adhered to it, would make life most agreeable[56]—an inherent danger arises when a social order is enshrined around collective solidarity rather than civil liberties. In the context of the TRC, people were asked to compromise their rights and face up to the duties that *ubuntu* required. Taken a step further, victims are expected to forgive and accept into the fold the perpetrator in the interests of traditional African values, and may feel guilty if they cannot.

The notion of *ubuntu* is not limited to Tutu and scholars of African traditions. Cynthia Ngeweu, mother of Christopher Piet, one of the Guguletu Seven (young men from Guguletu township executed by police in 1986), understands *ubuntu* this way: "This thing called reconciliation . . . if I am understanding it correctly . . . if it means the perpetrator, the man who has killed Christopher Piet, if it means he becomes human again, thus man. So that I, so that all of us, get our humanity back . . . then I agree, then I support it all."[57]

However, it has been suggested that *ubuntu* is a "current invention."[58] Does *ubuntu* hearken to an idyllic, precolonial idealized view of a past that may not have actually existed and cannot be resurrected? Richard Wilson believes that to see African law "as completely excluding revenge is an act of wishful romantic naivete."[59] He cites examples where traditional courts administered by Africans have applied the death penalty for certain categories of criminals (informers, witches, and car highjackers in the 1990s). However, Gunnar Theissen argues that while *ubuntu* may be exploited by politicians, "nation builders," and intellectuals to sell political compromise as an indigenous virtue, it actually does exist in African political culture. "The fact that the African non-metropolitan poor are [the] most willing [of all population groups] to grant amnesty [according to polls] supports this interpretation."[60] The universality of reconciliation in the major religious and philosophical traditions, including African tradition, suggests that the truth and reconciliation process upon which South Africa has embarked may serve as a guide to other countries dealing with a divisive past or the aftermath of ethnic bloodletting.

Notes

1. Fully 72.6 percent of South Africans identify themselves as Christians.

2. See Kuperus, *State, Civil Society, and Apartheid in South Africa.* See also Moodie, *The Rise of Afrikanerdom;* de Klerk, *The Puritans in Africa;* and Templin, *Ideology on a Frontier.*

3. Graybill, *Religion and Resistance Politics in South Africa.*

4. Smit, "Confession-Guilt-Truth-and-Forgiveness in the Christian Tradition," p. 96.

5. Niehaus, "Reconciliation in South Africa," p. 87.

6. Desmond Tutu, cited in Hollyday, "Truth and Reconciliation in South Africa."

7. Desmond Tutu, *No Future Without Forgiveness,* p. 81.

8. Ibid., p. 82.

9. For a Jewish perspective on the TRC, see Siffrin, Friedman, and Beller, "Can Reconciliation Take Root in Post-Apartheid South African Society?" See also Siffrin, Auerbach, and Friedman, "The Truth Commission."

10. TRC press release, "Archbishop Desmond Tutu's Address to the First Gathering of the Truth and Reconciliation Commission" (December 16, 1995).

11. "A Service of Dedication and Blessing of Commissioners of the Truth and Reconciliation Commission," p. 165.

12. TRC press release, "Archbishop Desmond Tutu's Address to the First Gathering of the Truth and Reconciliation Commission" (December 16, 1995).

13. Desmond Tutu, foreword to *To Remember and to Heal,* p. 8.

14. Roughly one-third came from the church, one-third from the health and mental health professions, and one-third from the legal system.

15. Boraine is also a former Progressive Federal Party leader in Parliament who resigned to set up the Institute for Democracy in South Africa (IDASA). It is no exaggeration to say that Boraine more than any other single individual is responsible for South Africa's TRC. He formed the IDASA offshoot that planned the 1994 conferences on "Justice in Transition," which debated the need for a truth commission, and he worked closely with Minister of Justice Dullah Omar to prepare the legislation for Parliament.

16. de Gruchy, "Redeeming the Past in South Africa."

17. Storey, "A Different Kind of Justice," p. 793.

18. Desmond Tutu, *No Future Without Forgiveness,* p. 82.

19. Meiring, *Chronicle of the Truth Commission,* p. 30.

20. du Boulay, *Tutu,* p. 54.

21. Hope and Young, *The South African Churches in a Revolutionary Situation,* p. 112.

22. Comment, King's College newsletter (December 1984), cited in du Boulay, *Tutu,* p. 60.

23. Cited in du Boulay, *Tutu,* p. 140.

24. Ibid., p. 163.

25. The buildings and property of FEDSEM were confiscated by the government in 1974.

26. SACC consists of twenty member churches and seven Christian organizations with observer status. Among the largest members are the mainline Protestant churches: Presbyterian, Methodist, Anglican, and Congregational. Member churches of SACC have 12 to 15 million adherents, 80 percent of whom are black.

27. Desmond Tutu, "Christianity and Apartheid," p. 40.

28. Ibid., pp. 45–46.

29. Ibid., pp. 41–42.

30. Desmond Tutu, *Hope and Suffering,* p. 51.

31. Desmond Tutu, cited in Maimela, "Political Priest or Man of Peace?" p. 47.

32. "General Secretary's Report, 1984," p. 5, cited in Maimela, "Political Priest or Man of Peace?" p. 47.

33. Desmond Tutu, "The Theology of Liberation in Africa," p. 166.

34. Cited in Naomi Tutu, ed., *The Words of Desmond Tutu,* p. 48.

35. Some white liberals thought it a mistake to award the Nobel Peace Prize to Tutu. Alan Paton, for instance, argued that the prize should go to someone whose concern was "to feed the hungry and not one who calls for economic pressure which could put a man out of a job and make his family go hungry." See Villa-Vicencio, "Archbishop Desmond Tutu," p. 1.

36. Sparks, *The Mind of South Africa,* p. 319.

37. du Boulay, *Tutu,* p. 168.

38. Desmond Tutu, "Spirituality," p. 163.

39. Cited in Villa-Vicencio, "The Conditions for Freedom," p. 31.

40. Desmond Tutu, "Where Is Now Thy God?" Trinity Institute, New York (January 8, 1989), cited in Battle, "The Ubuntu Theology of Desmond Tutu," p. 95.

41. Desmond Tutu, *No Future Without Forgiveness,* p. 84.

42. Ibid., p. 83.

43. Battle, *Reconciliation,* p. 5.

44. Desmond Tutu, "The Nature and Value of Theology" (undated), cited in Battle, "The Ubuntu Theology of Desmond Tutu," p. 104.

45. Lodge, *South African Politics Since 1994,* p. 99.

46. Ngubane, *Ushaba: A Zulu Umlando,* cited in Lodge, *South African Politics Since 1994,* p. 100.

47. Cited in Njongonkulu Winston Ndungane, "UTutu," p. 78.

48. Mahamba, "Ubuntu and Democracy," p. 7.

49. Mbiti, *African Religions and Philosophy,* pp. 108–110.

50. For a detailed discussion of *ubuntu,* see Battle, *Reconciliation.*

51. Mark Gevisser, "The Ultimate Test of Faith," *Mail & Guardian* (April 12, 1996).

52. Bhengu, *Ubuntu,* p. 5.

53. Ndungane, "UTutu," p. 79.

54. Niehaus, "Reconciliation in South Africa," p. 87.

55. Mokgoro, "Ubuntu and the Law in Africa," p. 52, cited in Lodge, *South African Politics Since 1994,* pp. 100–101.

56. Lodge, *South African Politics Since 1994,* p. 103.

57. Cited in Krog, *Country of My Skull,* p. 109.

58. See Richard Wilson, "The Sizwe Will Not Go Away."

59. Richard Wilson, *The Politics of Truth and Reconciliation in South Africa,* p. 11.

60. Theissen, "Common Past, Divided Truth," p. 24.

4

Forgiving the Unforgivable

As Desmond Tutu envisioned the working of South Africa's Truth and Reconciliation Commission (TRC), perpetrators would confess their sins and victims would offer their forgiveness. But many criticized the very framing of the issues in terms of repentance and forgiveness, which they saw as uniquely Christian concepts and thus alienating to South Africans who did not come from this faith perspective. One academic at a conference in Cape Town in July 1996 expressed horror at Bishop Tutu's thanking a mother for her "sacrifice" of her husband to the cause.[1] Not only academics but some victims as well have complained about "the imposition of a Christian morality of forgiveness."[2] One letter to the weekly newspaper *Mail & Guardian* expressed this common complaint: "I understand how Desmond Tutu identifies reconciliation with forgiveness. I don't, because I'm not a Christian and I think it grossly immoral to forgive that which is unforgivable."[3]

Ideally, perpetrators were expected to repent for their sins and victims to offer forgiveness, leading to reconciliation between individuals and ultimately for the nation at large. Tutu encouraged this process when he invited perpetrators to say they were sorry. He implored perpetrators to publicly apologize and accept the forgiveness that he believed would be forthcoming from their victims. In a Cape Town speech given in May 1977, Tutu urged political leaders to make pilgrimages to the sites of atrocities committed by their supporters and to apologize to the victims. He suggested that President Nelson Mandela go to Church Street in Pretoria, where a car bomb was exploded outside air force headquarters, on behalf of the African National Congress (ANC); that F. W. de Klerk represent the National Party (NP) at the site of the Boipatong massacre, where ANC supporters were hacked to death by police-aided Inkatha Freedom Party (IFP) members; that Stanley Mogoba of the Pan-Africanist Congress (PAC) call on the St. James Church in Kenilworth, where white worshipers were murdered; and that Mongosuthu Buthelezi of the IFP visit KwaMakhutha, the site of a massacre in which thirteen ANC supporters were killed by police who sided with the IFP. "This is a wonderful opportunity which will never return. All it requires is for somebody to say 'I am sorry. Forgive me.' We would all be amazed at the response."[4]

However, the Promotion of National Unity and Reconciliation Act, the law empowering the TRC, provided merely that amnesty be granted in exchange for full disclosure; remorse was not a requirement. Could victims forgive when the perpetrators had not apologized? There is a view that forgiveness is two-sided, requiring not only mercy on the part of the persecuted but also repentance on the side of the oppressor. Dietrich Bonhoeffer's notion of "cheap grace" is apposite: "Cheap grace is the preaching of forgiveness without requiring repentance . . . absolution without personal confession."[5]

The story is told that when the act was explained to the commissioners at the onset of the hearings, some of them started to cry when they realized that perpetrators did not have to show remorse.[6] Marius Schoon, whose wife and daughter were killed by a package bomb sent by agent Craig Williamson, has said: "there can be no indemnity, no forgiveness, without remorse. We see no signs of Craig being sorry. I mean, are we going to have a situation where people can qualify for indemnity just by saying, as if they were reeling off a grocery list, 'I killed this one, and poisoned that one and beat the shit out of the third one'?"[7] Beyers Naudé, head of the former Christian Institute (CI) and one of the leading Afrikaners to oppose apartheid, saw a merciful attitude on the part of the ANC leadership: "In some incredible way God has sown the seeds of a gracious attitude, of the spirit of *ubuntu,* in the hearts and minds of the whole African community." Yet, he too failed to see any admission of guilt on the part of the oppressors: "As far as I know, none of the leaders of the National Party ever said they were sorry about the system they created."[8]

Former president F. W. de Klerk resisted apologizing for actions of the previous National Party government. During the four years of negotiations leading up to elections, there was no reference made by the NP to the immorality of creating and maintaining a system of exploitation based on strict racial segregation. To de Klerk, apartheid was not inherently wrong, and no evil intent had motivated its architects. The motivation behind de

Klerk's reforms was not the belief that apartheid was wrong or sinful but simply that it had failed to work.[9] As the bill authorizing the TRC was debated, de Klerk continued to maintain that "everything in the so-called apartheid era wasn't bad."[10]

This attitude of denial did not change with the National Party's submission to the TRC. During his first presentation, de Klerk, speaking for the NP, denied that he or his cabinet had planned murders, tortures, or assassinations of opponents.[11] He maintained that while the NP accepted responsibility for political decisions taken when it was governing, it could not be held accountable for unauthorized actions by "maverick elements" committing cold-blooded murder, which he insisted was not the policy of his government. In the National Party's second submission, in response to a series of written questions posed by the TRC, de Klerk insisted that he was as shocked as anyone on hearing of acts committed by a "handful of operatives" in the police and military and could not accept that the government's policies gave security forces a "license to kill." When presented with a document that showed he was present at a cabinet meeting in 1986 when a decision was made to create a security force that would "eliminate" the state's enemies, de Klerk denied that "eliminate" meant "to kill," a statement the TRC commissioners found not to be credible.[12]

At subsequent amnesty hearings, former cabinet minister Adriaan Vlok, police commissioner Johan van der Merwe, and former Vlakplaas commander Eugene de Kock all testified that while P. W. Botha had given the actual orders for their deeds—bombing COSATU House (headquarters of the Congress of South African Trade Unions), Khotso House (headquarters of the South African Council of Churches [SACC]), and movie theaters playing *Cry Freedom* (about the life of Steve Biko)—de Klerk had known about these actions. In a strongly worded statement, de Klerk denied that he had lied to the TRC about his involvement. Nowhere had he said he denied *knowing,* de Klerk said; he had simply denied having any part in the decision. The Afrikaner newspaper *Beeld* editorialized, "It is a pity that a leader who played such a major role to achieve a peaceful settlement in the country minimized his contribution to reconciliation and an understanding of what went wrong, in this way."[13]

Commentators have noted that de Klerk may have ruined chances for reconciliation by refusing to come to terms with the past and by not responding to the politics of grace offered by the Truth and Reconciliation Commission. P. W. Botha, the former state president, also refused to apologize to the victims of apartheid. Botha was adamant: "I am not going to repent. I am not going to ask for favours. What I did, I did for my country, my God and my people and all the people of South Africa. . . . I am not asking for amnesty. I did not authorize murders, and I do not apologize for the struggle against the Marxist revolutionaries."[14] After defying three subpoenas to tell what he knew about the State Security Council (SSC), an organization set up during his presidency that had been implicated in masterminding the killing, torturing, and detaining of thousands of blacks, the former president was prosecuted for contempt.[15] Tutu pleaded with him to apologize:

> I speak on behalf of people who have suffered grievously as a result of policies carried out by the government that he headed. I want to appeal to him to take this chance provided by the court to say that he himself may not have intended the suffering to happen to people . . . [but] the government that he headed caused many of our people deep, deep anguish and pain and suffering. If Mr. Botha is able to say, "I am sorry the policies of my government caused you so much pain"—just that—that would be a tremendous thing.[16]

Botha told reporters, "I only apologize for my sins before God."[17] And Botha's lawyer added that his client had nothing for which to apologize.

Michael Lapsley, former pastor to the ANC in exile and now chaplain for the Trauma Center for Survivors of Violence and Torture, has argued: "The perpetrators have the audacity to tell the victims 'it is your job to forgive and forget' while at the same time refusing to acknowledge that they have been party to evil."[18] During the TRC hearings, Lapsley said:

> I lay sole responsibility for that [the letter bomb sent to him in Zimbabwe] with F. W. de Klerk. De Klerk knew of the hit squads—Frederick Van Zyl Slabbert [opposition leader in Parliament] himself told me that he told De Klerk about them—but De Klerk chose to do nothing about it. Forgive I will be able to, but then the asking of forgiveness must take place within the framework of repentance . . . but from the direction of De Klerk not a single sound of admission has come. And I also want to know, what is a person doing now to make up for what he or she destroyed in the past?[19]

In the TRC's final report, Tutu lamented the absence of a grand apology from the white leadership: "I still hope that there will be a white leader who will say, 'We had an evil system with awful consequences. Please forgive us. Without qualification.'"[20]

Is forgiveness possible without those acts of repentance? The South African theologians who penned the *Kairos Document* following the state of emergency in 1985 had argued that reconciliation is not possible without true repentance. For the *Kairos Document* theologians, reconciliation can only *follow* white repentance and a clear commitment to fundamental change.[21]

What has disturbed many TRC observers is this lack of any requirement to be remorseful in order to get amnesty, whereas in a court case, remorse would have been taken into consideration in sentencing. For these critics, "reconciliation" is just a code word for simple forgiveness on the part of victims, with all the movement coming only from the victims' side. But the reality is that perpetrators cannot be forced to repent, nor can victims be compelled to forgive. Nothing in the legislation required either forgiveness or repentance, although clearly Bishop Tutu yearned for both to happen. Indeed, many cases abound in which witnesses extended forgiveness, prompting observers to remark on the seemingly endless capacity of victims to forgive.

Beth Savage personified the willingness to forgive. Shot with an AK-47 at a Christmas party at King William's Town Golf Club in 1992, her body remains so full of shrapnel that she sets off the alarms at airport security. Her father, who had always opposed apartheid, went into a deep depression and died a broken man soon after the attack. Savage had this to say about her experience to the commissioners: "But all in all, what I must say is, through the trauma of it all, I honestly feel richer. I think it's been a really enriching experience for me and a growing curve, and I think it's given me the ability to relate to other people who may be going through trauma."[22] Ms. Savage indicated that she wanted to meet the soldier from the Azanian People's Liberation Army (APLA) who threw the grenade, with "an attitude of forgiveness and hope that he could forgive me too for whatever reason."[23] She had her wish fulfilled at Mr. Thembelani Xundu's amnesty hearing, and later told the press that she no longer had nightmares about the attack.

In 1993, APLA soldiers opened fire on 400 worshipers at St. James Church in Kenilworth, a Cape Town suburb, killing 11 and wounding more than 50. One of the three amnesty applicants involved in the attack on the St. James Church had this to say: "We are sorry for what we have done. It was the situation in South Africa. . . . We are asking from you, please to forgive us. All that we did, we can see the effects today." The other two applicants apologized as well. Dawie Ackerman, whose wife was killed in the attack, responded: "I want you to know that I forgive you unconditionally. I do that because I am a Christian, and I can forgive you for the hurt that you have caused me, but I cannot forgive you the sin that you have done. Only God can forgive you for that."[24] After the hearing, Ackerman and several other survivors met in a private meeting with their attackers. Each killer walked around the table and addressed each survivor in turn, asking personally for forgiveness.

Paul Williams, another victim of the massacre, who remains partially paralyzed, said: "I have now forgiven the one who shot me, unconditionally. I looked him in the eye and actually had a chat with him. It was a good experience for me. I saw that we could each forgive the other. . . . You have to remember, that I am a coloured man and I know where these guys are coming from. I know how they were wronged and how even my own group turned away from their suffering."[25]

One of the young killers, Gcinikhya Makoma, had been approached by a church member soon after his arrest in 1993. He sent the young parishioner away, threatening to send his comrades to get him.[26] The later empathy between victim and perpetrator was almost certainly an outcome of the TRC process.

Jeanette Fourie, whose daughter Lyndi was a victim of the Heidelberg Tavern killings in December 1993, testified at the amnesty hearings about the three APLA men who had killed her daughter:

> I am very sorry that I can't express my thoughts and feelings in Xhosa. I think you remember me. At the criminal trial, I asked the translator to tell you that I had forgiven you. Do you remember that?
>
> I shook your hands. Mr. Gqomfa was unwilling and he looked the other way, but I certainly shook Mr. Mabala and Mr. Madasi's hands. Nothing has changed. I still feel exactly the same way and I do forgive you because my High Command demonstrated to me how to do that by forgiving his killers. . . . I think that the reason for my being here this week and particularly today, which is very important to me, is to tell you that on that day, you ripped my heart out. Lyndi was one of the most precious people that this country could have produced. I resent being called a victim. I have a choice in the matter—I am a survivor. Lyndi was a victim—she had no choice. . . . I am happy that you are well. I hope that emotionally and psychologically you can be well because you have been programmed killers though you repeatedly said that you were acting under orders from your high command. You could not tell us how you felt while killing innocent people, which indicated to me that you may have been trained to "not feel" and I recognize how important that would be in a killing machine—to be unable to feel, but just to carry out orders indiscriminately. I have no objection to the granting of amnesty for you. . . . I thank you for being able to look me in the eye and for hearing my story.[27]

At the end of the hearing, the three young men asked to speak privately to Mrs. Fourie, who has recounted: "Gqomfa . . . [said] they wanted to thank me for my forgiveness; they would take that message of peace and hope to their communities and to their graves, whether or not they were given amnesty. Gqomfa said that if someone were to kill his child he didn't think he could forgive them. I was profoundly moved by their acceptance of my gift of forgiveness." Asked about their hatred for whites, Madasi said that his father had been killed by a white man. Mabala explained that others in his family were also killed by white security force members in a riot near East London. At the end of their meeting, a hug from Fourie for each of the men "indicated the depth of community we had entered into in this short while."[28]

But most of the survivors and victims' families from the Heidelberg Tavern massacre, according to Antjie Krog, seemed "ablaze with anger and neglect."[29] Roland Palm, whose Coloured daughter died in the attack, told the amnesty applicants, "The irony of her death is that she was not a white person who, according to APLA, were the legitimate targets of their death squads. I cannot begin to describe the rage I feel and have felt for the past years at her senseless killing. You simply ended Rolande's life as if she was a worthless piece of rubbish. You say you did so to liberate Azania. I say to you [that] you did it for your own selfish and criminal purposes. . . . My personality has changed. I have not been able, despite extensive therapy and counseling, to shed the anger, rage, guilt, feelings of revenge and helpless desperation at the system that allows murderers to escape punishment."[30]

Neville Clarence was left totally blind when a bomb exploded in front of the air force headquarters on Church Street in Pretoria in 1983, an attack by Umkhonto We Sizwe (MK) that killed 19 people and injured 217. At the amnesty hearings, he approached Aboobaker Ismail, the leader in charge of the operation, with these words: "I forgive you for what you have done. I came to the trial to share my feelings with you. I wanted you to know that I harbour no thoughts of revenge."[31] According to Piet Meiring, Ismail was deeply moved. Close to tears, he grasped the hand of the former air force officer and started to tell Clarence about his own colleagues who had lost their lives in the struggle. As a soldier, Clarence could understand Ismail's action, although they had been enemies in the past.[32]

Linda Biehl, mother of Amy Biehl, the American Fulbright scholar who was killed in Guguletu township near Cape Town in 1993 by members of the Pan-Africanist Students Organization (PASO)—the student wing of the PAC—explained her ability to forgive: "I don't think I have anything to forgive. I never truly felt hatred. Our family never felt anger or hatred, only incredible sadness." Each amnesty applicant made an apology at the hearing. "When I look closely at what I did, I realize it was bad," said applicant Ntobeko Peni. "We took part in killing someone we could have used to achieve our own aims. I ask Amy's parents, friends, relatives—I ask them to forgive me."[33]

Johan (Hennie) Smit, an Afrikaner, told the TRC about the killing of his eight-year-old son, Cornio, in a bomb blast at a shopping center in Amanzimtoti. He met the parents of the boy who had planted the bomb. "It was a great relief seeing them and expressing my feelings . . . that I felt glad that I could tell that I felt no hatred for them and no grudge. And there was no hatred in my heart."[34]

In an unusual turnaround, one victim even asked forgiveness from the perpetrators. At the amnesty hearings for Boy Diale and Christopher Makgale, killers of the government-appointed chief of the Bafokeng tribe in Bophuthatswana homeland, it was clear these two men felt little remorse; rather they felt they had done the Bafokeng tribe a favor by killing the government-appointed chief. After listening to the testimony, the chief's son sent a message to the commissioners, asking for a chance to speak: "I think I am beginning to understand why you hated him so. . . . Now I would like to stretch out my hands to you and ask your forgiveness for what my father did to you. Please forgive us! And, if you desire my family's forgiveness, we would be happy to give it."[35]

Kimpani Peter Mogoai, a former askari (someone who has "turned" from the resistance to be an informer), was involved in the murder of the PEBCO Three, three activists from the Port Elizabeth Black Civic Organization, based on the Eastern Cape. At his amnesty hearing, he said: "It is with my deepest remorse that I ask for forgiveness and hopefully wish to be reconciled with everybody once more and be part of a better and brighter future of South Africa."[36]

Colonel Horst Schobesberger, former chief of staff of the Ciskei Defense Force, made the following apology to the families of those shot dead in the Bisho massacre when homeland soldiers opened fire on ANC demonstrators in that city: "I say we are sorry. I say the burden of the Bisho massacre will be on our shoulders for the rest of our lives . . . but please, I ask . . . the victims to forgive us, to get the soldiers back into the community, to accept them fully, to try to understand also the pressure they were under then. This is all I can do."[37] The audience applauded.

However, there were perpetrators who seemed emotionless and unrepentant. Former commander Dan Mofokeng refused to apologize for the attacks by APLA followers on soft targets, such as the St. James Church, King William's Town Golf Club, and the Heidelberg Tavern. He said, "The leadership of APLA takes full responsibility for these operations; we do not regret that such operations did take place, and there is nothing to apologize for."[38]

A moving example of forgiveness is that of James Wheeler and Corrie Pyper, who asked for amnesty for the killing of Vuyani Papuyana, a student and taxi driver. Wheeler and Pyper, both in an intoxicated state on election day in 1994, decided to kill blacks in an effort to stop the election. Wheeler turned to Vuyani Papuyana's family, saying: "Can you forgive me? I cannot believe I was so shortsighted! I have decided never again to resort to violence to achieve a political objective. I hope that in the future, through my actions, I can contribute towards reconciling white and black people who still bear animosity to one another."[39]

Four years earlier, Pyper had asked the family for forgiveness. Nelson Papuyana said:

> I immediately knew that it was the best thing I have ever done: to face the man who murdered my son. The meeting helped me to overcome my emotional problems. Before that meeting I was convinced that I would never be able to forgive my son's murderer. In my wildest dreams I did not think that the meeting would become a situation where I would be the one trying to comfort the murderer and his wife. Mrs. Pyper was crying so much that she could not really talk. Mr. Pyper told me what had happened that night. He said that he still could not explain why he had done such a mindless thing. He repeatedly said that it had been an extremely mindless deed and that he was very sorry.[40]

Pyper had offered to pay for the funeral costs and offered 5,200 rand to the family. Said Mr. Papuyana: "I at first refused to accept it, but when he insisted I could see that it would relieve his pain if I accepted it. He felt better afterwards."[41] Piet Meiring comments, "A strange, wonderful country, ours—I thought—where the father of the murdered son embraces the perpetrator, the murderer, and his wife to comfort them."[42]

Brian Mitchell deeply regretted his actions as station commander of the New Hanover police. Mitchell had given the order in December 1988 to attack a house in the Trust Feed village in the New Hanover area of the Natal Midlands, where members of the United Democratic Front (UDF), engaged in a fight with Inkatha Freedom Party loyalists, were believed to be sleeping. Eleven people were killed including children, none of whom, it turned out, were UDF supporters. Mitchell's first attempt to meet with the community was rejected. When a meeting was finally arranged, it was clear that many were not willing to forgive the policeman. Mitchell pleaded: "I can never undo what I have done. I have no right to ask your forgiveness, but I ask that you will allow me to spend my life helping you to rebuild your village and put your lives together."[43] Jabuliswe Nguane, who had lost her mother and children in the attack, told journalists: "It is not easy to forgive, but because he stepped forward to ask forgiveness, I have no choice. I must forgive him." As Mitchell drove away from the community he had so harmed, the community called out, "Bye-bye, uhambe kahle [go well], Mitchell."[44] On his release from prison after receiving amnesty (he had been serving nineteen life sentences), Mitchell approached the Pietermaritzburg Agency for Christian Social Awareness in order to become involved in community work in the area.[45]

Eric Taylor faced the families of his victims, four activists from the Eastern Cape referred to as the Cradock Four, whom he had killed:

> I am here in response to God's prompting and I fully believe that He has forgiven me. I also applied for amnesty and although it is not a certainty, amnesty may be granted. But amnesty is a technical matter and will do nothing towards reconciliation. I have realised that the only way to find peace is to tell the families, wives, children, brothers and sisters that I am sorry for a lot that happened and to ask them if they can find strength through God to forgive.[46]

The son of Matthew Goniwe, one of the four, embraced the white policeman: "You murdered our father. But we forgive you!"[47]

Commenting on the amazing capacity of South Africans to forgive, Tutu exclaimed, "Sometimes God knocked your feet out from underneath you when things happened at the most unexpected times and places, and about the mercy and generosity and forgiveness he planted in people's hearts."[48] Still, one cannot realistically expect that all victims will readily forgive even when apologies are forthcoming. Another relative of one of the Cradock Four said: "I told God if He put you in front of me I would shake your hand. I appreciate what you have done here today. I am relieved, but not yet fully." The widow of Fort Calata, one of the Cradock Four, rejected Taylor's apologies: "You have teased our grief for nearly twelve years, and you think you can reconcile in fifteen minutes?"[49]

Before his amnesty hearing for the murder of civil rights attorney Griffiths Mxenge, Dirk Coetzee said: "I will have to live with my conscience for the rest of my life and with the fact that I killed innocent people. . . . In all honesty, I don't expect the Mxenge family to forgive me."[50] But after receiving amnesty for the killing, Coetzee lashed out at the Mxenge family for refusing to forgive him: "I've never seen them smiling and the like," he told state television. "Their faces show revenge and hatred." Coetzee said he felt sympathy for the children of the victim. "But for the brothers, I'm really getting fed up with their nagging and not falling in with the new South Africa."[51] Forgive, they would not. Mr. Mxenge's brother, Churchill, said: "President Mandela wishes that people will forgive and forget and life goes on. But unless justice is done, it is difficult for any person to think of forgiving."[52]

When Coetzee, who had also testified about roasting the corpses of murdered antiapartheid activists on a pyre while guzzling beer with his police buddies, turned to the families of those victims at his amnesty hearing, asking their forgiveness, the legal representative of Charity Kondile, mother of one of the victims, read her client's statement: "You said that you would like to meet Mrs. Kondile and look her in the eye. She asked me to tell you that she feels it is an honour . . . you do not deserve. If you are really sorry, you would stand trial for the deeds you did."[53]

Neither was the widow of Bheki Mlangeni, a well-known activist and lawyer who was killed by a package bomb, willing to forgive: "The murderers of my husband must be found and prosecuted! I understand that Eugene de Kock is asking for amnesty from you. I oppose that! He knew that people would die when he sent those explosives. Today I am a widow. I feel like an outcast because of a person who is asking for pardon."[54]

For Chris Ribeiro, whose parents, Fabian and Florence, were gunned down outside their Mamelodi home in December 1986, forgiveness was problematic: "If my parents' killers get amnesty, it will be like having my parents killed for the second time. . . . If the killers are not going to face the music, then I am not interested in the Truth and Reconciliation Commission."[55]

At times, Tutu gave the impression that Africans have some supernatural capacity at forbearance. At hearings of the Human Rights Violations (HRV) Committee, after individual suffering was valorized, the commissioners urged those testifying to forgive perpetrators and abandon any desire for retaliation against them. Richard Wilson writes: "Commissioners never missed an opportunity to praise witnesses who did not express any desire for revenge. . . . The hearings were structured in such a way that any expression of a desire for revenge would seem out of place. Virtues of forgiveness and reconciliation were so loudly and roundly applauded that emotions of revenge, hatred and bitterness were rendered unacceptable, an ugly intrusion on a peaceful, healing process."[56] Even before victims testified at hearings, they were guided by statement takers, many of whom were religious activists in church settings, to frame their stories in terms of forgiveness. One statement taker in the Vaal region, when asked how he responded to victims' feelings of revenge, described how he steered a victim's perspective in order to "uplift reconciliation."[57]

By constantly harping on the infinite capacity of Africans to forgive, did Tutu make it more difficult for victims to express their legitimate rage? Psychologist Nomfundo Walaza responds that anger is crucial for progress.[58] Yet we saw very little of this in the hearings. By encouraging victims to turn the other cheek, did the TRC do victims a disservice concerning their long-term healing? Audrey Chapman has argued that at the HRV hearings over which Tutu presided, more emphasis was placed on eliciting forgiveness from the victims than in securing knowledge of wrongdoing or apologies from the perpetrators.[59] The outward public displays of forgiveness may have had more to do with "Tutu's dominating presence" than with the genuine attitude of victims.[60] Graeme Simpson, director of the Center for the Study of Violence and Reconciliation in Johannesburg, noted: "If the Commission did offer an opportunity for dealing with wounds of the past and for healing, then it has to be acknowledged that expressions of anger and the desire for revenge (rather than forgiveness) on the part of victims, may in fact be more functional to the sort of substantive recovery best characterized by the shift in identity from 'victim' to 'survivor.'"[61] For Simpson, reconciliation can best be achieved by integrating the anger, sorrow, and trauma rather than subtly suppressing them.

Wilhelm Verwoerd recorded a conversation he had with a young woman: "What really makes me angry about the TRC and Tutu is that they are putting pressure on me to forgive. . . . I don't know if I will ever be able to forgive. I carry this ball of anger within me and I don't know where to begin dealing with it. The oppression was bad, but what is much worse, what makes me even angrier, is that they are trying to dictate my forgiveness."[62] Brandon Hamber believes that the anger of victims and families needed to be legitimized and space provided for people to express their genuine sadness and rage.[63] Forced forgiveness is destructive; only the individual herself or himself can choose to forgive or not to forgive. South Africans cannot forgive perpetrators on behalf of individual victims.

Jeffrie G. Murphy, in dialogue with Jean Hampton, has argued that resentment is tied to self-respect. He calls this "retributive hatred."[64] In response to Hampton, who urged victims to transcend their resentments, Murphy commented: "Jesus, being divine, perhaps had certain advantages that mere mortals lack."[65] Is it a vice to be willing to forgive, reflecting a lack of self-respect? Are there occasions when too much of a person is "morally dead" to be forgiven?[66] Or, as Hannah Arendt has argued, is "forgiveness the only power that can stop the inexorable streams of painful memories"?[67]

As difficult as it may be to forgive the enemy, Janet Cherry believes that the hardest of all to forgive is betrayal. How does one find mercy in one's heart toward a former ally who turned informer—an askari, a former resistance fighter who for money or to save his own life infiltrated the resistance? "An enemy met on equal terms," Cherry writes, "can be forgiven for the killing of a loved one or a comrade. One of your own side, whose betrayal led to such a death, cannot be so easily forgiven."[68] And what of black policemen who killed township youth? Or the youth who killed black councilors? This was and is a major obstacle toward reconciliation, as most perpetrators of killings were blacks in the resistance movements and Inkatha Freedom Party loyalists who are now living in the same neighborhoods as their victims and must be seen daily.

And where does forgiveness begin? One theological tradition asserts that it begins with the one who has been wronged, who forgives because he is forgiven by God. (In the TRC setting, this was often demonstrated when victims took the initiative in offering forgiveness to perpetrators even before or in the absence of an apology.) Another tradition holds that it begins with the perpetrator, who must confess and ask for forgiveness; the victim then grants it, and both sides are changed by the encounter.[69] (This was exemplified in the case of Brian Mitchell, who made the overture to his victims and was forgiven by the Trust Feed community.) Charles Villa-Vicencio has said that, "correctly understood, it is a cycle that begins with forgiveness . . . [but] it could be argued in the secular world of politics it does not really matter at which point one enters the cycle—as long as one stays on board for the entire journey."[70]

How sincere were these apologies? Joyce Hollyday had described how Paul van Vuuren, a security officer who murdered the parents of a five-year-old boy named Tshidiso, got together with the now fourteen-year-old boy. Van Vuuren's response to the boy was, "I don't know you. I owe you nothing."[71] Yet van Vuuren is now hailed as a reformed victimizer. Did he come to realize that an unrepentant attitude would not play well with the Amnesty Committee, despite the fact that remorse was not a technical requirement? At his amnesty hearing, van Vuuren said:

> I mean he sat there and he looked at me and I killed his father . . . and I can understand that he should hate me in his heart and his whole soul. . . . But I didn't even see him that night . . . so I feel so sorry for him. . . . I mean you can't get past that. I truly feel sorry for him. . . . If I could do something for him and he calls me and says do something for me, then I will do it. . . . And if he says take me to Cape Town then I will take him . . . but I mean, what the hell does one do?[72]

Captain Jacques Hechter expressed contrition for dozens of murders he committed as a security policeman in the northern Transvaal. Reading from a prepared text, he said: "I believed that what I did was in the interests of the Republic of South Africa, my religion, and my Christian convictions. Today I am uncertain where I stand. I am sorry about the loss of lives. I hope this will result in reconciliation in South Africa."[73] When writer David Goodman stopped him later in the afternoon and asked, "Do you really feel sorry for what you did?" Hechter answered, "Ach, I'm not fuckin' sorry for what I did. Look—I fought for my country, I believed in what I did, and I did a good job. They were my enemy at the time. That oke over there was a terr [said while motioning to a black activist waiting to testify]. I gave him the hiding of his life and that he'll never forget. I did my job well. And I'd do it again if the circumstances called for it. No, man. I'm not really fuckin' sorry for what I did."[74]

While some like Hechter feigned impassioned remorse, others offered but lukewarm apology. ANC luminary Winnie Madikizela-Mandela offered at best tepid regret at the conclusion of the special hearings into the activities of the Mandela United Football Club, a vigilante gang of young thugs who did her bidding in Soweto. These hearings looked into the kidnapping and murder of Stompei Sepei and the murder of Abu-Baker Asvat, the physician who had examined him after his assault. Although the testimony placing her at the center of these events was overwhelming, she vehemently denied any responsibility. At the end of the ninth day of testimony, after Tutu pleaded with Madikizela-Mandela to show some sign of contrition, she replied tersely: "I am saying it is true, things went horribly wrong. I fully agree with that and for that part of those painful years when they went horribly wrong . . . for that I am deeply sorry."[75] The hearings ended "on that false note," as one commentator put it.[76] Tutu later argued: "It may have been considered a lukewarm plea, but I am not sure that we are right to scoff at even what might appear a halfhearted request for forgiveness. It is never easy to say 'I am sorry.'"[77] Does the insincerity or perfunctory tone of the apology matter? Mark Bennett and Deborah Earwaker's study suggests that victims who receive even unconvincing apologies from a perpetrator most often accept them.[78]

Others did not bother with the charade. Former National Party presidents F. W. de Klerk and P. W. Botha, as well as Inkatha Freedom Party leader Mongosuthu Buthelezi, denied personal responsibility for any acts of violence and did not apply for amnesty. (They, along with Winnie Madikizela-Mandela, were implicated in taking part in and/or in being accessories to gross human rights abuses in the TRC's final report, with the exception that de Klerk had an agreement with the TRC to omit its charges against him pending a court case.) They remain unrepentant.

The expectation by Bishop Tutu and others from the faith community that perpetrators would express remorse and victims would find it in their hearts to forgive has not universally occurred. In fact, Ron Krabill maintains that the vast majority of victims and their families opposed the amnesty of their perpetrators, and the vast majority of perpetrators offered little remorse, regret, or apology.[79] Nevertheless, former Methodist bishop Peter Storey was not concerned with the lack of contrition on the part of many amnesty applicants. He has argued that forced repentance would have devalued those moments of apparently genuine repentance that did occur.[80] Whether amnesty applicants were remorseful or not, disclosure meant at the very least acknowledging the truth about what had happened.

Notes

1. "Fault Lines" conference, Cape Town, July 4–5, 1996.

2. Statement by Marius Schoon, whose wife and daughter were murdered by the explosion of a parcel bomb sent to his wife, Jeanette, in Lubango, Angola, where she was teaching at a branch of the national university. Cited in Villa-Vicencio, "Learning to Live Together," p. 14.

3. Harold Strachan, letter to editor, *Mail & Guardian* (July 25, 1997).

4. TRC press release, "Statement—Tutu Calls On Leaders to Visit Sites of Atrocities" (May 8, 1997).

5. Bonhoeffer, *Cost of Discipleship,* p. 47.

6. Cited in Krog, *Country of My Skull,* p. 165.

7. Mark Gevisser, "Hippie Who Became Staunch," *Mail & Guardian* (February 24–March 2, 1995).

8. Naudé and Winterfeld, "South Africa," p. 9.

9. Ottaway, *Chained Together,* p. 62.

10. Lynne Duke, "For de Klerk's Party, Apartheid Is Part of a Past Best Forgotten," *Washington Post* (October 30, 1995).

11. SAPA, "FW Apologises for Apartheid but Denies Sanctioning Assassinations" (August 21, 1996).

12. Transcript of the NP recall in Cape Town, May 14, 1997.

13. Cited in Meiring, *Chronicle of the Truth Commission,* p. 360.

14. "Botha: No Apology for Apartheid," *Newsday* (November 22, 1996).

15. Botha was found guilty and sentenced to a fine and a suspended prison sentence.

16. Lynne Duke, "South Africa's Botha Offers No Apologies," *Washington Post* (January 24, 1998).

17. Ibid.

18. Eddie Koch, "The Truth and Reconciliation Commission," *Mail & Guardian* (May 19–25, 1995).

19. Human Rights Violations (HRV) hearing, East London, June 10, 1996.

20. *Truth and Reconciliation Commission of South Africa Report,* vol. 1, chap. 1, "Foreword," p. 19.

21. *Kairos Document,* p. 11.

22. HRV hearing, East London, April 17, 1996.

23. Ibid.

24. Amnesty hearing, Cape Town, July 10, 1997.

25. Cited in Scheper-Hughes, "Un-doing," p. 167.

26. Scheper-Hughes, "Un-doing," p. 169.

27. Amnesty hearing, Cape Town, October 28, 1997.

28. Fourie, "A Personal Encounter with Perpetrators," pp. 234–235.

29. Krog, *Country of My Skull,* p. 227.

30. Amnesty hearing, Cape Town, October 28, 1997.

31. Amnesty hearing, Pretoria, May 6, 1998.

32. Meiring, *Chronicle of the Truth Commission,* pp. 339–340.

33. Amnesty hearing, Cape Town, July 8, 1997.

34. HRV hearing, Johannesburg, April 29, 1996.

35. Amnesty hearing, Phokeng, May 20–21, 1996.

36. Amnesty hearing, Port Elizabeth, November 12, 1997.

37. Bisho massacre hearing, Bisho, September 11, 1996.

38. Armed forces hearing, Cape Town, October 7, 1997.

39. Amnesty hearing, Pretoria, March 25, 1998.

40. Written statement by Vuyani Papuyana, amnesty hearing, Pretoria, March 26, 1998.

41. Ibid.

42. Meiring, *Chronicle of the Truth Commission,* p. 334.

43. Cited in Storey, "A Different Kind of Justice," p. 793.

44. *Truth and Reconciliation Commission of South Africa Report,* vol. 5, chap. 9, "Reconciliation," p. 395.

45. Ivor Powell, "Where Have All the Bastards Gone?" *Mail & Guardian* (June 15–22, 2000).

46. Cited in Meiring, *Chronicle of the Truth Commission,* p. 126.

47. Ibid.

48. Ibid., pp. 376–377.

49. Cited in Meredith, *Coming to Terms,* p. 91.

50. Cited in Gevisser, "The Witnesses," p. 32.

51. "Hit Squad Leader Goes Free in South Africa," *Boston Globe* (August 9, 1997).

52. Cited in Rosenberg, "Recovering from Apartheid," p. 88.

53. Antjie Krog, "The Parable of the Bicycle," *Mail & Guardian* (February 7–13, 1997).

54. HRV hearing, Johannesburg, May 2, 1996.

55. Cited in Coetzee, "Voice of Grief," p. 19.

56. Richard Wilson, "Reconciliation and Revenge in Post-Apartheid South Africa" (paper presented at the "TRC: Commissioning the Past" Conference), pp. 16–17.

57. Ibid., p. 19.

58. Walaza, "Insufficient Healing and Reparation," p. 251.

59. Chapman, "Coming to Terms with the Past," p. 24.

60. Ibid., p. 27.

61. Simpson, "A Brief Evaluation of South Africa's Truth and Reconciliation Commission," p. 21.

62. Cited in Wilhelm Verwoerd, "Forgiving the Torturer but Not the Torture," *Sunday Independent* (December 14, 1998).

63. Hamber, "How Should We Choose to Remember?"

64. Murphy and Hampton, *Forgiveness and Mercy,* p. 90.

65. Ibid., p. 94.

66. Ibid., p. 50.

67. Arendt, *The Human Condition,* p. 241.

68. Cherry, "Historical Truth," p. 140.

69. See Muller-Fahrenholz, *The Art of Forgiveness,* pp. 4–5.

70. Villa-Vicencio, "A Cycle of Healing," p. 11.

71. Cited in Hollyday, "Hearts of Stone," p. 44.

72. Cited in Krog, *Country of My Skull,* p. 93.

73. Amnesty hearing, Pretoria, February 25, 1997.

74. Cited in Goodman, "Why Killers Should Go Free," p. 176.

75. Winnie Madikizela-Mandela, "Mandela United Football Club" hearing, Johannesburg, December 4, 1997.

76. Meredith, *Coming to Terms,* p. 270.

77. Desmond Tutu, *No Future Without Forgiveness,* pp. 174–175.

78. Bennett and Earwaker, "Victims' Responses to Apologies," p. 458.

79. Krabill, "Review of *Long Night's Journey Into Day.*"

80. Storey, "A Different Kind of Justice," p. 793.

5

Amnesty: A Controversial Compromise

Amnesty may be understood as the secular counterpart of forgiveness. The view is shared by a minority of theologians and a majority from the legal/human rights community that South Africa's Truth and Reconciliation Commission (TRC) was wrong to offer amnesty to perpetrators. For them, what was needed was punitive, retributive justice, without which reconciliation would be impossible. Victims' pent-up anger had to be addressed and channeled in a constructive way, which required nothing short of a court of law.

Theologian Willa Boesak declared that at least those at the top who gave the orders—"the Magnus Malans of the world"—could not expect mercy. (Ironically, Magnus Malan—the former defense minister charged in connection with the creation, training, and deployment of a secret hit squad that massacred thirteen people in 1987—was tried in Boesak's preferred forum, a court of law, and was acquitted.) Boesak argued that whites expected blacks not to succumb to bitterness or anger and that this "unnatural . . . patience or reasonableness" was not Christian but a distorted ethos of submissiveness. The wrath of the marginalized reflects the wrath of God, and the evildoer must be punished. Boesak drew a distinction between *wraak* (revenge, vengefulness, blind destructive fury, vindictiveness) and *vergeldig* (recompense, requital, retribution, reward). The distinction was between subjective and objective punishment, the latter finding its fulfillment in a court of justice where God's rightful avenger would become the civil authorities.[1]

Wolfram Kistner has rejoined that there are two theological approaches to reconciliation and justice. The classical approach (Boesak's "theology of retribution") holds that the offender must be punished to make atonement. Kistner has suggested that whether or not an offender is punished should be determined by considerations of how healing and reconciliation can be promoted in the life of the offender and victim. This approach would offer a basis for renouncing punishment as long as such a renunciation served the purposes of reconciliation by reintegrating offenders into the society and healing victims.[2]

Arguments on Amnesty

It was in fact the renunciation of punishment—the amnesty provision—that was the most controversial aspect of the TRC. National surveys found that more than half of those interviewed believed perpetrators should be brought to trial.[3] One interesting argument for punishment came from Andrew Horne, who argued that punishment makes the offender feel better in the long run, relieving him of feelings of guilt.[4] (Perhaps *ubuntu* should be interpreted, then, as requiring punishment so that perpetrators can fully be reintegrated into the community with a clear conscience.) Many in the human rights community were disappointed with the South African decision to offer immunity from prosecution. From his studies of the former Eastern Bloc countries, John Borneman argued that a state's failure to seek retributive justice leads to cycles of violence and counter-violence.[5] Critics claimed that a failure to punish might lead to cynicism about the rule of law and a government's commitment to human rights.

Human Rights Watch said it was opposed in principle to the granting of indemnity, maintaining that governments have a duty under international law to prosecute those guilty of gross violations of human rights.[6] Human Rights Watch's position overstated the case, as international law contains few specific regulations dealing with prosecutions.[7] It is more accurate to say that international law *permits* prosecution, but as Daan Bronkhorst has pointed out, it is more the exception than the rule to prosecute those who have committed serious human rights abuses.[8] John Dugard has noted that the United Nations (UN) in many cases, including that of South Africa, has actually welcomed amnesties as a solution.[9] At the very least, it is the obligation of states to establish the truth about the past, but this does not require punishment of perpetrators.

Some have seen in the amnesty provision a complete surrender of justice in order to mollify whites. Michael Lapsley, former pastor of the exiled African National Congress (ANC) whose hands were blown off by security police, joined others in the human rights community who opposed the decision to offer immunity from prosecution. "No trials means no justice," he said.[10] A group of victims and victims' families, including the widow of Steve Biko, fought unsuccessfully to have that section of the Promotion of National Unity and Reconciliation Act allowing for amnesty with no prospect of future criminal or civil trials deemed unconstitutional. Court trials would have meant perhaps more justice for the Bikos and others who could have afforded to wage court battles, but it would have deprived millions of the possibility of knowing the truth. Reflected Lawrence Weschler, "I prefer more truth for more people."[11]

Defenders of amnesty pointed to the necessity of political compromise. The negotiation processes of all the major political parties in the early 1990s produced a variety of compromise agreements that found their way into the 1993 interim constitution. One of these revolved around the issue of apartheid-era crimes. The National Party (NP) demanded that its supporters be indemnified from criminal prosecutions through an amnesty agreement.[12] Dullah Omar, one of the ANC negotiators, explained: "The amnesty clause in our interim constitution is the result of political negotiations. . . . [W]ithout that amnesty provision, there would have been no political settlement. It was the one issue that stood in the way of democratic elections . . . and we had to concede that the amnesty problem would be dealt with after the elections."[13] The final clause of the interim constitution reads: "In order to advance such reconciliation and reconstruction amnesty shall be granted in respect of acts, omissions, and offenses associated with political objectives, and committed in the course of the conflicts of the past." The guarantee of amnesty thus became the basis for the Promotion of National Unity and Reconciliation Act passed by the Government of National Unity in 1995.[14]

Supporters of amnesty maintained that to bring the National Party on board, concessions were necessary, and that without the amnesty guarantee the NP would have walked out of negotiations altogether. Amnesty was a compromise the ANC was forced to strike because it did not ride victorious into Pretoria on tanks, but rather came to power through a negotiated settlement.[15] ANC member of Parliament (MP) Willie Hofmeyr has said:

> We had to accept very early on that we would not get complete justice. In the negotiation process, several compromises had to be made, and I would defend them very strongly in the interests of peace in this country. We could have chosen the revolution and overthrow route, but we chose the negotiations route, and that means having to live and work

> with and rebuild the country together with people who have treated us very badly in the past and against whom we have very strong feelings.[16]

Amnesty was important not only in bringing on board the prior regime, but also in keeping them on board. Marvin Frankel argued that if soldiers and police from a former regime were treated too harshly, or if the net of punishment were cast too widely, the perpetrators would feel victimized, and there might have been a backlash.[17]

Supporters of amnesty have pointed out that, unlike truth commissions in other parts of the world, South Africa's did not offer blanket amnesty but required disclosure on an individual basis. Knowledge about the past was seen as paramount, and identifying perpetrators was one of the TRC's key tasks. The daughter of murdered activist Sicelo Mhlawuli, one of the Cradock Four, explained at the TRC's first hearing: "We want to forgive but we don't know who to forgive."[18] Amnesty was the carrot to get perpetrators to come forward with the truth. Applicants were required to fill out a prescribed form that called for very detailed information, which was published in the *Government Gazette,* and all amnesty hearings were conducted in public. Those who refused to disclose fully the details of their deeds were subject to prosecution.

The original deadline for amnesty applications was December 14, 1996. It was first extended to May 10, 1997, to allow the Section 29 subpoena process, which had only been initiated in November 1996, time to encourage potential applicants to file so as to avoid prosecution. The extension also enabled perpetrators and their lawyers to see more of the decisions being handed down and to have a better idea of how the Amnesty Committee was applying the law, especially the proportionality requirement. To encourage more applications, the TRC later extended the deadline a second time, to September 30, 1997. It was argued that since the constitutional amendment extending the amnesty cutoff date for offenses from December 6, 1993, to May 10, 1994, had only become law in late August, some perpetrators might have decided not to submit their applications until they were sure that Parliament would approve the extension of the cutoff date.[19]

All Are Guilty

That no moral distinction was made by the TRC between the violence used to maintain an unjust system and the violence employed to oppose the system has been one of the major criticisms against the commission. To compare the limited excesses of the ANC, a liberation movement that was fighting for freedom, to the colossal atrocities that were committed by an illegitimate government in an effort to shore up white supremacy was tantamount to ignoring the distinction in size between a flea and an elephant, argues Michael Lapsley.[20]

Kader Asmal, Louise Asmal, and Ronald Roberts argue in their book *Reconciliation Through Truth* that nothing in the legislation authorizing the TRC *required* the commissioners *not* to make a distinction between acts committed by perpetrators and victims.[21] But Peter Storey, on the importance of hearing about atrocities committed by both sides, has argued: "The primary cancer will always be and has always been Apartheid. But secondary infections have touched many of Apartheid's opponents and eroded their knowledge of good and evil. And one of the tragedies of life is it's possible to become that which we hate most—a ruthless abuse of power and a latitude that allow our deeds to resemble the abuses we fought against."[22]

Highlighting Storey's point was the case of Winnie Madikizela-Mandela, former wife of Nelson Mandela. Although clearly a victim herself, as she had been shamed, held in solitary confinement, banned, and harassed by the police, Winnie was also implicated in human rights violations committed at her behest by the Mandela United Football Club. Likewise, the majority of incidents of violence in KwaZulu-Natal were between black followers of the Inkatha Freedom Party (IFP) and black supporters of the ANC—rival resistance movements. The TRC's final report revealed a complex picture of individuals who were often both victim and perpetrator. Tragically, the majority of killings were committed by blacks against other blacks, not by whites against blacks—one of the most disturbing truths that TRC researchers were forced to confront.

Because the ANC believed its struggle was a moral one against an apartheid system condemned worldwide as a "crime against humanity,"[23] it initially urged its members not to seek amnesty. ANC secretary-general Cheryl Carolus argued: "We believe that every single act we engaged in was morally justified."[24] Mathews Phosa, legal adviser to the ANC, was also telling ANC members that they need not apply for amnesty. However, Bishop Desmond Tutu threatened to resign from the TRC if the ANC tried to exempt itself from the provisions of the legislation requiring all individuals involved in gross human rights abuses to apply for amnesty in order to avoid prosecutions.[25] After a meeting between the ANC and TRC, differences were ironed out and the ANC said it would no longer discourage ANC members from applying for amnesty (although it did insist on vetting members' submissions).

Tutu insisted that the Amnesty Committee was concerned not with the morality of a politically motivated offense, but only with whether the applicant could be held criminally or civilly liable for his or her actions. Tutu's thinking was echoed by deputy chair Alex Boraine, who said: "No matter how just the cause may be, if there are violations of human rights, the liberation movements must accept responsibility for them."[26] Although the ANC was adamant that it had fought a "just war," a basic tenet of just-war theory distinguishes between justice of war (jus ad bellum) and justice in war (jus in bello). It does not follow that if the cause was just, the rules of justice in war—such as the rule that noncombatants not be killed—could be ignored.[27] The bombing of Magoo's Bar in Durban, which resulted in civilian casualties (three dead and sixty-nine injured), cannot be justified by jus in bello criteria even though MK's explanation for the selection of the bar was that it was a known watering-hole for off-duty military personnel.

To a large degree, the ANC did try to follow the jus in bello requirements. Oliver Tambo, the ANC leader in exile, signed the Geneva Convention, which bound the ANC to avoid civilian targets and was the first example of a guerrilla organization signing the protocol. Tom Lodge insists: "In comparative terms—with reference to the general conduct of liberation wars in other parts of the world—the ANC fought a clean war."[28] Observers believed that the issue of evenhanded amnesty had been accepted by the ANC, but this acceptance was belied by their angry reaction to the TRC's final report, which made a finding that while they had engaged in a legitimate struggle, the ANC had nevertheless committed gross violations of human rights for which they were morally and politically accountable. Deputy president Thabo Mbeki accused the TRC of an "artificial even-handedness" and attempted to interdict the publication of the report.

Applying the Amnesty Principles

The legislation provided that amnesty not be granted for crimes that were motivated by "personal gain, or out of malice, ill will, or spite." Commissioners had to assess the relationship between the act and the object pursued, "in particular the directness and proximity of the relationship and the proportionality of the act, omission, or offense to the objective pursued."[29]

To be political, an act had to have been committed by a member or supporter of a "publicly known political organization or liberation movement" or by an employee of the state, either acting "in furtherance of a political struggle (including both acts by or against the state and acts by one political organization or liberation movement against another) or with the object of countering or otherwise resisting the said struggle." The act had to have been committed "in the course and scope of his or her duties and within the scope of his or her express or implied authority."[30]

The first two cases before the Amnesty Committee, heard on May 20–21, 1996, and decided on August 30, 1996, granted amnesty to Boy Diale and Christopher Makgale for the murder on December 29, 1990, of Glad Mokgatle. Mokgatle had been appointed by Bophuthatswana president Lucas Mangope to be chair of the Tribal Council for the Bafokeng tribe, in which capacity he was to administer tribal affairs on behalf of a regime that the Bafokeng people, because they rejected incorporation into the Bophuthatswana homeland, had not accepted. Although Diale and Makgale had been convicted previously in a court of law for the murder, the committee concluded that since they had believed they were acting on behalf of the Bafokeng people in furtherance of their political struggle against an oppressive regime, the crime was associated with a political objective and therefore qualified for amnesty.[31]

The Amnesty Committee announced its second set of amnesty decisions on September 2, 1996, when it denied the applications of Johan van Eyk and Hendrik Gerber, who had been convicted for murdering Samuel Nganakga. The two applicants had been employed with Fidelity Guards in Johannesburg. They suspected that a third employee, Nganakga, had participated in a theft from the company. After torturing Nganakga by shocking his testicles, hanging him upside down from a tree, and setting a fire underneath him, they shot him dead when he tried to escape. Realizing they could get in trouble, they then burned and buried his body.

In their amnesty applications, van Eyk and Gerber argued that the deceased had had contacts with the Pan-Africanist Congress (PAC). But they were not able to show either the court or the Amnesty Committee any evidence that Nganakga had had political connections, nor could they show that they had been politically motivated to act as they did. Citing testimony indicating that the applicants had been in the habit of using torture to elicit information from suspects, the commissioners concluded that they had not acted in furtherance of political goals; they had suspected Nganakga of being a thief, nothing more.[32] (This case highlights the fact that many amnesty applicants were common criminals who were hoping that they could present their acts in political terms and so be freed from prison—about three-fourths of the 7,000 applicants were deemed liable for ordinary crimes rather than human rights violations and were denied amnesty.)

Brian Mitchell was the first former security force member to be granted amnesty. The former commander of the New Hanover police station, Mitchell had in April 1992 been sentenced to death for eleven counts of murder, and to three years imprisonment for each of two counts of attempted murder (the death sentence was later commuted to life imprisonment when the death penalty was banned). The Amnesty Committee noted that United Democratic Front (UDF) activists had sparked violence in the New Hanover area in October 1988 by attacking Inkatha youth. Mitchell, who had close links with the Joint Management Committee system (the government's counterrevolutionary mechanism), had considered it his duty to counter the ANC/UDF in his area. It was decided after talks with a superior officer and Inkatha leaders that special constables would assist in an attack on UDF activists in the Trust Feed area, targeting males between sixteen and thirty-five years of age who were involved in political violence. The constables launched the attack in the early hours of December 3, 1988, killing eleven people and wounding two others. Shortly after the incident, it was discovered that the constables had attacked the wrong house and that the people killed and injured were not the intended victims.

"Applicant was not at the scene and did not take part in the actual attack, but it is quite clear that the execution of the whole plan was directed by him in his capacity as the station commander of the area," the Amnesty Committee said. "It is also clear that the special constables acted on his instructions and were accountable to him." In granting amnesty, the committee concluded: "[The] applicant's offenses were part of the counterrevolutionary onslaught against the African National Congress and the United Democratic Front activists and [he acted] within the course and scope of his duties as an officer in the South African Police force."[33]

The decision to grant amnesty to Brian Mitchell was painful to the families of the victims. Their resulting anger was understandable, Tutu said, and was an indication that the TRC had not done enough to warn people about the price that had to be paid for stability in South Africa: "Amnesty is going to cause people a lot of heartbreak." The decision was announced on the very day Tutu was scheduled to deliver remarks to an Afrikaner group who had told him it believed no former security force members were likely to be awarded amnesty. "This was a wonderful coincidence. [It] pulled the carpet from under their feet," Tutu noted, "showing people that the Amnesty Committee was not biased."[34]

As of one week prior to the original amnesty deadline of December 14, 1996, only four decisions had been made.[35] No doubt it was the slowness in announcing decisions that had kept perpetrators from coming forward until they could see how judges were going to interpret the legislation.[36] Just what constituted "politically motivated acts"? What did "proportionality to objectives" mean? It was especially the ambiguity and murkiness surrounding these clauses that kept many perpetrators away. Those guilty of more serious crimes feared that they might not get amnesty, despite confessing, because of the proportionality clause, and so many stayed away in the gamble that they would not be caught.

Despite the paucity of decisions, amnesty applications were submitted in unprecedented numbers as the revised May 10, 1997, deadline approached. In just the final two months before this deadline, some 1,000 people applied. The steady stream of applications had became a virtual torrent, bringing the tally to 7,124. The PAC announced that its entire Azanian People's Liberation Army (APLA) high command of senior officers as well as some 600 cadres would apply (but more than 130 APLA/PAC applications were declared invalid because it was unclear which individuals were applying and what specific deeds had been committed). The ANC applied for amnesty for thirty-seven leaders, including then deputy president Thabo Mbeki and five senior cabinet members—Mac Maharaj, Alfred Nzo, Pallo Jordan, Dullah Omar, and Joe Modise—in applications that accepted joint responsibility for acts committed by followers. Although the committee granted them amnesty, the TRC itself challenged the amnesties in court because the committee had not followed the prescribed guidelines for full disclosure of individuals' acts. For instance, Wally Serote had applied for amnesty for "acts unknown to me unless stated otherwise by individual amnesty applicants." Peter Mokaba likewise applied for amnesty for acts "detailed by individual applicants who may implicate me."[37] A new Amnesty Committee convened to reconsider the applications and determined that, since no one personally had been involved in executing or ordering any actions constituting gross human rights violations, "their applications fall outside the ambit of the . . . act and accordingly they do not [need] to apply for amnesty."[38]

Constand Viljoen, a former defense minister and leader of the right-wing Freedom Front, applied for amnesty for preelection bombings and other acts of violence he ordered in the run-up to the 1994 elections. And Eugene Terre'Blanche, a leader of the Afrikaner Weerstandsbeweging

(AWB; Afrikaner Resistance Movement), applied for his tarring and feathering of Professor Floors van Jaarsveld in 1979, and for his part in the battle of Ventersdorp in August 1991 when he clashed with police during a meeting held by F. W. de Klerk in the town, resulting in three deaths.

One last-minute submission was the thousand-page application of Eugene de Kock, the jailed former police commander of Vlakplaas—the notorious base near Pretoria that had been the center of the government's death-squad operations. He had been convicted of eighty-seven charges of murder and sentenced to two life terms plus 212 years. According to George Bizos, it was not remorse but the knowledge that de Kock (nicknamed "Prime Evil") was going to reveal all in his amnesty application and bring down other members of the security police with him that encouraged so many policemen to apply in the last few days.[39] Conversely, since former defense minister Magnus Malan had been acquitted in a court trial and refused to apply for amnesty, the military was effectively off the hook. They knew their misdeeds would remain hidden so long as no one squealed, and accordingly there were few applications for amnesty from this group.[40]

Another applicant was Piet Koornhof, a former NP cabinet minister once responsible for forced removals and identity-pass laws. He called his amnesty application a "symbolic act of asking for forgiveness." Applying for amnesty, he said, was "a sign of feeling intensely sorry."[41] Koornhof was only the second NP cabinet member to file for amnesty (following Adriaan Vlok, former minister of law and order).

Noticeably absent from the total were applications from former presidents P. W. Botha and F. W. de Klerk, former deputy minister Magnus Malan (who spent the day of the deadline on the golf course), and IFP leader Mongosuthu Buthelezi, who said he would not apply because he never killed anyone or ordered anyone's death.[42] Missing too were applications from former members of the South African Defense Force (SADF). Former defense chief general Jannie Geldenhuys said he was tired of talk about the "apartheid military machine." He foresaw endless complications if all of the 300,000 SADF solders who took part in military operations during the apartheid years were to ask for amnesty. If only half applied, he maintained, the cost, time, and administrative implications would have been enormous.[43] But Bishop Tutu did not see these concerns as a problem for the TRC: "It's a problem for them. I'm not the one who's going to jail."[44]

While some of the "foot soldiers" of the old regime (especially police) came forward, few senior officials, including politicians and generals who had ultimate responsibility for implementing apartheid, applied. Many of them were continuing to play a prominent role in the new South Africa and no doubt were betting that the ANC government would lack the will to prosecute. Approximately 3,000 of the amnesty applications were from applicants already convicted of crimes and serving sentences, and very few were from members of the National Party, the Inkatha Freedom Party, or the former South African Defense Force. Nevertheless, individuals from these organizations were implicated in the TRC's final report.

Amnesty Versus Prosecution

Despite assumptions that courts of law produce more justice, it is not at all certain that Nuremberg-type legal prosecutions ensure more justice for victims. To equate "pure justice" with the court route and only something vastly inferior with the TRC route would be to create a false dichotomy.

In any criminal court proceeding, the aim of the defense team is to produce legal arguments to challenge and exclude from the record some of the most basic information used in persuasive storytelling. Witnesses are not permitted to tell their stories in their own way. Rather they are required to answer hostile cross-examinations posed by the defendant's attorney in an adversarial setting as opposed to the supportive forum that the TRC provided.[45] Richard Wilson writes that since the TRC was not a legal forum, there was "little interruption of narratives on violence by lawyers calling attention to picayune legal technicalities."[46] In many ways, the TRC process ensured respect for the human dignity of the witnesses, something that would not have happened in court proceedings. For example, a courtroom audience stands when the judge enters, whereas at the TRC hearings, the audience stood when the victims scheduled to testify entered the room. The empathetic counselors that Tutu provided for witnesses before, during, and after their testimony would not have been made available for them in a court of law. The TRC forum put the victim rather than the perpetrator on center stage.[47]

Also, traditional judicial courts require hard evidence in order to convict, and in the cases of perpetrators of atrocities in South Africa, much essential evidence had been destroyed (in its final report, the TRC pointed to shredded documents as the major impediment in its investigations). The burden of proof in a court trial is beyond reasonable doubt; inevitably, many of those accused would have been acquitted. Findings by the TRC, on the other hand, were made by a balance of evidence.

The prosecution of former defense minister Magnus Malan is illustrative: despite a seven-month trial and spending 7 million rand (plus 9 million rand for his defense, since the state was obliged to pay the legal bills of state employees), the attorney general of KwaZulu-Natal was not successful in securing a guilty verdict on the charge that Malan had ordered the hit-squad murder of thirteen people (mainly women and children) at a prayer meeting in KwaMukutha, a village south of Durban, in 1987.[48] (Malan later appeared before the TRC and, while denying some allegations, admitted to much more than his trial had revealed.) For Tutu, the Malan verdict proved that the TRC was a better forum for dealing with South Africa's past.[49]

At the time of Malan's acquittal, critics claimed that attorney general Tim McNally had mishandled the case. Fred Hendricks wondered if the attorneys general "[a]t the very least . . . lack the experience for securing prosecutions now that they do not have on their side a security establishment which could, under duress and torture, force confessions out of offenders."[50] Less cynically, Paul Van Zyl has suggested that the South African criminal justice system was virtually dysfunctional—from the capacity of police to investigate and arrest, to the ability of attorneys general to prosecute, judges to convict, and correctional facilities to imprison. Only 4 percent of those who committed crimes such as murder, armed robbery, rape, and serious assaults spent more than two years in jail.[51] Court trials, then, may not be appropriate in societies that are in transition from authoritarianism to democracy, or where there is a weak or nonexistent commitment to the rule of law.

Another advantage of truth commissions over prosecutions is that they can cover an extended period more quickly and efficiently than criminal trials. Says Richard Goldstone, a constitutional court judge and former prosecutor of the Rwandan and Bosnian war-crime tribunals: "If one had to bring to court all the perpetrators of human rights abuses during the last 40 years, there just would not be enough courts to deal with it."[52]

In the TRC setting, a perpetrator may have received amnesty, but at least there was a full accounting of what had happened. Trial defendants, on the other hand, often lie or invoke the right to silence, thereby compromising the historical record. On the success of the amnesty offer at getting to the truth, Bishop Tutu exclaimed at the time: "I am thrilled by the new information that has come in among applications about the Pebco Three and Cradock Four—and especially Steve Biko. We've never got this information before and the country deserves to have it. This uncovering more or less justifies the existence of the Commission."[53]

As amnesty applicants began to confess their deeds, the truth about many cases began to surface. Establishing the identities of everyone responsible for the various violations may have been only partially successful, but amnesty applicants named others in their affidavits who in turn were subpoenaed as witnesses or decided to apply for amnesty themselves lest they be prosecuted. History was recorded with South Africans coming closer to a common view of the recent past, which hopefully will prevent future revisionism. Michael Ignatieff's assertion that amnesty contributed to "reducing the number of permissible lies in circulation" is apt.[54]

Nevertheless, there has been criticism that the full truth did not come out. One high-profile case involving the killers of Steve Biko points to the limited success the TRC's Amnesty Committee had in uncovering the entire truth. The five amnesty applicants denied that they had intended to kill Steve Biko in police custody, calling his death an accident that occurred after he had hit his head against a wall following a scuffle with his interrogators. Their testimony disappointed many in the audience, who found their stories simply not credible, and not very much different from the versions they had recounted twenty years previously at an inquest.[55] George Bizos, the attorney representing the Biko family at the amnesty hearing, insisted that the five applicants had not made full disclosure. "Statements made at the inquest have merely been modified to try to explain away concrete evidence which did not fit in with the false evidence given at the inquest." Nor did he believe they had a political motive when they killed Biko. "Torturing helpless detainees for the purposes of exacting information to the point that they end up dead is not a political objective," he argued.[56] At the end of their amnesty hearings, no one had identified which of the five had delivered the fatal blow to the activist's head. The Amnesty Committee ultimately rejected their amnesty arguments and these men may ultimately be prosecuted, although after so many years the prospect seems unlikely.

The Biko case highlights the imprecision inherent in the application of the amnesty criteria. Amnesty was rejected because the commissioners did not believe there was full disclosure or that there was a political motive. Some observers were surprised by this decision, since killing the leader of the very highly political Black Consciousness Movement would seem obviously a political act.[57]

Another case in which the perpetrators did not reveal all was that of the PEBCO Three, leaders of the Port Elizabeth Black Civic Organization. They had been telephoned and asked to meet someone from the British embassy at the airport. They never returned. Security police applied for amnesty for abducting and torturing the PEBCO Three, but they presented three different versions of events. According to Gideon Nieuwoudt, the white security policeman from Port Elizabeth, the three had been taken to a remote farm, where they were interrogated but not tortured, and drugged before being shot. Their bodies were burnt, and their ashes thrown into the Fish River. But according to a black policeman and an askari, the men had been brutally tortured during interrogation, and then killed one by one in each other's presence. In Joe Mamasela's (the askari's) version, one of the three had confessed to being a paid informer of the National Intelligence Service (NIS). They kept him alive overnight to verify the story. An NIS officer confirmed that he had worked for them, but gave the go-ahead for the agent to be killed anyway on the grounds that he had not been of great use to them. The three different versions of course indicate that someone was lying.

Political Motive and Proportionality

In a controversial decision, the TRC in June 1998 granted amnesty to the killers in the St. James Church massacre, where PAC followers five years earlier had attacked parishioners at worship, killing eleven and injuring fifty-six. The killers were adjudged to have passed the "political motive" test. Members of the Amnesty Committee accepted that the killers had "believed they were advancing the struggle of the PAC which was waging a war against the National Party–led government."[58] Still, critics wondered how they possibly could have passed the "proportionality" test. How did the indiscriminate massacre of worshipers at a church (a multiracial church at that) fit any notion of proportionality?

Commenting on how political motive and proportionality were weighed, Nkosinathi Biko, son of Steve Biko, criticized the amnesties given to the killers of Fabian and Florence Ribeiro and Griffiths and Victoria Mxenge: "I am uncertain how the killers of Florence Ribeiro, a mother and housewife, could have gotten around the political motive requirement. I am equally uncertain how the killers of Mxenge, whose brutal murder is surpassed by few others, met the proportionality requirement."[59] Apparently the Amnesty Committee jettisoned all notions of proportionality. In an article written before the TRC began operation, Peter Parker explained that although the legislation establishing the TRC set out the Norgaard principles regarding proportionality and political motivation,[60] the Amnesty Committee was nonetheless instructed in applying them to take into account the criteria applied in the Indemnity Act of 1990 and Further Indemnity Act of 1992.[61] Since under the Further Indemnity Act a political act was anything a person believed or was told was political, one would have expected broad interpretation by the committee.

Another publicized amnesty hearing was that of the killers of Amy Biehl, the twenty-six-year-old American Fulbright scholar beaten and stabbed by a mob in August 1993. One of the four PAC members seeking amnesty for the murder, Ntobeko Peni, had argued that it was carried out with the approval of the regional executive of the Pan-Africanist Students Organization (PASO). Explaining the political motive, Peni said: "I rose against the government and in the process a white woman was killed." Testifying at his amnesty hearing, Peni said: "The order was we should make South Africa ungovernable, burn down government vehicles—and every white person we came across was an enemy."[62] Fellow amnesty petitioner Mangezi Manqina explained: "I stabbed Amy Biehl because I saw her as a 'target,' a 'settler.'" Peni rejected Judge Andrew Wilson's suggestion that this was a mindless, savage attack with no political motivation: "Our killing Amy Biehl had everything to do with politics—the unrest at the time and international attention helped bring South Africa to where we are today."[63]

The committee granted amnesty to Amy Biehl's killers, again emphasizing the political motivation: "One of the applicants said during evidence that they all submitted to the slogan 'One Settler, One Bullet.' To them this meant every white person was an enemy of the black people. At that moment, to them, Amy Biehl was a representative of the white community. They believed that by killing white civilians, APLA was sending a serious political message to the government."[64] This decision in particular was controversial because the leadership of the PAC had denied giving an order to kill Amy Biehl. The applicants instead relied on the implied authority of political speeches. Biehl's parents, who had traveled from California to attend their daughter's killers' amnesty hearing, did not oppose the amnesty application, saying they believed in the importance of the process South Africans had chosen to heal themselves. And what of proportionality? Was killing an innocent white foreign student proportionate to the political aims? Since the Biehl family did not oppose amnesty, one cannot rule out the possibility that extraneous factors influenced the decision.

Amnesty was also granted in the case of the Heidelberg Tavern attack, killings by APLA members of patrons at a Cape Town bar. The Amnesty

Committee decided that the three applicants who had killed four people and wounded five others met the requirements for amnesty because "they were acting on behalf of APLA, a publicly-known organisation. . . . [They] did not act for personal gain or out of personal malice, ill-will or spite . . . and . . . they had no personal knowledge of the victims."[65] The decision made no mention of proportionality.

It should not be surprising that full disclosure became the only criterion for amnesty. If amnesty was the carrot to induce perpetrators to come forward, it would have done no good to insist that they also meet the other requirements. As Fred Hendricks has observed: "Amnesty has to appear to be working, if it is to act as an incentive to perpetrators. The only sure way in which it would appear to be working is if state criminals and other perpetrators are actually allowed to (literally) get away with murder."[66]

If amnesties were granted in these cases, why were they not for Clive Derby-Lewis and Janusz Walus, convicted killers of Chris Hani? New National Party spokesperson Jacko Maree criticized the decision at the time: "The danger exists that the Amnesty Committee may be tempted to apply different norms and standards depending on who the applicants are and what the political pressure may be."[67] Killing Chris Hani, a charismatic political leader and secretary-general of the Communist Party second in popularity only to Nelson Mandela, was clearly a political act. Although the Conservative Party (CP) did not authorize the killing, its leader, Ferdi Hartzenberg, testified during the hearing that Derby-Lewis and Walus could have interpreted militant talk by party leaders at the time as a sanction to use violence in promoting CP aims. "I said some strong things myself which could have been interpreted as an instruction to do something," Hartzenberg said. He suggested that articles in the CP newspaper *Patriot* that spoke of taking up arms were a reflection of party policy. "I think these contributed to their actions. We were living in a time of high tensions, and people could have argued it was the right time to act."[68] This was hardly different from the testimony of the PAC that their slogan "One Settler, One Bullet" could have incited the students to kill Amy Biehl. But the Amnesty Committee did not see it that way. Its main finding was that the two applicants had failed to prove that the killing was politically motivated: "The CP has never adopted, propagated or espoused a policy of violence or assassination of political opponents."[69]

The committee also found that Derby-Lewis and Walus had failed to make full disclosure. Where they tripped up was in their testimony of a list of high-profile names that had been given to them by Derby-Lewis's wife, a journalist. They insisted that this was not a "hit list," a statement the committee found not to be credible. The commissioners felt Derby-Lewis and Walus were not disclosing all, perhaps in an attempt to shield Mrs. Lewis, who had not applied for amnesty. Also, they were vague about the acquisition of the weapon, again possibly to protect others. Communist Party secretary-general Blade Nzimande said, "We would like to say to them that we know that there was a wider conspiracy in the murder of Chris Hani."[70]

To contribute to the truth about the past, full disclosure was paramount, and full disclosure clearly trumped all other criteria for amnesty. Hendricks asserted: "If there is even a hint that part of the story has been distorted or hidden, the Amnesty Committee has not granted amnesty."[71] Unfortunately for many amnesty applicants, they claimed not to remember what they did. Police captain Jeffrey Benzien, when facing one of his victims at his amnesty hearing, denied remembering him. He denied also ever using a broomstick to sodomize victims as his victims had claimed.[72] (In a sense, the victim was revictimized, for instead of having his pain acknowledged, it was trivialized.)

Were these examples of actual memory loss or simply lies? Psychologists in South Africa have attempted to explain this phenomenon as memory impairment brought on by trauma, a symptom of post–traumatic stress syndrome.[73] Nevertheless, it was to the advantage of amnesty applicants to disclose fully so that they would receive amnesty. Most amnesty applicants gave long descriptions of who had given the orders, in order to meet the political motive requirement, followed by grisly details of their deeds, in order to meet the full disclosure mandate. As a result of this process, the TRC established that certain people were directly involved in specific human rights violations, "an accomplishment that no other similar commission has achieved."[74]

As discussed in Chapter 4, critics have also made much of the fact that there was no requirement for remorse in the TRC legislation. As political analyst Stephen Friedman, director of the Center of Policy Studies in Johannesburg, has complained: "They don't even have to say that they are sorry or that they would not do it again."[75] Friedman believes it would have been better if amnesty applicants had been required to show repentance and possibly to commit themselves to some kind of community service. For James Gilligan, remorse is the more important component; he has argued that it is an index of the likelihood of recidivism.[76]

Judged by Nicholas Tavuchis's definition of apology—"To apologise is to declare voluntarily that one has *no* excuse, defense, justification or explanation for an action (or inaction)"[77]—hardly anyone, especially in leadership, truly apologized during the hearings. Leaders and followers alike hedged and qualified their apologies to the point of meaninglessness. A newspaper headline at the time reflected this: "Ag, we're sort of sorry," it said.[78]

A Second Amnesty?

The day after the amnesty deadline,[79] Minister of Justice Dullah Omar stated that attorneys-general would be duty-bound to prosecute perpetrators of apartheid-era crimes who had not applied to the TRC if sufficient evidence to prosecute existed.[80] Omar's statement was some consolation to the critics of amnesty, who saw it as an obsequious attempt at white appeasement. But more recently, Omar has said that any decision to prosecute would have to take into account "the national interest."[81] In its final report, the TRC recommended that where amnesty had not been sought or had been denied, prosecutions should be considered, and it submitted to the office of the national director of public prosecutions a list of 100 alleged perpetrators.[82] (Apparently, the TRC was split on how vigorously to support prosecutions, with Tutu advocating not to go ahead, and others supporting the prosecutions of at least some key perpetrators.)[83]

President Thabo Mbeki has hinted at a second amnesty and asked for a review of the TRC legislation to allow people to be granted amnesty without having to apply individually. Soldiers of the old SADF and those involved in KwaZulu-Natal violence should qualify, he has said.[84] But new justice minister Penuell Maduna denied that the government was contemplating a change to a general amnesty: "Those who failed to apply for amnesty when they had the chance only have themselves to blame."[85] Human Rights Watch also warned against a second amnesty: "Granting repeated amnesties can lead to a culture of impunity, and that is exactly what South Africa needs to avoid," said Peter Takirambudde, director of its Africa division.[86] Mandela himself spoke strongly against a second amnesty, pledging "to resist a general amnesty with every power I have."[87] The idea of an indiscriminate pardon does not square with the government's avowed commitment to rebuilding the rule of law and a human rights culture. Neil Kritz points out that the failure to prosecute will effectively emasculate the South African model of threatening prosecutions for those who do not come forward.[88]

Barney Pityana, head of the Human Rights Commission, feels differently about post-TRC prosecutions:

> [I]t is difficult to square this belief of the Commission in restorative justice with its strong call for the prosecution of those who were not granted amnesty or who failed to apply for amnesty. . . . They would simply raise the hopes of the victims, commit resources that are required to finance other pressing national priorities like the levels of crime. . . . Those who have escaped the net of the TRC must receive forgiveness by the nation. In that way we can all make the much-delayed beginning and construct our lives into the future. We cannot afford the futility of the Magnus Malan trials.[89]

At the time of this writing, no general amnesties have been given. Neither have any unsuccessful amnesty applicants been prosecuted. In her comparative study of truth commissions, Priscilla Hayner states that prosecutions are "very rare" after a truth commission report is published.[90] It is unlikely that any of those found guilty of human rights violations without amnesty—including P. W. Botha, Magnus Malan, Mongosuthu Buthelezi, or Winnie Madikizela-Mandela—will be prosecuted.

Notes

1. Boesak, "Truth, Justice, and Reconciliation," pp. 65–69.
2. Kistner, "The Biblical Understanding of Reconciliation," p. 89.
3. Rickard, "Fierce Emotions As S. Africa Seeks Peace," p. 12.
4. Horne, "Reflections on Remorse in Forensic Psychotherapy," p. 23.
5. Borneman, *Settling Accounts,* p. 5.
6. "South Africa: Threats to a New Democracy." For a hard-line view on the duty to prosecute, see especially Orentlicher, "Settling Accounts."
7. The Nuremberg principles of the 1945–1946 military tribunal against the Nazi war criminals asserted that crimes against humanity could be tried in an international court because they offended humanity itself. The Genocide Convention of 1948 (Article 4) provides that genocide is a punishable crime. The Apartheid Convention of 1973 classifies apartheid as a crime against humanity and provides for prosecution in a court of law in one of the states involved, or in an international criminal tribunal. The Convention Against Torture of 1985 requires that states submit cases to the competent authorities for prosecution, but does not require that actual prosecution take place. The Fourth Geneva Convention (Article 146) states that parties shall bring persons alleged to have committed serious breaches before its own courts, or hand them over to another High Contracting Party.

8. Bronkhorst, *Truth and Reconciliation,* p. 91.

9. Dugard, "The Third Manfred Lachs Memorial Lecture," p. 4.

10. Cited in Eddie Koch, "The Truth and Reconciliation Commission," *Mail & Guardian* (May 19–25, 1995).

11. Weschler, cited in Steiner, ed., *Truth Commissions,* p. 52.

12. The NP government had enacted the 1990 Indemnity Act, allowing for nonprosecution for returning exiles, and the Further Indemnity Act of 1992. The Promotion of National Unity and Reconciliation Act superseded the Further Indemnity Act, which was viewed as the government giving itself self-amnesties, reminiscent of the Punto Final (Full Stop) legislation in which the Argentinian military introduced a self-amnesty.

13. Dullah Omar, "Opening Address," reporting the TRC conference, Johannesburg, March 1–2, 1996.

14. Although the National Party favored a blanket amnesty, the ANC insisted on conditional amnesty—amnesty offered to perpetrators on an individual basis in exchange for full disclosure.

15. Tina Rosenberg's view is that Mandela's government was so popular that it probably could have reversed the constitutional provision of amnesty but chose not to because its leaders genuinely believed in reconciliation. See Rosenberg, "Recovering from Apartheid," p. 91.

16. Cited in Gevisser, "Truth and Reconciliation," pp. 920–921.

17. Frankel, *Out of the Shadows of the Night,* pp. 103–104.

18. Human Rights Violations (HRV) hearing, East London, April 16, 1996.

19. SAPA, "Amnesty Application Deadline Extended to September 30" (September 1, 1997).

20. Cited in Boraine, Levy, and Scheffer, eds., *Dealing with the Past,* p. 29.

21. Asmal, Asmal, and Roberts, *Reconciliation Through Truth,* pp. 14–15.

22. Cited in Krog, *Country of My Skull,* p. 248.

23. The UN Security Council stated in 1976 that "apartheid is a crime against the conscience and dignity of mankind." In 1984, the Security Council passed Resolution 556, which declared apartheid to be "a crime against humanity." The United States abstained from voting.

24. SAPA, "TRC Members Not Morally Neutral: Tutu" (March 7, 1997).

25. SAPA, "Cabinet to Discuss Extending Amnesty Cut-Off Date" (October 25, 1996).

26. SAPA, "TRC Members Not Morally Neutral: Tutu" (March 7, 1997).

27. The ANC's position led to a debate on just-war theory in South Africa sponsored by the Western Cape office of the TRC on May 6, 1997.

28. Tom Lodge, "Taking Great Pains to Justify a 'Clean War,'" *Mail & Guardian* (August 23–29, 1996).

29. Promotion of National Unity and Reconciliation Act (no. 34 of 1995).

30. Ibid.

31. TRC press release, "The Decision and Reasons of the Amnesty Committee in the Matter of Boy Diale and Christopher Makgale" (August 30, 1996).

32. TRC press release, "Decision and Reasons Therefore in the Matter of Johan van Eyk (First Applicant) and Hendrik Gerber (Second Applicant)" (September 2, 1996).

33. TRC press release, "Application #2586/96—Applicant: Brian Mitchell: Decision and Reasons, Therefore" (December 10, 1996).

34. SAPA, "Amnesty Will Cause Heartbreak" (December 11, 1996).

35. Krog, *Country of My Skull,* p. 118.

36. Coming forward to disclose their crimes and request amnesty has not kept individuals from being indicted. This undoubtedly increased perpetrators' uneasiness about the truth process.

37. www.woza.co.za/dp90.htm (December 4, 1997).

38. SAPA, "ANC Leaders Need Not Apply for Amnesty" (March 4, 1999).

39. Bizos, *No One to Blame?* p. 236.

40. Christie, *The South African Truth Commission,* p. 140.

41. SAPA, "7,700 Amnesty Applications Received by Midnight Deadline Saturday" (May 10, 1997).

42. SAPA, "Amnesty Committee Faces Monumental Task" (May 11, 1997).

43. SAPA, "Truth Commission Hostile Against SADF, Says Former Chief" (March 15, 1997).

44. SAPA, "Amnesty Applications Stream In" (December 11, 1996).

45. Although the commissioners worked under time constraints and attempted to hear ten to twelve witnesses a day, their efforts to get witnesses to stick to their presubmitted testimony and not to stray off track, and to tell only what was relevant, went unheeded. Even when told to start at a certain point, the witnesses invariably said they would start somewhere else in the story—much earlier—and then did just that.

46. Richard Wilson, "The Sizwe Will Not Go Away," p. 16.

47. As a result of a lawsuit, *DuPreez and Van Rensburg vs. TRC,* the TRC was required to give twenty-one days' notice to anyone named as a perpetrator in a victim statement. This finding impacted negatively on the sensitive, supportive atmosphere for victims, who ran the risk of confrontation and cross-examination from the accused.

48. Ironically, the state would foot the bills of former government officials and functionaries prosecuted in the courts, because they were claiming their innocence, but not the legal bills of those going the TRC route, because these people were admitting their guilt—another disincentive for coming forward. However, if subpoenaed, the TRC was authorized to offer legal assistance.

49. SAPA, "Malan Verdict: Truth Body Better Bet Than Court Says Tutu" (October 11, 1996).

50. Hendricks, "Amnesty and Justice in Post Apartheid South Africa," p. 6.

51. Van Zyl, "Truth and Reconciliation in South Africa," pp. 651–652.

52. SAPA, "Failure to Deal with the Dark Past Spells Disaster: Goldstone" (August 14, 1997).

53. Cited in Krog, *Country of My Skull,* p. 156.

54. Ignatieff, "Articles of Faith," p. 113.

55. Alex Russell, "We Didn't Intend to Kill Biko," *The Daily Telegraph* (September 11, 1997).

56. Cited in Meredith, *Coming to Terms,* p. 82.

57. The *Citizen* editorialized: "The Amnesty Committee says the killing of Mr. Biko was 'not an act associated with a political objective.' Extraordinary.

How much more political can you get?" See "Amnesties Not Even," *Citizen* (February 22, 1999).

58. Amnesty hearing decision, June 11, 1998.

59. Biko, "Amnesty and Denial," p. 195.

60. The principles adopted by the Amnesty Committee, including "the proportional relationship between the act and any political objective," were adopted from those set forth by Carl Aage Norgaard, president of the European Commission of Human Rights, for use in the 1989 settlement in Namibia.

61. Parker, "The Politics of Indemnities, Truth Telling, and Reconciliation in South Africa," p. 6.

62. Amnesty hearing, Cape Town, July 8, 1997.

63. Ibid.

64. Amnesty hearing decision, July 28, 1998.

65. Amnesty hearing decision, July 15, 1998.

66. Hendricks, "Amnesty and Justice in Post Apartheid South Africa," p. 9.

67. SAPA, "Hani's Killers Face Life Imprisonment After Amnesty Denied" (April 7, 1999).

68. Amnesty hearing, Benoni, December 3, 1997.

69. Amnesty hearing decision, April 7, 1999.

70. SAPA, "SACP Leader Calls for Investigation Into Hani Murder to Be Reopened" (April 11, 1999).

71. Hendricks, "Amnesty and Justice in Post Apartheid South Africa," p. 11.

72. Benzien was granted amnesty. Because he admitted to so many violations, and even demonstrated the "wet bag" method of torture to the TRC, his inability to remember sodomizing a victim was overlooked.

73. Krog, *Country of My Skull,* p. 78.

74. Ronald Slye, review of Jeffery Anthea's *The Truth About the Truth Commission,* in *Southern African Review of Books* (November 1999), www.uni-ulm.de/~rturrell/sarobnewhtml/trcindex.html.

75. SAPA, "South Africans Find Truth and Reconciliation a Tall Order" (August 25, 1997).

76. Gilligan, "The Agenbite of Inwit," p. 34.

77. Tavuchis, *Mea Culpa,* p. 17 (original emphasis).

78. Villa-Vicencio, "Restorative Justice," p. 74.

79. The deadline was extended once again to September 30, 1997. Since the constitutional amendment extending the amnesty cutoff date from December 6, 1993, to May 10, 1994, had only become law in late August 1997, it was believed that some perpetrators might have decided not to submit their applications until they were sure that Parliament would approve this extension.

80. SAPA, "AGs Now Duty-Bound to Prosecute Apartheid-Era Criminals: Omar" (May 11, 1997).

81. Cited in Meredith, *Coming to Terms,* p. 322.

82. *Truth and Reconciliation Commission of South Africa Report,* vol. 5, chap. 8, "Recommendations," p. 309.

83. Chapman, "Coming to Terms with the Past," p. 26.

84. According to Alex Boraine, Mbeki in a private interview with Mandela warned of dire consequences if members of the security forces had to risk prosecution. See Boraine, "Truth and Reconciliation in South Africa," p. 143.

85. SAPA, "No General Amnesty, Maduna Says" (June 28, 1999).

86. SAPA, "Human Rights Watch Applauds Decision to Deny ANC Leaders Amnesty" (March 6, 1999).

87. SAPA, "Mandela Rejects Blanket Amnesty" (December 6, 1998).

88. Cited in Shea, "Are Truth Commissions Just a Fad?" p. 35.

89. Pityana, "Reconciliation After the TRC."

90. Hayner, "Fifteen Truth Commissions—1974 to 1994," p. 600.

6

Storytelling

Individual Stories

"The psychologies of remorse, guilt, catharsis, and closure compete today with the theologies of reconciliation, forgiveness, and redemption," wrote one analyst.[1] Yet it was not the competition but rather the synthesis of psychological and theological insights that marked the work of South Africa's Truth and Reconciliation Commission (TRC). One commentator has called this the "psycho-religious" model of healing.[2] A South African journalist put it this way: "Judicial commission? Church service? Theatre? Group Therapy?"[3] A bit of all of the above. Theological insights that were the foundation of the TRC are supported by psychological concepts.

Both theology and psychology speak of the importance of telling one's story. Storytelling is central to the various faiths, and it is the narrative element that has made the hearings of the Human Rights Violations (HRV) Committee compelling. "While the importance of narrative has been a central issue in much contemporary theology and ethics, this theory is rarely demonstrated with as much power as it is in the TRC hearings," assert theologians H. Russel Botman and Robin Petersen.[4] Some 2,000 victims (a representative sample of over 20,000 persons who made submissions) were invited to tell their stories in a safe, supportive environment.

Previously, victims had been tormented with self-blame, the sense that somehow they had deserved what happened to them, or guilt for the fact that their political activity had caused suffering for their families. It is important that victims be allowed to tell their stories, because survivors often feel misunderstood and ignored, their sacrifice unacknowledged, their pain unrecognized, and their identity lost. Theologian Robert Shreiter writes that individuals cannot survive without a narrative of identity. Through torture and coercion, oppressors attempt to substitute another narrative so that people will acquiesce in their subjugation. If the original narrative is suppressed, the lie will be accepted as truth. Victims can only overcome suffering by overcoming the narrative of the lie and embracing a redeeming narrative.[5]

South Africa's Black Consciousness Movement of the late 1960s and 1970s had stressed this point: blacks through daily intimidation and subjugation had internalized a sense of inferiority and the acceptance of an inferior status preached to them by whites. Certainly, counter-ideologies had appeared over the years to combat the false ideology of Afrikanerdom. Still, it is a nearly universal phenomenon that victims often blame themselves. Survivor Albie Sachs, commenting on the importance of storytelling to the process of identity reclamation, has said: "We need to feel that basically we did right, that we did not deserve what was inflicted upon us. This gives us a sense of rightness to the world, not just to us but to the future."[6]

For Judith Herman, "The fundamental premise of the psychotherapeutic work is a belief in the restorative power of truth-telling."[7] Speaking of testimony as a therapeutic technique, Guus van der Veer explains, "The point of departure of this method is to encourage the traumatized person to describe his traumatic experiences in as much detail as possible, as though he was giving evidence as witness for the prosecution."[8] And A. J. Cienfeugos and C. Monelli endorse the view that testimony has significant therapeutic value for victims of political repression and torture.[9]

Psychology teaches us that sharing stories in a supportive setting leads to healing, whereas suppressing them leads to anxiety, stress, and depression. Johnny de Lange aptly described the atmosphere for victims at HRV hearings as having been "a soft place to deal with hard issues."[10] Through the TRC, "people who have nurtured their subjugated stories in the confines of their hearts and hearths—offstage—now have an opportunity to articulate and own their stories on stage. What was hidden is now becoming public."[11]

Richard Wilson made note of the script that was followed at the HRV hearings: at the conclusion of the testimony, the chair asked the audience to stand and observe a minute of silence for the nation's fallen heroes. The message that was communicated was that people had not died in vain, but as heroes for the liberation of the nation. The commissioners then thanked the victims for their sacrifice.[12] Elaine Scarry observed in *The Body in*

Pain that the process of telling and observing one's story being heard allows survivors to become subjects again.[13] Harvard professor Martha Minow says, "Tears in public will not be the last tears, but to know one's tears are *seen* may grant a sense of acknowledgment that makes grief less lonely and terrifying."[14] Commissioner Mary Burton agreed that giving public testimony had been healing for many survivors: "The right to be heard and acknowledged, with respect and empathy, did contribute to a process of healing in many cases."[15] Many victims spoke afterward of the therapeutic effect of voicing their pain publicly, often for the first time, and of having their contribution to the struggle acknowledged.

Speaking about the healing potential of storytelling, Lukas Baba Sikwepere said after testifying to the TRC about being blinded by police bullets: "I feel that what has been making me sick all the time is the fact that I couldn't tell my story. But now it feels like I got my sight back by coming here and telling you the story."[16] One man said in reference to the psychological value of testifying: "When the officer tortured me at that time in John Vorster Square, he laughed at me: 'You can scream your head off, nobody will ever hear you!' He was wrong. Today there are people who hear me."[17]

But perhaps the cathartic value of testifying and the benefit of having one's sacrifice acknowledged were overemphasized by the media and by the commissioners. As long as there had been crying, commissioners said that healing had occurred, which led to some critics calling the TRC the "Kleenex Commission." Many victims, after the initial relief, found themselves months later reexperiencing the trauma and despondency. Yazir Henry writes about his experiences after testifying: "After my testimony, I could not interact with anybody other than the members of my immediate family. It felt as if I had spent everything that was inside me and the slightest bit of external pressure would finally and completely crush me."[18]

Tom Winslow, assistant director of the Trauma Center for Survivors of Violence and Torture in Cape Town, has said that some witnesses came away more embittered. For Winslow, the TRC "opened the patient up and then walked away."[19] According to Trudy de Ridder, the trauma center's director, after victims experienced an initial sense of relief at having unburdened themselves, "there [was] a return and intensification of symptoms associated with the original violations as well as the onset of new symptoms that may [have been] related to an actual retraumatisation caused by retelling the story."[20] Some 50–60 percent of the victims seen by the trauma center had suffered serious difficulties after testifying.[21]

Symptoms related to post–traumatic stress syndrome, such as confusion, nightmares, loss of appetite, and sleeplessness, often appeared afterward.[22]

Brandon Hamber has reported that little long-term mental health follow-up was actually provided to the victims by the TRC. He writes: "The adrenaline-filled and cathartic experience of testifying publicly . . . often initially masked the long-term or deeper psychological issues that were at play."[23] It is harmful to ask people to tell their most painful experiences one time and then just leave them to cope with stirred-up memories that had been buried. Most therapists in a clinical setting would avoid pushing a patient to speak of extreme trauma too quickly, yet TRC witnesses were encouraged to tell their stories in one sitting, typically lasting about an hour.[24] Grahame Hayes argues that the TRC operated under a simplistic view of healing (under a banner that read "Revealing Is Healing"), but that real healing "takes time and it involves hard work, not just the expression of painful emotions. Healing doesn't come all at once, and maybe, in hindsight, the revealing shouldn't have come all at once either."[25]

Dan Stein cautions that later psychodynamic models diverge from earlier cathartic models of psychotherapy used to treat post–traumatic stress syndrome, which argued for the importance of verbalizing past traumas. These later models emphasize the importance of the relationship "between the testifying victim and his or her listeners." Stein believes that having to testify about trauma to an unempathetic audience may result in "secondary traumatisation."[26] Many of those listening to the stories at home on television were not sympathetic (as polls indicated) and felt that black victims were exaggerating. Barney Pityana, head of the Human Rights Commission, also questions whether victims' dignity was restored when they told their stories in the glare of television cameras. He writes: "I would suggest that such a spectacle was not necessarily ennobling but demeaning of their human dignity."[27]

Furthermore, there was a need for continued psychological support, which most victims unfortunately did not get,[28] not surprising given that there were so few psychiatrists practicing in rural areas. In the Northern Province, for example, for a population of 5.3 million, there were no clinical psychologists in the public health services, and only three in private practice.[29] The TRC has been criticized for not providing sufficient follow-up services to those who testified.[30] One critic said: "The TRC is essentially a legal structure. The healing stuff was tacked on at the end. When funding becomes tight in the TRC, the first thing they cut is psychological services."[31] Hamber cautions that the unavailability of psychiatric care is a problem with this kind of process, and even where available, people who feel overwhelmed with their daily lives (with social problems and poverty) do not prioritize mental health care.[32]

Often overlooked in analyses of the TRC was the benefit of confronting perpetrators at their amnesty hearings. The relations of power were challenged as perpetrators were cross-examined by victims or victims' families. This may well have been more psychologically beneficial to people than speaking about their suffering in HRV hearings. Winslow has commented: "By taking control of the amnesty process . . . these survivors of gross abuses directly sought the answers that would heal their memories and prevent a repetition of the same torture in the future. The victims assumed the role of the interrogators, and the torturer appeared at the mercy of his inquisitors."[33] The amnesty hearings were a "ritual of empowerment," in which people who had been "treated like rubbish" were treated like citizens.[34] Once-feared torturers who had seemed invincible now appeared as cowering shells of their former selves, often breaking down into tears. Smangaliso Mkhatshwa, deputy minister of education in Nelson Mandela's cabinet, met his former torturers at one hearing. When he had been interrogated and tortured by them, "these men were God Almighty. I was scared of them. They were very powerful people. Suddenly now that I see them here, they are very ordinary human beings."[35]

Psychology also speaks of the benefit of the confessional narrative. Psychotherapy is based on the notion of the couch as confessional, and patients are urged "to tell the truth."[36] Hence, sharing stories can be of therapeutic value for perpetrators as well. Piet Meiring has noted that when a perpetrator after much anguish and embarrassment testified to the Amnesty Committee and unburdened himself, it was as if a cloud had been lifted. After testifying about his role in the bombing of Khotso House, headquarters of the South African Council of Churches, Adriaan Vlok said: "I had a lump in my throat—and thanked the Lord."[37] This opportunity given to perpetrators to explain their motives and perspectives was unique among truth commissions.[38] Feeling that an attempt had been made to "hear" them and understand them may have been the turning point of the reintegration of the perpetrator into society. George Bizos argues that for perpetrators, "to be understood is a form of forgiveness."[39]

Theologians James Cochrane and Gerald West have written of the need for "dangerous memories" and "subjugated knowledges" to be recovered, aroused, and expressed. Without expression, memories that are sufficiently intense will engender not only personal but also social brokenness.[40] These stories, then, had significance not only for victims but for perpetrators and bystanders as well. Speaking of the narratives that came forth from the hearings of the HRV Committee, West has said: "I need the stories of the TRC to be placed next to mine so that I can acknowledge my own part in our past and so that I may become more whole."[41] H. Russel Botman notes that these stories impinged on our own well-known stories, broadening our horizons: "Every time [we] hear the stories, the contemporary miracle happens; the deaf begin to hear!"[42]

Storytelling is significant because it is a way for victims, perpetrators, and bystanders to construct a common memory of the past.[43] H. Richard Niebuhr in *The Story of Our Life* writes: "Where common memory is lacking, where people do not share in the same past, there can be no real community, and where community is to be formed common memory must be created."[44] Quoting theologian Dietrich Ritschl, Dirkie Smit writes: "We love only those with whom we are prepared to share our story and in whose story we want to have a share. Only those who share memories and hopes really belong together."[45] The TRC offered the opportunity to participate in each other's humanity in story form. A South African journalist who covered the TRC writes: "For me, the Truth Commission microphone with its little red light was the ultimate symbol of the whole process: here the marginalized voice speaks to the public ear; the unspeakable is spoken."[46]

The authors of *Reconciliation Through Truth* argue that through the stories emanating from the TRC, South Africans faced unwelcome truths in order to "harmonise incommensurable world views" so that conflicts and differences stood "at least within a single universe of comprehensibility."[47] TRC cochair Alex Boraine insisted that South Africans needed a "common memory to remind us what our society was like and the dark era we have passed through."[48] Reconciliation required that there be some general agreement between both sides of the wrongs that had been committed. The sheer number of stories ensured that it would be impossible for South Africans to deny what had happened during the apartheid years. Antjie Krog is convinced that these narratives alone are enough to justify the existence of the TRC: "Because of these narratives people can no longer indulge in their separate dynasties of denial."[49] This exercise in creating a shared memory of the past may preempt future political efforts by conservative whites to form organizations, write revisionist histories, and introduce curricula that deny the realities of the apartheid past.

However, the National Party (NP) was very wary of the TRC's effort to uncover the past, and argued in effect to let bygones be bygones. Former president F. W. de Klerk urged South Africans to look not to the past but to the future, for national unity required moving forward, he insisted. Donald Shriver, on the other hand, argues that remembrance is essential: "Forgiveness begins with a remembering and a moral judgment of wrong, injustice, and injury. . . . Absent a preliminary agreement between two or more parties that there is something from the past to be forgiven, forgiveness stalls at the starting gate."[50] Shriver argues that the Christian injunction is not to "forgive and forget" but to "remember and forgive."[51] A consensus about the wrongs inflicted is a prerequisite. H. Richard Niebuhr reminds us: "We cannot become integrated parts . . . until we each remember our whole past, with its sins . . . and appropriate each other's past."[52] Karl Barth called Christian confession of faith an exercise in name giving.[53] In order to give a name, to be in agreement, to concur, to admit the other is right, those parts of the past of which one is unaware—for whatever reason (including denial and self-deception)—must be made known. For instance, a victim's story of torture at the hands of the security force challenged the official police story that they had been defending the country from terrorists. Listening to a victim's narrative of pain, the perpetrator was invited to share the victim's experience of the truth and to make it his own, making confession possible. Hence, encouraging the perpetrators to remember the past correctly, to see it through the eyes of their victims, was seen as vital.

From Victims to Masterminds

A shift from individual stories to collective narratives took place late in 1996, as political parties were invited to make submissions. Unique among truth commissions, political parties and other organizations such as the South African Defense Force (SADF) and State Security Council (SSC) agreed to make submissions to the TRC so that their understanding of developments in South Africa during the thirty-four-year period under investigation could be shared.

When political parties were called to give account of their human rights violations, they obfuscated. While party leaders seemed keen on apologizing for what they called "excesses," none claimed that murder and torture were the official policies of their parties. De Klerk, speaking for the National Party, denied that he or members of his cabinet had ever planned murders, tortures, or assassinations of opponents.[54] While accepting the National Party's overall responsibility for political decisions taken when it was governing, he insisted that it could not be held accountable for the unauthorized actions of people who had committed cold-blooded murder. That had not been the policy of his government, he maintained. "No President can know everything which takes place under his management," he insisted.[55]

In the National Party's second submission (party recall), de Klerk insisted repeatedly in response to a series of written questions submitted by the TRC that he was as shocked as anyone to hear of acts committed by a "handful of operatives" in the police and military. He could not accept that the government's policies might have given security forces a "license to kill." When presented with a document showing that he had been present at a 1986 cabinet meeting at which a decision was made to create a security force that would "eliminate" the state's enemies, de Klerk denied that "eliminate" meant "to kill," a statement the TRC commissioners found not credible.[56] Desmond Tutu lamented the fact that de Klerk had "spurned the opportunity to become human."[57]

The African National Congress (ANC) revealed more about National Party violations than did the National Party itself. It highlighted the government's invasion of three countries in the 1980s, the attempted assassinations of two prime ministers, the support of dissident movements in Mozambique and Angola, the disruption of oil supplies to six countries, the attack of railroad routes to several countries, and the overall economic damage to the region.[58]

The ANC was less forthcoming about its own acts, however. Speaking for the ANC, then deputy president Thabo Mbeki dismissed the notion that it had been official ANC policy to attack civilians or to "necklace" government collaborators (the practice of placing a lighted, gasoline-soaked tire around the neck of an enemy), but admitted that "excesses" had occurred especially in the ANC exile camps, including the execution of thirty-four cadres in Angola accused of mutiny, murder, and rape.[59] In fact, the ANC had held its own commissions of inquiry into the human rights abuses at the camps,[60] "the only example of an opposition group formally investigating and publicly reporting on the dark side of its own past."[61] It conceded that over time it had became "increasingly difficult to maintain the highly disciplined and restrained approach to the use of violence."[62] Nevertheless, its overall argument was that because it had waged a just struggle, by definition that precluded it from having engaged in gross violations of human rights.

The ANC was more straightforward in its second party submission (party recall) of May 1997, and more willing to accept the distinction between jus ad bellum and jus in bello. The ANC conceded that in the mid-1980s it had placed less emphasis on avoiding civilian casualties at all costs. When pressed by the TRC, the ANC admitted to lapses and slippages in its principled positions—to assassinating informers who betrayed the struggle, violating women's human rights (including rape), arming township self-defense units in the early 1990s (in retrospect, "a mistake"), and bombing companies involved in worker disputes.[63] The ANC confessed that it had waited too long to condemn necklacing. The ANC also accepted responsibility for the 1983 bombing of air force headquarters in Pretoria, which had been authorized by ANC president Oliver Tambo,[64] for dozens of land mine explosions, and hundreds of limpet mine explosions, throughout the country, and for attacks on police officials and black council members. Some of its actions—such as the bombing of Ellis Park Stadium in Johannesburg—had been against its policy of not hitting purely civilian targets, but were explained by the "blurring of the lines" between military and civilian targets in the 1980s. Political analyst Tom Lodge has noted that more came out about the behavior of the liberation movements from the party hearings than about the previous regime, since the National Party admitted to little.[65] Still, the ANC was vague about the chain of command, who did what and who gave the orders. Antjie Krog asserts that the ANC did not deal openly with its role in the death squads against Inkatha Freedom Party (IFP) supporters in KwaZulu-Natal in the 1980s.[66]

Pan-Africanist Congress (PAC) leader Clarence Makwetu took responsibility for acts of guerrilla violence by the Azanian People's Liberation Army against white civilians, and for the murder of American Amy Biehl by members of the Pan-Africanist Students Organization, but he denied that orders were given by the organization's leadership. He disavowed responsibility for many of the acts attributed by the government and the press to the PAC.[67]

In a presentation that lasted five hours, Mongosuthu Buthelezi, speaking for the Inkatha Freedom Party, painted the ANC as the main aggressor in KwaZulu-Natal. He charged the ANC with assassinations of 420 IFP leaders, and denied that his party had ever authorized any acts of violence for political purposes.[68] Eight months later, he was still insisting that "IFP leadership never chose the path of violence nor planned or executed any violent action." He went on to say that his apology was for the fact that "our followers were drawn into the violence."[69]

The political party hearings were followed in October 1997 by special hearings of the SADF and the SSC. General Constand Viljoen, a former SADF chief, testified: "You really erred in your assumption, and the expectations you created in public, that the SADF was guilty of gross violations of human rights on a substantial scale."[70] Former defense minister Magnus Malan admitted to having set up the Civil Cooperation Bureau (CCB) to "disrupt the enemy" but denied having authorized the assassination of antiapartheid activists. He admitted approving cross-border raids against enemy targets in southern Africa but would not apply for amnesty for those operations, as he considered them legal actions of the state.[71] Of their testimony, Boraine said, "I find it almost unbelievable that . . . there can be no acknowledgment or acceptance that the SADF, in implementing a policy of apartheid, could bear no responsibility for a single death."[72]

It was harder for the police generals to deny knowledge, as dozens of policemen had submitted amnesty applications admitting to murder, torture, and bombing on a large scale. Nevertheless, General Johan Coetzee and General Johan van der Merwe argued that "eliminate" did not mean "to kill" (just as de Klerk had argued earlier), although they admitted the word could have been "misconstrued."[73] Major Craig Williamson, a former police spy, explained that the vague language was intentionally all-encompassing "to allow those at the top to avoid having blood on their hands."[74]

At the hearing of the State Security Council, the organization wherein senior generals and politicians met to set policy on dealing with the opposition, Adriaan Vlok, a former police minister, agreed that the language used by the SSC—to "eliminate," "take out," "neutralize"—was open to misinterpretation by the ranks.[75] Former foreign minister Pik Botha and deputy police minister Roelf Meyer spoke of their omission in not reining in the security forces. Leon Wessels, a former deputy police minister, went the furthest in acknowledging responsibility: "It was foreseen that . . . people would be detained, people would be tortured. . . . I don't believe I can stand up and say, 'Sorry, I didn't know.'"[76]

Does Denial Mean Failure?

Do the denials by de Klerk that the National Party ever authorized human rights violations against political opponents, or fueled black-on-black violence (between ANC and IFP supporters), signify that the TRC was unsuccessful? And what of the Dutch Reformed Church's tepid apology and refusal to explicitly acknowledge the link between its teachings and apartheid (discussed in Chapter 10)? Should one conclude that the TRC was a failure?

Psychologist Sean Kaliski argues that even the denials from the highest levels are a positive step. He says that denial is a first step akin to the initial step in the stages terminally ill patients experience: denial, rage, bargaining, depression, and finally acceptance. Kaliski says that white Afrikaners especially feel exposed: "If you personalise it: a very proud person who is publicly exposed for being a scoundrel will almost never respond with humility and contrition; they will almost always respond with anger and outrage." He adds that he would be concerned if whites overnight had integrated information that overturned their whole world. "It will take decades, maybe generations, for people to assimilate the truths of this country's past. But there will be no grand release—every individual will have to devise his or her own personal method of coming to terms with what happened."[77]

Theologian Denise Ackermann agrees that to hear the truth, we must unlearn almost everything we think we know, which is a lengthy process.[78] The "conversion of the memory," suggests H. Richard Niebuhr, is never completed but is ongoing.[79] The departure of the National Party from the TRC in July 1997, following what it considered hostile questioning of de Klerk during the National Party's submission,[80] and the noncooperation of the Inkatha Freedom Party,[81] which accused the TRC of a pro-ANC bias and repeatedly called for scrapping the TRC—together composing one-third of the electorate—ran the risk that some South Africans unable to reconcile themselves with uncomfortable historical facts might find themselves in a kind of psychological exile with their unconverted, unredeemed memories.[82]

Nevertheless, because of the TRC all South Africans have heard something of what happened during the dark years of apartheid. Political scientist Andre du Toit asserts: "In whatever way they may still be interpreted or explained, the sheer number and gravity of political atrocities in our recent past can no longer be doubted or ignored. This is already a historical achievement for the TRC."[83] Whites have moved from the position of denying that these things happened to denying they knew anything about them. Many whites who claim amnesia about the past have been forced to confront themselves with the questions "What did we do?" and "What did we not do?"

Still, most whites have remained indifferent. The *Mail & Guardian* reported in February 1997 that as a result of complaints by white radio listeners who objected to hearing TRC-related stories, such stories were broadcast during non-prime-time hours (after 8 P.M.), "when most of the farmers are no longer listening."[84] Also, few whites watched television journalist Max du Preez's weekly *TRC: Special Report,* the highest-rated public affairs broadcast thanks to its 1 million black viewers. A poll by the South African Broadcasting Corporation revealed that white viewership of the program was consistently lower than that by blacks, Coloureds, or Indians over the two years.[85] The whites "don't want to deal with the truth," explains investigative journalist Jacques Pauw.[86] The Afrikaans press, especially in its newspapers *Rapport* and *Die Burger,* denounced the TRC as the "Lying and Confessing Commission" and the "Truth and Provision Commission," and did very little to encourage Afrikaners to engage seriously with the hearings.

Very few whites attended any of the HRV or amnesty hearings, a cause of much concern to the commissioners. A black minister at the first HRV hearing held on the eastern Cape exclaimed: "There must be some mistake! Where are the Whites we wanted to talk to, with whom we wanted to be reconciled?"[87] Eli Wiesel, who has spent his life documenting Nazi atrocities, remarked that victims suffered more profoundly "from the indifference of the onlookers than from the brutality of the executioner."[88] One middle-class white woman sent a statement to the TRC that shed some light on why whites did not attend hearings. She explained: "It is not denial that keeps me away. It is a deep and overwhelming sense of shame. . . . I find it almost impossible to look you in the face."[89] But, whether willingly or not, the past was being confronted, and a new social memory for South Africa was being created. Interpretations of the past that were previously suppressed have now been legitimized.

Notes

1. Scheper-Hughes, "Un-doing," p. 157.
2. Hayes, "We Suffer Our Memories," p. 32.
3. David Beresford, "Theatre of Pain and Catharsis," *Mail & Guardian* (April 19, 1996).
4. Botman and Petersen, introduction to *To Remember and to Heal,* p. 12.
5. Shreiter, *Reconciliation,* pp. 34–35.
6. Cited in Dowdall, "Psychological Aspects of the Truth and Reconciliation Commission," p. 35.
7. Herman, *Trauma and Recovery,* p. 181.
8. van der Veer, *Counseling and Therapy with Refugees,* p. 150, cited in de la Rey and Owens, "Perceptions of Psychosocial Healing and the Truth and Reconciliation Commission in South Africa," p. 259.
9. Cited in de la Rey and Owens, "Perceptions of Psychosocial Healing and the Truth and Reconciliation Commission in South Africa," p. 269.

10. de Lange, "The Historical Context, Legal Origins, and Philosophical Foundations of the South African Truth and Reconciliation Commission," p. 25.
11. West, "Don't Stand On My Story," p. 6.
12. Wilson, "Reconciliation and Revenge in Post-Apartheid South Africa," (paper presented at the "TRC: Commissioning the Past" conference), pp. 15–16.
13. See Scarry, *The Body in Pain.*
14. Cited in Shriver, "Bridging the Abyss of Revenge," p. 1171 (original emphasis).
15. Cited in Hamber, "Past Imperfect," p. 5.
16. *Truth and Reconciliation Commission of South Africa Report,* vol. 5, chap. 9, "Reconciliation," p. 352.
17. Cited in Meiring, *Chronicle of the Truth Commission,* p. 50.
18. Henry, "Where Healing Begins," p. 169.
19. Cited in Charles Villa-Vicencio, "Don't Blame Me, I Just Live Here" (unpublished paper), p. 3.
20. de Ridder, "The Trauma of Testifying," p. 32.
21. Suzanne Daley, "In Apartheid Inquiry, Agony Is Relived but Not Put to Rest," *New York Times* (July 17, 1997).
22. Hayner, *Unspeakable Truths,* p. 141.
23. Hamber, "The Burdens of Truth," p. 21.
24. Hayner, *Unspeakable Truths,* p. 139.
25. Hayes, "We Suffer Our Memories," p. 47.
26. Stein, "Psychiatric Aspects of the Truth and Reconciliation Commission in South Africa," p. 455.
27. Pityana, "Reconciliation After the TRC."
28. Most victims had someone to brief and debrief them before and after testifying. These people were not trained psychologists or social workers. Statement takers had even less background in psychology.
29. Hamber, "The Burdens of Truth," p. 15.
30. Nevertheless, the TRC is the only truth commission that attempted to set up a system of referrals or follow-up for witnesses. See Hayner, *Unspeakable Truths,* p. 146.
31. Andrew Schackleton (Quaker Peace Center), cited in van der Merwe, Dewhirst, and Hamber, "Non-Governmental Organisations and the Truth and Reconciliation Commission," p. 69.
32. Hamber, "The Burdens of Truth," p. 13.
33. Winslow, "The Road to Healing?" p. 25.
34. Ignatieff, "Digging Up the Dead," p. 92.
35. Rickard, "Fierce Emotions As S. Africa Seeks Peace," p. 11.
36. Gilligan, "The Agenbite of Inwit," p. 34.
37. Cited in Meiring, *Chronicle of the Truth Commission,* p. 372.
38. The *Sunday Independent* singled out the chapter on motives and perspectives of perpetrators as the most important chapter in the report; Jeremy Gordin, "Beyond Mere Blame: Commission's Report Forges a Moral Framework for the Future," *Sunday Independent* (April 4, 1998). See *TRC Final Truth and Reconciliation Commission of South Africa Report,* vol. 5, chap. 7, "Causes, Motives, and Perspectives of Perpetrators."

39. Bizos, *No One to Blame?* p. 238.

40. Cochrane and West, "War, Remembrance, and Reconstruction," p. 25.

41. West, "Don't Stand On My Story," pp. 10–11.

42. Botman, "Narrative Challenges in a Situation of Transition," p. 39.

43. H. Richard Niebuhr, cited in Smit, "Confession-Guilt-Truth-and-Forgiveness in the Christian Tradition," p. 98.

44. Ibid.

45. Dietrich Ritschl, cited in Smit, "Confession-Guilt-Truth-and-Forgiveness in the Christian Tradition," p. 98.

46. Krog, *Country of My Skull,* p. 237.

47. Asmal, Asmal, and Roberts, *Reconciliation Through Truth,* p. 46.

48. "Reaction Strengthens Against Secrecy Compromise on Truth Commission," *SouthScan* (December 9, 1994).

49. Krog, *Country of My Skull,* p. 89.

50. Shriver, *An Ethic for Enemies,* p. 7.

51. Ibid.

52. H. Richard Niebuhr, cited in Smit, "Confession-Guilt-Truth-and-Forgiveness in the Christian Tradition," p. 100.

53. Karl Barth, cited in Smit, "Confession-Guilt-Truth-and-Forgiveness in the Christian Tradition," p. 102.

54. NP hearing, Cape Town, August 21, 1996.

55. Ibid.

56. Transcript of the NP recall in Cape Town, May 14, 1997.

57. Cited in Krog, *Country of My Skull,* p. 158.

58. ANC hearing, Cape Town, August 22, 1996.

59. Ibid.

60. However, no one was named or held personally accountable. See Hayner, "Fifteen Truth Commissions—1974 to 1994," p. 626.

61. Priscilla Kayne, cited in Frost, *Struggling to Forgive,* p. 154.

62. ANC hearing, Cape Town, August 22, 1996.

63. Transcript of ANC party recall in Cape Town, May 12–13, 1997.

64. The ANC insisted, however, that the attack did not contradict the ANC policy to avoid civilian casualties, faulting instead the government for placing strategic installations in high-density civilian areas.

65. Tom Lodge, cited in Eddie Koch, "Military 'Third Force' Walks Free," *Mail & Guardian* (May 16–22, 1997).

66. Krog, *Country of My Skull,* p. 125.

67. PAC hearing, Cape Town, August 20, 1996.

68. IFP hearing, Cape Town, September 5, 1996.

69. SAPA, "Buthelezi Accuses Tutu of Theatrics" (May 9, 1997).

70. Armed forces hearing, Cape Town, October 8, 1997.

71. SAPA, "Malan Admits Setting Up CCB, Ordering Raids" (May 7, 1997).

72. Cited in Meredith, *Coming to Terms,* p. 167.

73. Armed forces hearing, Cape Town, October 9, 1997.

74. Ibid.

75. SSC hearing, Johannesburg, October 14, 1997.

76. Ibid.

77. Sean Kaliski, cited in Antjie Krog, "Unto the Third or Fourth Generations," *Mail & Guardian* (June 13–19, 1997).

78. Ackermann, "On Hearing and Lamenting," p. 51.

79. H. Richard Niebuhr, cited in Smit, "Confession-Guilt-Truth-and-Forgiveness in the Christian Tradition," p. 100.

80. The National Party returned in September 1997 after Marthinus van Schalkwyk replaced de Klerk as party head.

81. The IFP is a mainly Zulu party with its main support in KwaZulu-Natal. As a rival to the ANC, its Zulu followers (supported and armed by the government) were pitted against Zulu supporters of the ANC in KwaZulu-Natal, which became a virtual killing field in the 1980s and 1990s.

82. Asmal, Asmal, and Roberts, *Reconciliation Through Truth,* p. 51.

83. Andre du Toit, "No Rest Without the Wicked," p. 9.

84. Claudia Braude, "Media Should Get the Truth Out," *Mail & Guardian* (February 7–13, 1997).

85. Theissen, "Common Past, Divided Truth," p. 11.

86. Cited in ibid.

87. Cited in Meiring, *Chronicle of the Truth Commission,* p. 374.

88. Cited in Meiring, "The Baruti Versus the Lawyers," p. 128.

89. Leslie Morgan, written submission to the TRC, June 27, 1997.

7

Women's Testimony Before the TRC

Ranking internationally as a country with one of the highest numbers of women in Parliament,[1] South Africa has taken the lead among African nations in articulating gender rights as vital human rights. In the post-apartheid constitution, the government committed itself to the abolition not only of race inequality but also of the gender inequality that had previously characterized the nation. Initiatives early in Nelson Mandela's administration that focused on women's rights included the Commission on Gender Equality, which monitors, investigates, and reports on issues of gender in civil society; the Office on the Status of Women, which is responsible for mainstreaming gender in all government departments; and the introduction of the Women's Budget Initiative (WBI), which analyzes the impact of the national budget on women.

Given the government's strong support for women's rights, it came as a surprise to many observers that women's voices were not being heard by South Africa's Truth and Reconciliation Commission (TRC), and that the nation as a result was getting a skewed look at the nature of human rights violations that had been committed.

Women's Experiences of Repression

The 1960s were the decade of entrenchment of separate development. Forced removals (to remove "black spots" from white areas) proceeded apace, and many blacks were "endorsed" out to the homelands under the government's influx control system. Families were torn apart under the migrant labor system, since women along with their children were prevented from joining their husbands in the towns. Single-sex hostels that housed the male workers (in mining and other industries) made it impossible for rural wives to maintain family life.[2]

The 1960s also witnessed the end of nonviolent protest. After the Sharpeville massacre of March 1960, during which sixty-nine people (including eight women) were shot dead during peaceful identity-pass protests, the government instituted a state of emergency and banned both the African National Congress (ANC) and the Pan-Africanist Congress (PAC). Following the bannings, the ANC embarked on armed struggle through its military wing, Umkhonto We Sizwe (MK), and the PAC embarked on armed struggle through the Azanian People's Liberation Army (APLA). During this decade the state developed more sophisticated psychological methods of interrogation. Solitary confinement in indefinite detentions without trial was combined with psychological and physical torture. Sleep deprivation, forcing a detainee to stand for long periods, and repeated assaults were among the methods used to break down prisoners' resistance.[3]

Women's resistance during this and earlier decades was secondary to men's. Cultural norms discouraged women's active participation in the liberation movements. One common view is that African men discouraged their wives' participation in politics because they feared that if their wives were imprisoned, they would have to tackle domestic chores, including taking care of babies.[4] Cheryl Walker suggests that women's activism disturbed men in the ANC because it conflicted with "their deeply rooted views on the junior position women should occupy in society at large and within the national movement in particular."[5]

By the 1970s the Black Consciousness Movement, a movement initiated by intellectuals schooled under Bantu education in all-black institutions, was in full sway. Led by Steve Biko, it included a number of women intellectuals and professionals, including nurses, social workers, teachers, and medical doctors, who were nonetheless marginalized within the movement because of prevailing norms.[6] It was adult women who gave significant support to the youth in the movement, especially after the Soweto uprising, when children were shot for defying the requirement that high school courses be taught in Afrikaans.

During the 1970s many African women migrated to informal settlements near the major industrial centers and were subject to raids and harassment by the state authorities. Employers seeking to cut labor costs began to hire more women in the commercial sector, especially in the low-salaried manufacturing sector, and some women found themselves in positions of leadership in the burgeoning trade union movement, although the most highly visible labor and community leaders were men.[7] Women trade unionists were among those rounded up, detained, and assaulted. Methods of torture had by this time assumed a more violent form. Women were increasingly treated in as brutal a manner as their male colleagues, as interrogators combined physical torture with sexual torture, including electric shocks to the genitals and the breasts.

In the 1980s a strong mass movement emerged under the United Democratic Front (UDF), the coalition of workers, civics, students, and women's organizations that came together to oppose the new constitution, which had granted limited rights to Coloureds and Indians but continued to exclude Africans from meaningful political participation. Women were active in rent and consumer boycotts, and in work stay-aways as trade unionists.[8] The Congress of South African Trade Unions (COSATU) continued to attract female members, although few made it to the top level of leadership. In 1988, for instance, only eight of eighty-three office bearers at the national level in COSATU's affiliates were women.[9]

State repression became more violent, with the state continuing to support reactionary forces within the homelands. The ANC stepped up its guerrilla attacks, and women increasingly were drawn into the violence as activists themselves—women were soldiers and commanders in MK[10]—or on behalf of their sons and husbands as the core of the Detainees' Parents Support Committee (DPSC) bringing public attention to the detentions and making private concerns a political issue.[11] During the states of emergency in the late 1980s, women in women's organizations linked to the UDF were detained in large numbers.

Methods of sexual torture also increased during the 1980s. During interrogation, sexual tactics were used against detainees, including body searches, vaginal examinations, rape and forced intercourse with other prisoners, and pushing foreign objects into women's vaginas.

Economic Oppression

During these three decades of apartheid, women experienced repression in distinct ways. While apartheid defined all blacks as secondary citizens, black women were assigned an even lower status through both customary and common law and other social mechanisms. They experienced what has been termed the "triple oppression" of race, class, and gender.[12]

Women, who had primary responsibility for child care and support, were disadvantaged in their access to the labor market. Influx control ensured that most women would remain in the reserves, which led to massive overcrowding and the undermining of peasant agriculture and thus the increased dependence on migrant remittances. However, many men found partners in the cities and started new families, which led to less money sent to the wives in the homelands. Women in the urban areas also faced hardships. They were limited to low-paying domestic work or farm labor, or the better-paying but illegal activities of beer-brewing and prostitution.[13] While men's lives were hard under apartheid, women suffered even greater economic burdens and social restrictions.

Sexual Exploitation

Societal norms also subjected women to treatment as sexual objects. Black women were oppressed not only by white men but also by black men within the resistance. Abuse of female MK soldiers in MK camps in Zambia, Angola, and Tanzania (including acts of rape, euphemistically called "gender-specific offences") made up part of the ANC's testimony at its two submissions to the TRC.[14] General Andrew Masondo, a former political commissar for the ANC in exile, explained that since there were 22 women to 1,000 men in the camps, the "law of supply and demand" spoke for itself.[15] He himself was accused of using his position as head of the Angolan camp to abuse and exploit young, ignorant women and girls—a charge he vehemently denied. The names of the perpetrators were not disclosed in the ANC's submission, and they chose to be part of a collective amnesty application submitted by the ANC for all acts they may have committed, instead of applying individually with full disclosure as the Promotion of National Unity and Reconciliation Act required.[16]

As the objects of sexual competition between men, women became the target of political violence. Many women were victims of the so-called necklace, a gasoline-soaked tire thrown around the neck of an adversary. For a woman, it was often her status as an enemy's wife or girlfriend that made her the object of this particularly gruesome method of killing. Groups punished women of rival political groups by means of gang rape. During the early 1990s women were often the victims of attacks by groups of armed men, especially in KwaZulu when competition between the United Democratic Front and Inkatha Freedom Party (IFP) was intense. It was these types of acts that the TRC recognized as human rights abuses.

How the TRC Dealt with Gender

The history of South African women's oppression is worth noting not only for historical purposes, but also as a guide for how to assess the TRC's treatment of women. Clearly, many courageous women contributed politically and militarily to the struggle for democracy,[17] but the majority were not directly involved, providing instead logistical and emotional support.[18] They suffered most brutally from the socioeconomic consequences of apartheid, and their efforts need to be acknowledged. Unfortunately, the guidelines of the legislation authorizing the TRC mandated compensation only for victims of *gross* human rights abuses, which were defined as the "killing, abduction, torture, or severe ill treatment" of any person by a person acting with a political motive.[19] Millions of ordinary people, especially women, who suffered from the structural violence of apartheid but who were not victims under this narrow definition, were not eligible to receive any compensation. One of the most serious legacies of apartheid has been poverty, whose main victims are women.[20]

Indirect Victims

It was noted early on in the TRC process that when women testified, they talked largely about abuses inflicted upon their male relatives—sons, husbands, brothers, and fathers—even though they too had been victimized, both directly and indirectly. In the first week of the TRC hearings in the Eastern Cape, the widows of the Cradock Four came to speak about their murdered husbands. While they had also been harassed and arrested, their own stories were not solicited but rather were treated as incidental by the commissioners, almost as a postscript. According to Beth Goldblatt and Sheila Meintjes, "Our society constantly diminishes women's role and women themselves then see their experiences as unimportant."[21]

Women's reluctance to see themselves as resisters, as primary agents, is not surprising given their inferior status both within society at large and within the liberation movements; patriarchy has been described as the one truly nonracial institution in South Africa.[22] One journalist explains that some of her colleagues had wanted to publish serious stories on gender issues but were prevented by their male editors, since such issues were seen as insignificant.[23] The media coverage of women witnesses tended to focus on what they wore. Even their tears went unreported; it was the image of men weeping that legitimized the suffering and made headlines.[24] Women's interest in speaking out was further eroded by both the TRC's and the media's portrayal of them as "secondary victims," which perhaps gave them the impression that their own stories were unimportant.

The definition of "victim" in the Promotion of National Unity and Reconciliation Act—while eliminating most women who suffered economically and socially under apartheid—did include relatives or dependents of the victims. This was important, because it recognized that wives, mothers, sisters, and daughters had suffered violations of human rights even if they themselves had not been not the objects of torture. The act took notice of the fact that the detention, imprisonment, exile, or death of a member of a poor family might have meant the difference between starvation and survival for those remaining who had lost a breadwinner. A detainee's wife lost more than simply her husband's income, because she was often unable to find work for herself because of her spouse's political activities, coupled with high levels of unemployment. Implicit in the legislation was the recognition that the loss of a husband was a profound cultural loss for the wife, for whom widowhood meant the loss of status. According to member of Parliament (MP) Jesse Duarte, "The minute her spouse or her partner was taken away, that was the end of her."[25] The broad definition of "victim" recognized too that it was difficult, if not impossible, to separate the psychological pain of a mother who watched her child violated from the pain of the child itself. Both were victims in need of rehabilitation.

Speaking Out

The TRC was criticized for locating women in the private realm as supporters of men, but not in the public realm as resisters of oppression. According to Fiona Ross's coverage of the first five weeks of hearings involving 204 witnesses, six out of every ten deponents were women but over 75 percent of their testimonies, and 88 percent of men's, were about abuses to men. Only 17 percent of women's testimonies and 5 percent of men's were about abuses to women. Fully 25 percent of all cases involved women speaking about their sons, 11 percent were women speaking about their husbands, and 8 percent were women speaking about their brothers. Just 4 percent of the cases involved men speaking about their sons. There were no cases at all of men speaking about their wives or sisters.[26]

Under pressure from women's organizations, and following a submission on "Gender and the Truth and Reconciliation Commission" by

University of Witwatersrand researchers Goldblatt and Meintjes, the TRC attempted to refocus its efforts on women. For instance, the commissioners amended the form used for statements, cautioning women: "Important: Some women testify about violations of human rights. Don't forget to tell us what happened to you yourself if you were the victim of a gross human rights abuse."[27] The TRC also decided that each region would hold at least one hearing dedicated to women and their own experiences of detention, torture, and loss. The TRC accepted recommendations from Goldblatt and Meintjes that women be allowed to tell stories on behalf of other women; that groups of women be permitted to come together and tell their stories as a collective; that hearings be held in camera; and that commissioners receive training on gender-related issues.

It was suggested that women be permitted to tell their stories before a panel of female commissioners in a meeting hall where only women were allowed to attend, since it was felt that the presence of male commissioners and reporters inhibited women in their testimony.[28] Three such women-only hearings were held by the TRC, the first in Cape Town to coincide with National Women's Day, on August 7, 1996, the next on October 25, 1996, in Durban, and the last in Johannesburg on July 28–29, 1997. Regrettably, no women's hearing took place in the fourth region, the Eastern Cape, even though it was recognized as the site of the most human rights violations, and a place where treatment in prisons had been particularly brutal.

Silencing Women

TRC press releases and media coverage of the special women's hearings were limited, arguably because violations against women were not regarded as sensational given the "almost commonplace nature in our society" of sexual assault.[29] Given the sparse coverage of the all-women hearings—compared to the saturation coverage given the other special-events hearings on business, the judiciary, the media, and so forth—many female victims were probably unaware of the more supportive environment afforded to them and did not avail themselves of this opportunity to testify in a safe space.[30]

Cultural norms also prohibited women from testifying. Women were ashamed to speak of their torture. Comparative studies of women victims have indicated that firsthand accounts were often "laconic and euphemistic."[31] David Morris's observation that "suffering tends to make people inarticulate,"[32] and Jean Franco's explanation that "pain destroys language,"[33] resonate in a country where sexual assault is common knowledge and "women are afraid to talk about these assaults."[34]

Many high-ranking women in government who had been rape victims during the apartheid years may have worried how they would be perceived if they came forward with their stories. Bridget Mabandla, the deputy minister of the Department of Arts, Culture, Science, and Technology, had said in a press interview that she had been tortured in prison but that she would not testify before the TRC.[35] Clinical psychologist Nomfundo Walaza ponders: "If you knew that a particular Minister had been raped—what would go through your mind when you saw her on television?"[36] Given the general assumption of South Africans that sexually abused woman somehow deserved it, many women chose not to speak out.

Duarte has described how women abused by political opponents were viewed as colluding with their captors: "If women said they were raped, they were regarded as having sold out to the system in one way or another."[37] And women raped by their comrades in MK camps resisted pointing the finger for fear of discrediting the movement, especially since some of the rapists presumably were ruling in the ANC-dominated government. By highlighting abuses committed against them by men in their own organizations, they would give credence to the view that the atrocities committed by the government are morally equal to the "excesses" that occurred on the other side in self-defense.[38] By speaking out, a victim might hurt herself. Walaza argues: "Another deterrent is that some of the rapists hold high political positions today—so if you spoke out you would not only undermine the new Government you fought for, but destroy your own possibilities of a future."[39]

One woman who did come forward to testify about sexual abuse by MK comrades was Nita Nombango Mazibuko, who testified that she was detained, raped, and tortured by colleagues in exile following an accusation that she was a government spy. She claimed in her testimony that two weeks after she had given a written submission to the TRC, she received a phone call from the ANC premier of Mpumalanga, Mathews Phosa, who tried to stop her from testifying. After she testified that a comrade had "cut through my genitals and . . . he . . . also pour[ed] Dettol over my genitals,"[40] Phosa threatened to sue her and she recanted her testimony.[41] This episode no doubt had a chilling effect on other women. In fact, by July 1997 only 9 of 9,000 women victims had admitted to having been raped, although the number was believed to have been much higher.[42] In the TRC's final report the database numbered just 140 rape cases.[43]

In a provocative essay on women's testimony before the TRC, Fiona Ross writes that women had spoken through their silences and that silence is a "legitimate discourse of pain." It is we who need to learn to listen to the silence, she insists.[44] Put differently, we need to pierce that which destroyed or constrained women's voices. Despite women's reluctance to speak openly, it nevertheless remains imperative that women speak out about their abuse. Although women are reticent to talk about their own suffering, it is important to highlight the abuse of women, to explore these issues openly, to lift the veil of silence. Only by speaking out have women begun the healing process. "Exposing the wounds and having them acknowledged creates the possibility for the healing process to start," writes Mamphela Ramphele on the importance of speaking out. Ramphele asserts that the individual "derives dignity out of the acknowledgment of her pain and is thus in a better position to feel worthy of the suffering, and available to the possibilities of healing."[45] Women's private suffering needs to be made "visible as social suffering, enabling them to stake their historical claims and thereby restore their dignity."[46]

For many victims, the TRC hearings afforded the first opportunity to tell anyone of their abuse during the apartheid years. Two women at the Johannesburg women's hearing, Thandi Shezi and Kedebone Dube, testified that this had been the first time either woman had told anyone of their rapes. Ms. Shezi, who was gang-raped by the police, testified: "I thought I'd done something that I deserved to be treated like that."[47] Ms. Dube, who was raped by Inkatha Freedom Party supporters, had told her family only that she had been kidnaped.[48] A woman testifying anonymously at the Durban hearing stated that she had told no one of being gang-raped by IFP members as her husband watched, explaining: "Sometimes I feel like I invited the trouble myself."[49]

For those women who were not raped, there had been the constant fear that they would be. Zubeida Jaffer recounted to the TRC her terror during interrogation when one policeman urged a fellow officer to "rape her, just rape her."[50] In addition to rape, women suffered a variety of other violations that also centered on their sexuality. Many women testified that they had been degraded during their menstruation periods, forced to stand without benefit of sanitary pads with blood running down their legs.[51] Women were sometimes made to disrobe in front of male warders, and were fondled by doctors and police officers who proceeded to apply electric shocks to their nipples and vaginas.[52]

Often their role as mothers was exploited. Pregnant women were threatened with miscarriage through beatings. Zubeida Jaffer had to decide whether to save the life of her unborn baby by giving the police the information they sought. She decided against giving the information, believing it would be "a heavy burden for a child to carry that her mother gave this information so that she could live."[53] Fortunately, her baby was not harmed. Sheila Masote was not so fortunate; she miscarried after being kicked during interrogation.[54] Women also had their nursing babies taken from them in prison. Joyce Ranken testified that "being forced to abandon my baby son, Nkosinatie, was untenable torture." To add to her pain, a three-year-old Afrikaner toddler was brought around to remind her of her own child at home.[55] Another woman whose nursing baby was removed from her in prison was played tapes of her baby's cries in order to pressure her to give information.[56] Other women were told that their children had died. Many began to experience guilt that their political activities had terrible consequences for their families.

What many women experienced as the most painful part of their detention was that their political bona fides were dismissed. One woman testified that the "drawing away from your own activism, from your commitment as an actor . . . was perhaps worse than torture."[57] Rather, women activists were taunted as unpaid prostitutes.[58]

Many women could not bring themselves to testify. Thenjiwe Mtintso, the first chair of the Commission on Gender Equality, praised the courage of other women testifying but admitted that she could not bring herself to talk publicly about the sexual abuse she had experienced.[59] Given the TRC's initial reluctance to focus on women's experiences, and the cultural norms that not only relegated women to second-class status but also encouraged women's self-blame, women's experiences were not always heard.

Though incomplete, women's stories nevertheless will add to the historical understanding of the repression during the apartheid era and, most importantly, help to raise consciousness about equality in the future in a country where gender violence remains a major problem. Dennis Davis argues that "together with race, gender . . . is the fundamental justification for treating people as less than human under the apartheid order. For society to realise what women went through in the past might raise consciousness about equality in the future."[60]

In the TRC's final report, the commissioners confirmed the initial impression that women were reticent to speak about their own violations. Although more than half of all deponents (54.8 percent) were women, only 43.9 percent of women identified themselves as victims (still, this was an increase of self-proclaimed victims from the first five weeks of hearings that Ross's study analyzes, which can be attributed in part to the decision of the TRC to hold special women's hearings). Eighty-five percent of women victims identified themselves as the object of "severe ill treatment."[61] These statistics can be explained in part by the fact that women were perceived as less of a threat to the apartheid state than men, and they were thus less often the victims of murder, abduction, and torture.[62]

In its findings, the TRC enumerated the kinds of abuses suffered by women at the hands of both the government and liberation movements:

> The state was responsible for the severe ill-treatment of women in custody in the form of harassment and the deliberate withholding of medical attention, food and water. Women were abused by the security forces in ways which specifically exploited their vulnerabilities as women, for example rape or threats of rape and other forms of sexual abuse, threats against family and children, removal of children from their care, false stories about illness and/or death of family members and children, and humiliation around biological functions such as menstruation and childbirth. Women in exile, particularly those in camps, were subjected to various forms of sexual abuse and harassment including rape.[63]

One curiosity is that while rape victims identified themselves as victims of "severe ill treatment," this was one type of violation to which no individual amnesty applicants confessed responsibility.[64] Not a single member of the former security forces or of the former liberation movement applied for amnesty for rape or other sexual violations. That was probably because they felt that rape would not have fallen within the guidelines, as an act not only had to have had a "political" motive but had to have been performed "without malice." Is it possible to rape without malice? Probably not. Keeping the comrades occupied probably would not have met the standards. Also, in addition to being "political," there had to have been some "proportionality" between means and ends.[65] Some suggest that another reason that rape was not acknowledged by perpetrators was its common occurrence in South Africa, which had and has the highest rape statistics in the world. Sadly, it is not considered a gross violation of human rights.

For whatever the reason, we have the anomaly of victims but no perpetrators. Women were deprived of the opportunity of hearing their perpetrators confess, and of the healing that comes from that acknowledgment. There was tremendous pressure from Archbishop Desmond Tutu for victims to forgive their assailants. But forgiveness can become a tool in the manipulation of power relations, making the oppressed even more a victim of injustice. Can one in fact forgive when there has been no apology? According to Trudy de Ridder: "The process is vulnerable to the accusation that it has put survivors at risk in the interests of national healing and reconciliation."[66] Women in particular were sacrificed for the greater good of nation building.

Beyond the TRC

Although the exposure that the TRC gave to women's voices and to the particular ways women had suffered under apartheid had been limited, in its final report as part of its mandate to establish "as complete a picture as possible of the causes, nature, and extent of gross violations of human rights," the commissioners did demonstrate some sensitivity to women's denial of basic economic rights in their lack of access to housing, education, health and welfare resources, freedom of movement, and choice of residence. However, they insisted that their mandate was to focus narrowly on *gross* violations defined as "killing, abduction, torture, or severe ill treatment." The TRC admitted that the definition of "gross" human rights violations it had adopted[67] resulted in a blindness to the types of abuses predominantly experienced by women, who were clearly apartheid's major economic victims.[68]

The Promotion of National Unity and Reconciliation Act required the TRC to make recommendations for preventing violations of *all* human rights (not just those violations deemed "gross"), and the need to promote gender equality was articulated in the TRC's final report. It urged the government to accelerate the closing of the gap between the advantaged and disadvantaged, the vast majority of the latter of whom were black women.[69] The report reminded South Africans that the TRC was but one step in the national effort of reconciliation, which it described as "a complex long-term process." It called upon the government and all individuals to continue the efforts at building a human rights culture.[70] It is vital that other forums address the issue of gender justice in the future. As Sheila Masote succinctly stated at the women's hearings in Johannesburg, "When you have packed your bags as a TRC, there is this work that's still to be done."[71]

In choosing to focus solely on *gross* human rights violations, South Africa's Truth and Reconciliation Commission did a grave disservice to the many female victims of apartheid, and it remains for the government through its policies to enlarge the concept of women's rights as human rights.[72] President Thabo Mbeki, Mandela's successor, pledged in his election victory speech to strengthen women's rights in South Africa: "The women of our country have mandated us to continue with the struggle for their upliftment and emancipation."[73] To highlight his commitment to women's rights, he immediately announced a cabinet with double the number of female members of the previous administration.[74] Pregs Govender, chair of the Parliamentary Joint Standing Committee on the Improvement of the Quality of Life and Status of Women, has pointed out that this is not just the government's responsibility, but also civil society's challenge. She argues that "change will depend on each institution in society. The media, the religious organizations, the educational institutions, business, the NGO's, community organizations, and trade unions each have to take responsibility for ensuring they address the beliefs and practices they hold which continue to oppress and exploit women."[75]

Notes

1. In South Africa's first democratic government, 24 percent of all members of Parliament (MPs) (and 33 percent of MPs in the African National Congress) were women, a consequence of the quota adopted by the African National Congress for its party in the 1994 elections.

2. Bernstein, *For Their Triumphs and for Their Tears,* pp. 11–17.

3. Goldblatt and Meintjes, "Gender and the Truth and Reconciliation Commission."

4. Ramphele, "The Dynamics of Gender Within Black Consciousness Organizations," pp. 224–225.

5. Walker, *Women and Resistance in South Africa,* p. 196.

6. Ramphele, "The Dynamics of Gender Within Black Consciousness Organizations," p. 219.

7. Bernstein, *For Their Triumphs and for Their Tears,* pp. 36–39.

8. Madlala-Routledge, "What Price for Freedom?" pp. 66–67.

9. Cock, *Colonels and Cadres,* p. 29. Not much changed in the 1990s. Dan Connell points out that women's rise to leadership in COSATU is hampered by their effectively working a double shift—paid employment coupled with the main responsibility for home and family—which leaves little time to serve as shop stewards, the first rung up the ladder. See Connell, "Strategies for Change," p. 201.

10. About 20 percent of soldiers in MK in the 1980s and 1990s were women. See Cock, *Colonels and Cadres,* pp. 156–174.

11. Goldblatt and Meintjes, "Gender and the Truth and Reconciliation Commission."

12. Zama, "Theories of Equality," p. 57.

13. Holmes, "Selling Sex for a Living," p. 39.

14. Promotion of National Unity and Reconciliation Act (no. 34 of 1995) required that all acts of human rights abuses—including those of the resistance movements—be acknowledged.

15. Cited in Sooka, "Gewalt gegen Frauen: Vergessener Teil der Wahrheit," p. 88.

16. The High Court directed the TRC to review the collective amnesties granted to the ANC. A new committee decided that based on their applications, no one had committed a gross human rights violation, and therefore these ANC members did not need to apply for amnesty.

17. Regarding political contributions, see Russell, *Lives of Courage.* Regarding military contributions, see Terbourg-Penn, "Black Women Freedom Fighters in South Africa and in the U.S."

18. See van Vuuren, *Women Against Apartheid.*

19. Promotion of National Unity and Reconciliation Act (no. 34 of 1995).

20. See Human Rights Watch, *Violence Against Women in South Africa,* pp. 14–18.

21. Goldblatt and Meintjes, "Gender and the Truth and Reconciliation Commission."

22. Sachs, "Judges and Gender," p. 1.

23. Caroline Massey, "It's Going to Be Very Easy to Rape You," *Agitate Magazine* (1996), www.agitate.co.za.

24. Olckers, "Gender-Neutral Truth," p. 66.

25. Cited in Goldblatt and Meintjes, "Gender and the Truth and Reconciliation Commission."

26. Ross, "Existing in Secret Places," p. 8.

27. *Truth and Reconciliation Commission of South Africa Report,* vol. 4, chap. 10, "Special Hearing: Women," p. 283.

28. Seven of seventeen commissioners were women, although the chair and deputy chair as well as the directors of the research and investigative units were men.

29. Goldblatt and Meintjes, "Gender and the Truth and Reconciliation Commission."

30. Goldblatt and Meintjes, "Dealing with the Aftermath," p. 10.

31. Franco, "Gender, Death, and Resistance," p. 110.

32. David Morris, "About Suffering," p. 28.

33. Cited in Goldblatt and Meintjes, "Gender and the Truth and Reconciliation Commission."

34. Goldblatt and Meintjes, "Gender and the Truth and Reconciliation Commission."

35. Meiring, *Chronicle of the Truth Commission,* pp. 190–191.

36. Cited in Krog, *Country of My Skull,* p. 182.

37. Cited in Goldblatt and Meintjes, "Dealing with the Aftermath," p. 11.

38. Goldblatt and Meintjes, "Dealing with the Aftermath," p. 12.

39. Cited in Krog, *Country of My Skull,* p. 182.

40. Transcript of Johannesburg women's hearing, July 29, 1997.

41. "Apology to Phosa Denied," *Mail & Guardian* (August 8, 1997).

42. Transcript of Johannesburg women's hearing, July 29, 1997.

43. *Truth and Reconciliation Commission of South Africa Report,* vol. 4, chap. 10, "Special Hearing: Women," p. 296.

44. Ross, "Existing in Secret Places," p. 28.

45. Ramphele, "Political Widowhood in South Africa," p. 109.

46. Ibid., p. 114.

47. Thandi Shezi, transcript of Johannesburg women's hearing, July 28, 1997.

48. Kedebone Dube, transcript of Johannesburg women's hearing, July 29, 1997.

49. Transcript of Durban women's hearing, October 25, 1996.

50. Transcript of Cape Town women's hearing, August 7, 1996.

51. Joyce Ranken, transcript of Johannesburg women's hearing, July 29, 1997.

52. Evelyn Masego Thunyiswa, transcript of Human Rights Violations Committee hearing, Mmabatho, July 8, 1996.

53. Zubeida Jaffer, transcript of Cape Town women's hearing, August 7, 1996.

54. Sheila Masote, transcript of Johannesburg women's hearing, July 28, 1997.

55. Joyce Ranken, transcript of Johannesburg women's hearing, July 29, 1997.

56. Shirley Gunn, transcript of Cape Town women's hearing, August 7, 1996.

57. Thenjiwe Mtintso, cited in Goldblatt and Meintjes, "Gender and the Truth and Reconciliation Commission."

58. Transcript of Johannesburg women's hearing, July 28, 1997.

59. Thenjiwe Mtintso, transcript of Johannesburg women's hearing, July 28, 1997.

60. Cited in Caroline Massey, "It's Going to Be Very Easy to Rape You," *Agitate Magazine* (1996), www.agitate.co.za.

61. *Truth and Reconciliation Commission of South Africa Report,* vol. 4, chap. 10, "Special Hearing: Women," pp. 285–286.

62. Goldblatt, "Violence, Gender, and Human Rights."

63. *Truth and Reconciliation Commission of South Africa Report,* vol. 5, chap. 6, "Findings and Conclusions," p. 256.

64. The only amnesty applications the TRC received relating to sexual offenses came from persons already in custody who had been convicted in a criminal court for rape. These were rejected because they were clearly not political rapes.

65. The proportionality principle was based on Professor Carl Aage Norgaard's rules, which were used in the settlement in Namibia. Norgaard himself did not believe that rape could be considered a political act.

66. de Ridder, "The Trauma of Testifying."

67. The category of "severe ill treatment" included the following acts: rape and punitive solitary confinement; sexual assault, abuse, or harassment; physical beating resulting in serious injuries; shooting and injuring people during demonstrations; burnings (including those caused by fire, petrol, chemicals, and hot liquids); injury by poison, drugs, or other chemicals; mutilation (including amputa-

tion of body parts, breaking of bones, pulling out of nails, hair, or teeth, and scalping); detention without charge or trial; and banning or banishment (a punishment inflicted without due process, consisting of [a] the restriction of a person by house arrest, prohibition from being in a group, prohibition from speaking in public, or being quieted; or [b] the enforced transfer of a person from one area to another without the right to leave; deliberate withholding of food and water to someone in custody with deliberate disregard for the victim's health or well-being; deliberate failure to provide medical attention to ill or injured persons in custody; or the destruction of a person's house through arson or other attacks that made it impossible for the person to live there again).

68. *Truth and Reconciliation Commission of South Africa Report,* vol. 4, chap. 10, "Special Hearing: Women," p. 288.

69. *Truth and Reconciliation Commission of South Africa Report,* vol. 5, chap. 8, "Recommendations," p. 308.

70. Ibid., p. 349.

71. Sheila Masote, transcript of Johannesburg women's hearing, July 28, 1997.

72. For a review of how the government is pursuing gender equity, see Goetz, "Women in Politics and Gender Equity in Policy." See also Connell, "Strategies for Change."

73. ANC press release, "Women's Mandate Highlighted in Thabo Mbeki's Election Victory Speech" (June 3, 1999).

74. South Africa now has eight female cabinet members (out of twenty-eight) and eight deputies (out of thirteen). Women are in charge of "nontraditional" portfolios such as foreign affairs, public service, minerals and energy, and communications.

75. Govender, "Parliamentary Joint Standing Committee on the Improvement of the Quality of Life and Status of Women," p. 4.

8

Innocent Bystanders?

Michael Lapsley has said there are three kinds of stories to tell: "What was done to me; what I did; and what I didn't do."[1] Although most white South Africans did not engage in acts of torture or murder, there were nonetheless degrees of responsibility. South Africans have become fond of quoting German philosopher Karl Jaspers, who wrote about the four levels of guilt: criminal, political, moral, and metaphysical. Those who actually gave the orders or executed the crimes are criminally guilty. Political guilt extends to all citizens except those who actively resisted. Moral guilt covers those who "conveniently closed their eyes to events, or permitted themselves to be intoxicated, seduced or bought with personal advantages or who obeyed from fear." Metaphysical guilt is "not a case of some, or the majority, or many or most, but all who are guilty."[2] The majority of South Africans were not perpetrators but individuals who fall into the latter three categories. Mamphela Ramphele, the mother of Steve Biko's child, has asked: "Who [were] the real criminals? The policemen who physically committed acts of torture, or the generals who sent them, the politicians who presided, or the silent voters who didn't stand up to say 'No' loudly enough."[3]

The issue of bystanders is especially important when one considers how little white South Africans have felt responsible for the apartheid system. Just weeks before the Truth and Reconciliation Commission (TRC) began hearings, a poll conducted by the Center for the Study of Violence and Reconciliation (CSVR) indicated that 44 percent of white respondents did not feel apartheid was unjust. In fact, every third respondent felt that apartheid had done more good than harm. Only 14 percent felt that those who had supported the National Party (NP) were in some way responsible for the repression of black communities.[4] Yet those who carried out abuses against Africans believed they alone should not be held responsible.

Dirk Coetzee's testimony was striking for its indictment of schools and churches that had trained him to be a loyal follower of the National Party willing to commit criminal acts in defense of apartheid. Once the commander of a ruthless hit squad, Coetzee sought and received amnesty for incidents of torture, abduction, and murder, including the brutal killing of human rights lawyer Griffiths Mxenge, who was stabbed forty times. Testifying to the Amnesty Committee, Coetzee said that his indoctrination had begun when he was just a child, and that his strict Afrikaans and religious upbringing had shaped his beliefs and made it easy for him to rationalize his actions. Coetzee told the committee that through church, school, and Afrikaner youth organizations, he had been taught that "God had given South Africa to the Afrikaners," and that defending South Africa against the "communist onslaught" was an act of patriotism.[5]

Likewise, former security police spy Major Craig Williamson implicated all organs of society in his submission at the armed forces hearings:

> Our weapons, ammunition, uniforms, vehicles, radios and other equipment were all developed and provided by industry. Our finances and banking were done by bankers who even gave us covert credit cards for covert operations. Our chaplains prayed for our victory and our universities educated us in war. Our propaganda was carried by the media and our political masters were voted back into power time after time with ever increasing majorities.[6]

Coetzee and Williamson were but two of the thousands of apartheid's henchmen with whom society shared responsibility for their crimes.

The TRC may have had particular significance for the many white South Africans who insisted they did not know much of what had been done in their name by the likes of Coetzee and Williamson. Willie Hofmeyr, member of Parliament for the African National Congress (ANC), believes that there may have been a number of whites who were genuinely sorry for what had happened during the apartheid era and who would have welcomed the opportunity to come to terms with their consciences.[7] Ugandan scholar Mahmood Mamdani explains that in South Africa there may have been few actual perpetrators, but there were many beneficiaries.[8]

One criticism of the TRC was that, by focusing on gross human rights violations, most whites could merrily go on their way secure in the knowledge that they certainly never did anything like that. According to Charles

Villa-Vicencio: "Many South Africans, not the least white South Africans who have enjoyed the fruits of apartheid—without ever having directly tortured anyone or pulled a trigger in defense of privilege—find it difficult to bring themselves to acknowledge any sense of moral responsibility for the gross violations of human rights that have been exposed through the Truth and Reconciliation Commission."[9] This denial was made easier by the public portrayal of perpetrators as "evil-looking Nazis with thick Afrikaans accents," according to *Cape Times* reporter Steven Robins.[10]

The TRC ignored the massive denial of human rights experienced by millions of ordinary people—the violence of identity-pass laws, Group Areas, and forced removals. The hearings became a warning against police torturing people, but were silent about the injustice of allowing people to be poor, exploited, or pushed around.[11] Mamdani believes that it was important "to teach beneficiaries not only of the abuses for which they bear no personal responsibility but also of the structural injustice of which they have been direct beneficiaries, and therefore bear direct responsibility."[12] By identifying themselves with victims (with arguments that "the government misled us"), beneficiaries therefore did not take their own responsibility seriously.[13]

Perhaps the TRC's most important goal—and at the same time its most difficult goal—was to implicate society at large. To move beyond demonizing a few torturers toward indicting all of society, the TRC set up special hearings—outside the purview of the regular work of the three committees—on the role of the media, the medical profession, and the judiciary. Other hearings followed on the role of business and of the faith community, which suggests that reconciliation was envisaged not just between victims and perpetrators, but between victims and beneficiaries as well. Villa-Vicencio, the TRC's research director, has explained: "We are trying to enable South Africans of all levels to acknowledge their guilt. There are different levels, but the bystander is still part of it."[14]

Health Hearings

Hearings on the health sector were the first in a series that looked at how the different professions colluded with the apartheid system. One of the first cases reviewed had to do with the death in detention of Steve Biko, the leader of the Black Consciousness Movement. During police interrogation, he sustained a head injury (probably through torture, although the policemen in their amnesty hearing denied this, arguing instead that he had hit his head against a wall during a scuffle). The district surgeons in charge, Dr. Benjamin Tucker and Dr. Ivor Lang, failed to record his injuries or to insist that Biko, who was naked and manacled to an iron grill, be kept in a more humane environment. Dr. Tucker acquiesced in the police's wish to transfer him to Pretoria Central Prison hundreds of miles from East London. Biko died on the floor of the cell naked and alone. The case was referred to the South African Medical and Dental Council (SAMDC) for probable misconduct on the part of the doctors. The SAMDC exonerated the doctors, and their decision was supported by the Medical Association of South Africa (MASA), the doctors' "trade union." Eight years later, the SAMDC decision was reversed by the South African Supreme Court, and Drs. Tucker and Lang were found guilty of improper conduct.[15]

Nearly all district surgeons were torn between their loyalty to the state, and their professional commitment to patients. The submission by the American Association of the Advancement of Science criticized district surgeons for violating their code of professional ethics by turning a blind eye to the torture and ill-treatment of detainees.[16] The TRC commissioners concluded that many district surgeons had violated their patients' human rights by examining them with security officers or prison warders in the room. District surgeons overlooked the torture and assault of detainees that had been commonplace during the states of emergency in the mid-1980s.[17] The submission by the Department of Health said: "District surgeons had a firm belief that the detainees were the enemy of the State and that it was the right thing to do to assist the police in getting the information out of the detainees, as they were trying to overthrow the government."[18]

One district surgeon who refused to look the other way was Dr. Wendy Orr, one of the seventeen TRC commissioners. As a district surgeon during the tumultuous 1980s, she lodged a complaint with the Port Elizabeth Supreme Court to prevent police from assaulting detainees. She was ostracized by her colleagues for her action, barred from seeing detainees, and ultimately resigned. This example indicates that although there was societal pressure to support the state in all aspects, individuals did not always succumb. There was the possibility to act ethically.

The TRC also accused the Department of Health of helping to develop healthcare legislation that discriminated on the base of race. For instance, hospitals and ambulances were assigned to different races. If an ambulance for whites arrived at the scene of an accident only to find that the victim was black, the driver would leave, and another ambulance of the right color assignment would have to be summoned. Likewise, if an

African patient turned up at a white hospital for treatment, he or she would be turned away.

One of the most serious problems was the unequal distribution of resources. The Department of Health made sure that most funds went to white areas, despite the poverty and greater numbers of the black population. Per capita medical funding for whites was four times what it had been for blacks. Other criticisms of the Department of Health had to do with unequal salaries for black and white doctors.[19]

Testimony was also heard from the South African Medical Services (SAMS), which was the medical service of the South African Defense Force (SADF). Like the district surgeons, these healthcare professionals had been expected to follow the orders given by military superiors, which often conflicted with standards of professional medical ethics and human rights. They were expected to treat enemy victims of torture in South West Africa (now Namibia) so that they could be tortured another day.[20] These medical personnel were also implicated in developing chemical and biological weapons for military use. The commissioners felt that the SAMS testimony was evasive: many questions were deferred because they related to supposed "classified" operations.[21] In later investigations into the SADF's secret chemical and biological weapons program, information surfaced on the shady world of deadly chemicals, poisonous tee shirts, screwdrivers with poisoned pens, and a pill to make black women infertile.[22]

Although some of the submissions were less than forthright, the TRC heard stories from amnesty applicants of human rights abuses committed by medical professionals. Some were implicated in developing more effective methods of torture, advising police on how to poison people in a way that would be undetectable, and falsifying records to disguise the cause of death of detainees and prisoners who had been tortured.[23] Professor Michael Simpson testified that it had been doctors who had advised police how to administer electric shock without leaving any marks. A particularly reprehensible action was physicians' willingness to turn over medical records to the police without the consent of patients. The police used these files to locate political activists. One doctor testified that he had advised his patients to give phony addresses so there would not be a paper trail for the police to follow. Again, this was the exception rather than the rule for physician behavior.[24]

The health-sector hearings were significant in helping to paint a picture of the context in which human rights abuses occurred. For the medical community, it was a "painful ethical voyage from wrong to right."[25] In its final report, the TRC concluded that "the health sector, through apathy, acceptance of the status quo and acts of omission, allowed the creation of an environment in which the health of millions of South Africans was neglected, even at times actively compromised, and in which violations of moral and ethical codes of practice were frequent, facilitating violations of human rights."[26] The editors of *An Ambulance of the Wrong Colour* warned that "scapegoating a few health professionals as 'bad apples,' 'mad scientists,' or crazed extremists has been far easier than overhauling an entire system."[27] However, they contended that those responsible were not heinous villains but rather ordinary healthcare providers doing their jobs within a system "that hid its flaws behind a veneer of professionalism."[28]

Unfortunately, human rights violations have not been confined to the apartheid past. "The complexities of HIV/AIDS, the persistent evidence of torture and death in police custody of 'common' criminals and the continuation of solitary confinement in the new C-MAX prison are challenges that confront us even now."[29]

Business Hearings

Desmond Tutu opened the business hearings with these words: "We want to hear your story. We are not so naive not to be aware that governments are powerful, and often room to manoeuvre by business is restricted. You know that wonderful story Jesus tells of the publican and the Pharisee. The publican is vindicated, because all he says is I have sinned, I am a sinner. I acknowledge who I am rather than engaging in the self-justification the Pharisee indulged in."[30]

Despite Bishop Tutu's plea to reject self-rationalization, that is in effect what the business community attempted to do during its three days of hearings in November 1997. Business organizations such as the Steel and Engineering Industries Federation of South Africa (SEIFSA), the South African Chamber of Business (SACOB), the Afrikaner Handelsinstituut (Afrikaner Institute for Commerce; AHI), the Council of South African Banks (COSAB), the Textile Federation, and the Johannesburg Chamber of Commerce and Industry articulated the view that apartheid hurt business and that they could be considered victims too. This position was shared by the Anglo-American Corporation and by Old Mutual, two mega-businesses in South Africa.

Strongly rejecting this view were the African National Congress, the Congress of South African Trade Unions (COSATU), and the South African Communist Party (SACP), all of which made submissions on the role of business in propping up the apartheid regime. They argued that the real victims were black workers, and that businesses were responsible for the denial of health and safety measures, medical aid, and pensions.

In its final report, the TRC distinguished three levels of culpability. The first order of culpability was "direct involvement with the state in the formulation of oppressive policies or practices that resulted in low labour costs or otherwise boosted profits."[31] The mining industry clearly fell within this category, as it played a critical role in advancing cheap labor policies. The mining companies influenced legislation (Natives Land Acts of 1913 and 1936) that forced black workers into the wage system by forcing them off their land, maintained a "color bar" that kept black wages artificially low, insisted on monopolistic recruiting practices through the Chamber of Mines, provided subhuman living conditions in the compounds, and brutally repressed trade unions. Testimony from other groups pointed to the dismal health and safety record of the mines. COSATU's submission drew attention to the health hazards associated with the use of asbestos and polyurethane in mines long after the dangers of such substances had become known.[32] The commissioners concluded that "the mining industry bears a great deal of moral responsibility for the migrant labour system and its associated hardships."[33] They added: "The failure of the Chamber of Mines to address this squarely and to grapple with its moral implications is regrettable and not constructive."[34]

The second order of culpability included "those businesses that made their money by engaging directly in activities that promoted state repression." Crucial to the determination of second-order culpability was that people had to have known that their products or services would be used for morally unacceptable purposes.[35] The Armaments Development and Production Corporation (ARMSCOR) and other businesses that provided armored vehicles to the police during the mid-1980s were included in this category. Against ARMSCOR's argument that procurement is a normal activity of governments for defense purposes, the commissioners insisted that "once the army rolled into the townships in the 1980s the scales should have fallen from the eyes of all perceptive South Africans."[36]

Another example of second-order culpability concerned the provision of covert credit cards to undercover policemen, which had been brought to the attention of the TRC by Major Craig Williamson, a former police spy who had testified that banks provided the Civil Cooperation Bureau with such cards.[37] The TRC noted: "The particular banker involved may not have had direct knowledge of why specific cards were being used. However, there was no obvious attempt on the part of the banking industry to investigate or stop the use being made of their facilities in an environment that was rife with gross human rights violations."[38]

The third order of culpability was described as "ordinary business activities that benefitted indirectly by virtue of operating within the racially structured context of an apartheid society." White farmers fell into this category. Farmers were early beneficiaries of the Natives Land Acts, which captured for them African workers for commercial farming who otherwise would have continued to practice subsistence farming on their own land. "This means that, at the very least, representatives of commercial agriculture need to acknowledge (not least to themselves) the extent to which white farmers and their families benefitted (irrespective of their political views) from their privileged access to the land, which excluded virtually all other potential farmers."[39] As white farms became more mechanized, and black labor was no longer needed, black families were forcibly resettled into the impoverished homelands "if not at the explicit request of the agricultural sector, certainly with its implicit support."[40] The farming community was also criticized for its failure to educate black children living on their farms. "This failure to educate children in a modern economy is itself a human rights abuse," the commissioners concluded. The TRC also admonished farmers for taking advantage of the farm prison system, which provided them with free prison labor and resulted in many human rights abuses.[41] Unfortunately, no representatives of commercial agriculture participated in the business hearings.

Nicoli Nattrass has argued that for the TRC, third-order culpability implies guilt by association. The fact of prospering under apartheid is equated with responsibility for it. "Thus, irrespective of whether a firm treated its workers well, protested against apartheid and supported the anti-apartheid movement, the firm is in effect held to be as culpable for apartheid as a racist firm which abused its workers and bankrolled right-wing activities."[42] The only way business could have avoided condemnation by the TRC would have been to disinvest entirely from the South African economy. Because the TRC held that all businesses benefited from apartheid, it recommended that all companies should pay a wealth tax as restitution.

English-Speaking Businesses Victims Too?

To what degree did Afrikaner businesses have a privileged relationship with the government that benefited them over English-speaking businesses? According to Professor Sampie Terreblanche, several Afrikaner corporations such as Rembrandt and the South African National Life Assurance Company (SANLAM) grew spectacularly due to lucrative favors and inside information received from the NP government.[43] The Anglo-American Corporation confirmed that the special relationship between the NP and Afrikaner businesses hurt its ability to do business. As an example, it cited that its bid for Samancor was rejected on political grounds.[44] The South African Breweries (SAB) also complained that "English-speaking business leaders often felt marginalised under apartheid, having little or no influence over government policy. . . . [I]n a real sense, such businesses were also victims of the system."[45]

COSATU rejected this self-identification as "victim" on the part of English-speaking businesses, saying that while the NP government explicitly set out to nurture Afrikaner businesses, its overall policy climate created the conditions for the rapid accumulation of capital by all white capitalists.[46] Terreblanche concurred: "White politicians and business people were most of the time, from say 1910 to 1994, hand in glove with each other to protect their mutual interests in the maintenance of the structures of white power, privilege and wealth on the one hand and the structures of black and mainly African deprivation, discrimination, exploitation and poverty on the other hand." He added: "Apartheid proved to be good for every white business."[47] The real victims, of course, were black businesses. Under Group Areas, Africans were not allowed to buy land in white areas. They were not able to own businesses in white areas either. The Bantu Education Act also limited their ability to acquire skills necessary to be successful in business.

An argument was presented by some businesses that apartheid was antithetical to capitalist development, and for that reason they had opposed apartheid policies. For instance, job reservation for white workers had kept labor costs high, Group Areas had kept black workers far from places of employment, and substandard education for Africans through the Bantu Education Act had hurt those businesses, especially in manufacturing, which had needed a stable, well-trained workforce. AHI testified that Harry Oppenheimer and Anton Rupert, representing the capital of English-speaking businesses and Afrikaner businesses respectively, established the Urban Foundation in 1976 to push for reform in influx control, housing, and black landownership.[48]

This view of business as progressive was disputed by other submissions, which called it a selective reading of history. Only when the economy matured and required a stable, more educated workforce had business spoken to government about reforming the system. The SACP argued, "The idea that the private sector's chief sin . . . was that it failed to 'speak out against a system that was against economic logic' is spurious. . . . Resisting the growth of black trade unionism, and calling in the police during strikes, is thus seen as evidence of collaboration with the apartheid system against democratization."[49]

One defender of business, Ann Bernstein, the director of the Center for Development and Enterprise, a probusiness research and lobby organization, argued that business "is not the place to protect human rights. . . . Corporations are not institutions established for moral purposes."[50] This thought was echoed by SANLAM: "Any notion that business could have acted as a watchdog of the government as far as human rights violations are concerned is totally unrealistic and should be dispelled."[51] Predictably, the TRC took exception to this view: "It would be a sad day for the nation, faced as it is with the opportunity for renewal, if business were to dismiss social concern, business ethics and moral accountability in labour relations as being of no direct concern to itself."[52]

One submission that owned up to complicity was that of the Development Bank of Southern Africa (DBSA), which admitted that by providing development loans to homelands and by advising officials, "the Bank was an integral part of the system and part and parcel of the apartheid gross violation of human rights."[53] No such admission was forthcoming from those businesses that participated in the network of Joint Management Committees, which coordinated the work of all government departments in dealing with points of unrest.

Two other sectors—media and faith communities—deserve special attention because, as the TRC highlighted in its final report, they "exerted immense influence, not least of which was their capacity to influence the ideas and morals of generations of South Africans."[54] They are the subject of the following chapters.

Notes

1. Lapsley, "Tears, Fears, and Hope," p. 1.
2. Jaspers, *The Question of German Guilt,* p. 31.
3. Mamphela Ramphele, cited in Boraine and Levy, eds., *The Healing of a Nation?* pp. 35–36.
4. CSVR poll conducted in May 1996.
5. Amnesty hearing, Durban, November 5, 1996.

6. Memorandum submitted to the TRC in armed forces hearing, Cape Town, October 9, 1997, cited in *Truth and Reconciliation Commission of South Africa Report,* vol. 4, chap. 2, "Institutional Hearing: Business and Labour," p. 24.

7. Eddie Koch and Gaye Davis, "Firing Up the Truth Machine," *Mail & Guardian* (July 26–August 3, 1995).

8. Mamdani, "Reconciliation Without Justice," p. 5.

9. Charles Villa-Vicencio, "Don't Blame Me, I Just Live Here" (unpublished paper), p. 1.

10. Cited in Hollyday, "Truth and Reconciliation in South Africa," p. 77.

11. The TRC, while acknowledging that forced removals may come under the category of "severe harm," maintained that because of limited funds and time limitations, only human rights violations, such as torture and murder, would come under the its purview.

12. Cited in Maluleke, "The Truth and Reconciliation Discourse," p. 111.

13. Mamdani, "A Diminished Truth" *(Siyaya),* p. 40.

14. Cited in Rosenberg, "Recovering from Apartheid," p. 95.

15. Health hearing, Cape Town, June 17, 1997.

16. Health hearing, Cape Town, June 18, 1997.

17. *Truth and Reconciliation Commission of South Africa Report,* vol. 4, chap. 5, "Institutional Hearing: The Health Sector," pp. 114–115.

18. Health hearing, Cape Town, June 18, 1997.

19. *Truth and Reconciliation Commission of South Africa Report,* vol. 4, chap. 5, "Institutional Hearing: The Health Sector," p. 156.

20. Health hearing, Cape Town, June 17, 1997.

21. *Truth and Reconciliation Commission of South Africa Report,* vol. 4, chap. 5, "Institutional Hearing: The Health Sector," p. 125.

22. Ibid., p. 126.

23. Ibid., pp. 128–129.

24. Health hearing, Cape Town, June 18, 1997.

25. Asmal, Asmal, and Roberts, *Reconciliation Through Truth,* p. 47.

26. *Truth and Reconciliation Commission of South Africa Report,* vol. 5, chap. 6, "Findings and Conclusions," p. 250.

27. Baldwin-Ragaven, de Gruchy, and London, eds., *An Ambulance of the Wrong Colour,* p. 208.

28. Ibid., p. 208.

29. Ibid., p. 13.

30. Business hearing, Johannesburg, November 11, 1997.

31. *Truth and Reconciliation Commission of South Africa Report,* vol. 4, chap. 2, "Institutional Hearing: Business and Labour," p. 24.

32. Business hearing, Johannesburg, November 13, 1997.

33. *Truth and Reconciliation Commission of South Africa Report,* vol. 4, chap. 2, "Institutional Hearing: Business and Labour," p. 33.

34. Ibid., p. 34.

35. Ibid., p. 25.

36. Ibid., p. 37.

37. Submission to armed forces hearing, Cape Town, October 9, 1997.

38. *Truth and Reconciliation Commission of South Africa Report,* vol. 4, chap. 2, "Institutional Hearing: Business and Labour," p. 26.

39. Ibid., p. 29.

40. Ibid.

41. Ibid.

42. Nattrass, "The Truth and Reconciliation Commission on Business and Apartheid," p. 389.

43. Business hearing, Johannesburg, November 11, 1997.

44. Business hearing, Johannesburg, November 13, 1997.

45. *Truth and Reconciliation Commission of South Africa Report,* vol. 4, chap. 2, "Institutional Hearing: Business and Labour," p. 30.

46. Business hearing, Johannesburg, November 13, 1997.

47. Business hearing, Johannesburg, November 11, 1997.

48. Business hearing, Johannesburg, November 12, 1997.

49. *Truth and Reconciliation Commission of South Africa Report,* vol. 4, chap. 2, "Institutional Hearing: Business and Labour," p. 22.

50. Business hearing, Johannesburg, November 12, 1997.

51. Business hearing, Johannesburg, November 13, 1997.

52. *Truth and Reconciliation Commission of South Africa Report,* vol. 4, chap. 2, "Institutional Hearing: Business and Labour," p. 54.

53. Business hearing, Johannesburg, November 12, 1997.

54. *Truth and Reconciliation Commission of South Africa Report,* vol. 5, chap. 6, "Findings and Conclusions," p. 249.

9

Media Hearings

A free and independent press is an indispensable ingredient of a vibrant democracy. That it was feeble if not entirely nonexistent in South Africa during the apartheid era was highlighted by special hearings on the media held by the Truth and Reconciliation Commission (TRC) in September 1997. Conflicting pictures of the media emerged from the three days of these hearings. One picture was that of reporters colluding with the government to enforce and entrench apartheid, perpetrators themselves of human rights violations against Africans. Another picture was that of journalists as objects of government attacks, victims themselves of apartheid.

Clearly the media, representing different sectors, was not a monolithic entity and was characterized by both collusion and resistance. Included were the South African Broadcasting Corporation (SABC), a willing government lackey owned and operated by the National Party; the Afrikaans press, a loyal advocate of the government's positions; the English-speaking press, a liberal opponent of apartheid in theory if not always in practice; and the "alternative" press, a small but important voice of resistance against government policies and most subject to attack.

South African Broadcasting Corporation

The official mouthpiece of the National Party from 1948 until the democratic elections in 1994, the SABC neglected its human rights obligations as the public broadcaster to report the truth. Its biased reporting of the news and stereotypical portrayal of blacks were intended to put the government in a positive light and the resistance in a negative one.

Broadcasters operated under provisions that forbade anything that would "disturb the peace . . . undermine the economy . . . promote revolutionary objectives . . . or directly or indirectly lead to transgressions of the law."[1] Therefore, it could not report the views of "terrorist" organizations like the African National Congress (ANC). Images that put the security forces in a favorable light were the only ones shown. For instance, footage of township violence involving the police and security forces never saw the light of day.[2]

By manipulating the news, the SABC brainwashed a substantial section of the white community into believing the government's version of affairs and supporting its policies and practices. John Van Zyl, director of the Media Monitoring Project, testified that the SABC violated the rights to information and free speech of South African citizens.[3] Other witnesses claimed that the SABC had been a "willing partner," often exceeding the wishes of its apartheid bosses.

The Afrikaans Press

Similar criticisms were lodged against the Afrikaans newspapers. The Freedom of Expression Institute (FXI), composed mainly of white editors and reporters from the English-speaking newspapers, summarized the role of the Afrikaans press in a written submission to the TRC: "The Afrikaans newspapers were official organs of the National Party and slavishly propounded its policies especially in regard to the implementation of apartheid."[4] There was no official response from the Afrikaans press, as the Nasionale Pers (Naspers; National Press), the publisher of the majority of Afrikaans newspapers, declined to make a submission. One explanation for the lack of official response from the Afrikaans press was provided by Max du Preez, a former editor of the Afrikaans newspaper *Vrye Weekblad,* who suggested that the Afrikaans press was not forthcoming because if the level of corruption were revealed to the public, these newspapers would lose credibility with readers, leading to a decline in readership and lost revenues.[5]

While no Afrikaans publishing company or publication submitted a statement,[6] several weeks after the hearings a group of 127 Afrikaner journalists from the major newspapers, including *Beeld, Die Burger,* and *Rapport,* provided a statement to the TRC in which they acknowledged and apologized for their role in upholding the apartheid state. The reporters admitted that a close relationship had developed between Naspers and the National Party, with the publishing group acting as a National Party mouthpiece. These newspapers formed an integral part of the power structure that implemented and maintained apartheid through support of the National Party in elections and referendums.

The submission stated: "I . . . did not properly inform readers of the injustice of apartheid, did not oppose these injustices vigorously enough and, where I had knowledge of these injustices, too readily accepted the National Party government's denials and reassurances."[7] Although not directly involved in committing human rights abuses, the reporters said they nevertheless regarded themselves as morally co-responsible for what had happened in the name of apartheid because they had helped maintain a system in which these abuses could flourish. The journalists concluded with an apology to those who suffered as a result of their actions and pledged their commitment to preventing the past from being repeated. Although the number of signatories was small compared to the total number of Afrikaner journalists, the gesture was symbolically important in a country where Afrikaners continued to live in denial about their complicity. Bishop Desmond Tutu, chair of the TRC, praised the submission as "a very significant contribution to reconciliation and the process of healing in our land."[8]

English-Speaking Press

According to the FXI, the English-speaking press had supported the opposition party, the United Party, and had opposed the National Party government "with varying degrees of vigour."[9] Yet their focus was on the excesses of apartheid rather than on the policy itself. In time, the English-speaking press supported the more liberal Progressive Party, which broke off from the United Party, and advanced the policy of a qualified black franchise.

During the apartheid era, the English-speaking press was thoroughly infiltrated by agents of the government whose goal was to disseminate propaganda and disinformation. Government agents hired or coerced journalists to report on the conduct of their colleagues. John Horak, a former policeman who was planted at the *Rand Daily Mail* as a journalist, testified that editors were well aware that government spies were in their midst, and estimated that half of all newsrooms harbored government collaborators.[10] Horak's handler, Craig Williamson, a former spy, explained that the intelligence services used reporters to gather information on the activities and whereabouts of black leaders because reporters often had better access to sources in the liberation movement, and they planted stories favorable to the government, especially concerning the police and military services.[11]

With close to 100 acts on the statute books, the English-speaking press operated under a host of censoring regulations with limitations on reporting police activities, defense force activities, energy matters, oil purchase and transportation details, prison conditions, pretrial detentions of prisoners and their appearances in court, and even trade figures. The "205 Process," which required journalists to reveal their sources, had a chilling effect on most of them. And the threats of prosecution for printing "subversive" statements likewise intimidated reporters from printing the truth. The Suppression of Communism Act, the Terrorism Act, the General Law Amendment Act, and the Internal Security Act were so ambiguous, labeling any opposition as "communism," "terrorism," or "sabotage," that journalists were unclear on how far they could legally go in opposing the system.

Nevertheless, during the hearings it was argued that many yielded to the threats without testing the limits of what they could get away with. Fearing government harassment, banning, or imprisonment, journalists actually went further than the law required. A spokesman for the Independent Newspapers, one of two major publishers of English-language newspapers, said that the press believed it could not quote prisoners or publish their pictures. Journalists thought they could not publish ANC statements since the ANC was a banned organization, while in fact they could have published statements as long as they were not provided by banned individuals. The spokesman indicted the English-speaking press for not taking the time to explore the opportunities that were legally available and testing the boundaries of the law.[12]

Because the laws were so vague and the penalties so severe, journalists and editors were intimidated into degrees of self-censorship. The newspaper industry set up the National Press Union (NPU) to rule on breaches of conduct and levy fees against offending reporters and editors, which had an inhibiting effect on their reporting the news. The NPU signed agreements with both the defense force and police service in which they agreed to meet with these sectors to discuss what could and could not be reported. Newspapers printed the official "sanitized version of the truth" rather than their own reporters' firsthand accounts.[13] For instance, when troops were engaged in fighting the Popular Movement for the

Liberation of Angola (MPLA) in Angola in 1975, the press obligingly reported the government's version that South African troops were not engaged. Under the agreements, the press liaised with the police and military, and reported what they were told to report. In justifying the press's actions, the NPU president testified that their feeling was that "some news was better than no news."[14] The Independent Newspapers explained to the TRC that the goal was to publish as much as possible without getting shut down.

Still, whereas the Afrikaans newspapers had never opposed the National Party or the security forces on any important issue, the English-speaking press, though compromised, had a much better record at exposing the truth than the Afrikaans press. While it did not do enough to fight the system, it at least was not in collusion with the government.

Black Independent Press

The black independent press was the focus of the third day of media hearings. The black press was an expression of the activism in the wake of the Black Consciousness Movement of the 1970s. It was one of the few forums where black voices could be heard and offered journalists a rare opportunity to work in a nondiscriminatory environment. While the English-speaking press had opposed apartheid in its editorial pages, it nevertheless practiced apartheid in the newsroom. English-language newspapers hired blacks, but they were paid considerably less than their white counterparts, "ghettoized" by consignment to reporting exclusively on "black issues" ("sensationalism, sex, and soccer"), and permitted to write only for township editions of the major newspapers.[15] In addition to paying blacks less than whites, English-language newspapers practiced "petty apartheid" in the workplace, segregating restrooms and canteens by race.

As the most vocal voice for change, the independent press sought to counter the view in the mainstream press of the resistance as "terrorist" or "communist-inspired." The black press stood alone in exposing security-branch and hit-squad activities. Not surprisingly, as strong critics of the government's policies, reporters from the alternative press were subjected to the most severe forms of harassment from the state, including banning, detention, and torture.

Although the most successful medium at maintaining journalistic integrity, the black press nevertheless came under criticism at the TRC hearings for a lack of objectivity. Clearly black reporters saw themselves first as blacks, and secondarily as reporters. One witness criticized the black press for advocacy over fairness. For instance, only atrocities committed by the police, and never the resistance, were reported. The Independent Newspapers spokesman explained that black reporters were under pressure from activists to portray them uncritically, and reporters were threatened for noncompliance.[16]

Media Freedom Beyond the TRC

In its final report, the commission concluded that "state restrictions on the freedom of the media played an important role in facilitating gross violations of human rights."[17] All the media, with the exception of the alternative press, had violated the public's basic right to information on what was being done on their behalf and for their benefit in the name of apartheid. The press suppressed information, cooperated with security forces, and practiced apartheid in its own operations. By keeping the public in the dark, they contributed to a climate in which human rights abuses against blacks could and did prevail. The question of whether purveyors of ideologies such as media practitioners were as culpable as direct perpetrators of human rights abuses—the assassins and torturers—is an important one. Joe Thloloe, managing editor of the *Sowetan* from 1988 to 1994, argues that the effects of a compromised press "were probably more devastating to the nation than all the bullets."[18]

Is there any danger that the press could once again be reduced to a government mouthpiece as it was in the dark days of apartheid? During his presidency (1994–1999), Nelson Mandela often castigated reporters for criticizing ANC/government policy and not playing their role in "nation building." Under Thabo Mbeki's administration, the media has come under fire by the government-appointed Human Rights Commission (HRC), which has accused it of racism and ordered editors through subpoenas and threat of imprisonment to come and give account of themselves to the commission.[19]

That racism still exists in South Africa, including in the media, is denied by no one. But a government commission acting as a czar of public expression is frightening if one believes that free expression is a prerequisite of a flourishing democracy. The Freedom of Expression Institute weighed in against the HRC's hearings, describing the commission as "the very essence of censorship."[20] Former HRC member Rhoda Kadalie blast-ed the commission's decision to serve subpoenas on more than thirty journalists: "These subpoenas are nothing but a gross violation of freedom of expression and an attempt to prescribe to the press what they should be thinking and writing."[21] And commissioner Sheena Duncan, a well-known antiapartheid activist since the 1950s, resigned from the HRC, saying: "In those [apartheid] days it was claimed that all was justified by the creation of the image of an enemy labeled communism. Now it seems the HRC has embarked on a process claiming justification in the name of racism." The rights to equality and human dignity, she continued, cannot be protected by the violation of the "right to freedom of expression which includes the freedom of the press and other media."[22]

There is something disturbing about a new democracy demanding minutes of editorial meetings, threatening searches of offices and seizure of documents, and threatening jail for editors for noncompliance. Fortunately the HRC has wisely decided to back down, but the incident raised concerns about the government's commitment to freedom of expression.[23] Despite the spotlight that the TRC put on the media's behavior during apartheid, the current vendetta against the press suggests the new regime is taking a few too many lessons from the old.

Notes

1. SABC policy guidelines, cited by Louis Raubenheimer, media hearing, Johannesburg, September 15, 1997.
2. Bheki Khathide, media hearing, Johannesburg, September 15, 1997.
3. Media hearing, Johannesburg, September 15, 1997.
4. Written submission by the FXI to the TRC on "The Role of the Media in the Apartheid Years and Associated Matters."
5. Media hearing, Johannesburg, September 17, 1997.
6. Instead, Naspers provided the TRC with a copy of "Oor Grense Heen," its official history.
7. Written submission by Naspers to the TRC.
8. TRC press release, "TRC Receives Submission Signed by 127 Journalists from Nas Pers" (September 16, 1997).
9. Written submission by the FXI to the TRC.
10. Media hearing, Johannesburg, September 16, 1997.
11. Ibid.
12. Media hearing, Johannesburg, September 17, 1997.
13. Jon Qwelane, media hearing, Johannesburg, September 17, 1997.
14. Jolyon Nutall, media hearing, Johannesburg, September 16, 1997.
15. Written submission by the FXI to the TRC.
16. Media hearing, Johannesburg, September 17, 1997.

17. *Truth and Reconciliation Commission of South Africa Report,* vol. 4, chap. 6, "Institutional Hearing: The Media," p. 18.

18. Jacqueline Zaina, "Editors Debate Probe by Truth Body," *Business Day* (January 21, 1997).

19. Subpoenas were issued to the editors of the Johannesburg *Sunday Times,* the *Mail & Guardian,* and two other Cape Town papers. One of the complaints lodged against the *Mail & Guardian* included the "over-representation of alleged corruption and incompetence among Black people and under-representation of Whites for similar alleged offenses"; see "What the HRC Wanted," *Mail & Guardian* (February 25–March 2, 2000). Another has to do with a story titled "African War Virus Spreads to Caprivi," presented alongside pictures of unidentified bodies, that "contributed to the de-personalisation of Black deaths and represented them as just another statistic"; see "What Our Lawyers Answered," *Mail & Guardian* (February 25–March 2, 2000).

20. Response of the FXI to the HRC's "Inquiry into Racism in the Media," March 30, 2000.

21. Rhoda Kadalie, "Defy Barney's Thought Police," *Mail & Guardian* (February 18–24, 2000).

22. Evidence wa ka Ngobeni, "Sheena Duncan Quits Over Racism Probe," *Mail & Guardian* (February 25–March 2, 2000).

23. While freedom of expression is enshrined in the Constitution, the ANC government is just one member of Parliament short of the two-thirds majority necessary to rewrite the document.

10

Wounded Healers: The Churches Respond

Despite the contribution that Christian theology can make toward understanding reconciliation and, more important, the responsibility the churches had in legitimating apartheid, church response to South Africa's Truth and Reconciliation Commission (TRC) was initially minimal. Formal responses came early on from the Research Institute on Christianity in South Africa (RICSA) at the University of Cape Town, the theological faculty at the University of the Western Cape, and church leaders from the South African Council of Churches (SACC).[1] But support from denominations and individual churches was weak. Etienne de Villiers, professor of ethics at the University of Pretoria, has made the point that the TRC could only function successfully if the Dutch Reformed Church (DRC) and other Afrikaner churches lent their support: "If the political parties of the Afrikaner, the Afrikaans newspapers, and, in particular, the Afrikaans churches withdraw their support and encourage Afrikaners to refuse any co-operation with the TRC, the TRC will surely not succeed in its objectives."[2]

White churches—especially white Afrikaner churches—were mainly uninvolved in the process. The Northern Province Council of Churches issued a statement in December 1996 critical of these churches' minimal assistance in statement taking, preparation for hearings, and counseling victims.[3] The Dutch Reformed Church—or the Nederduitse Gereformeerde Kerk (NGK)[4]—early on declined to make a submission, promising to review the issue later.[5] In August 1997 the DRC issued not a submission but a document written for the World Alliance of Reformed Churches, *The Story of the Dutch Reformed Church's Journey with*

Apartheid, 1960–1994. The DRC therein acknowledged that it had laid down the scriptural basis for apartheid as early as 1943, relying on texts that indicated God's desire for separate peoples to maintain their separateness, such as the story of the Tower of Babel, the events at Pentecost, and scriptures about the purity of the people of Israel.[6] The DRC further admitted that after 1948, when the National Party (NP) came to power, the Dutch Reformed Church had frequently urged the government to implement apartheid policies, recommending for instance the ban against mixed marriages and the establishment of Group Areas for the different races. The DRC insisted, however, that the church had been firm in its belief that apartheid should be implemented fairly, and that it should benefit all race groups. It called apartheid a well-intentioned system that degenerated into an oppressive one when it took on the character of ideology. However, apartheid as a political system went further in practice than simply acknowledging the right and freedom of all peoples and cultural groups to stay true to their own values, the DRC conceded. Through years of reflection on the part of the church, the conviction grew that "a forced separation and division of peoples cannot be considered a Biblical imperative."[7]

The DRC denied that it had failed to criticize the National Party's policies. It said it had not raised its concerns about Group Areas and the Immorality Act, but rather had chosen to use its privileged position with the government to oppose abuses behind closed doors.[8] "However, the church was hesitant to insist on the repeal of the Acts concerned and usually simply requested that they be applied with compassion and humanity," the DRC stated.[9] In retrospect, the DRC admitted that there had been occasions when its "prophetic voice should have spoken more clearly to the then government."[10]

Regarding its support of the South African Defense Force (SADF) with chaplains,[11] the DRC argued that it had been and still was convinced that the war waged on the borders and later internally was a just struggle. For the church, the war was about survival and protection of the Christian faith.[12] Since the war was viewed as a total onslaught from communist forces (Cuba and the Soviet Union), "the outspoken atheism of these forces was by implication a threat to religious freedom."[13] Had the chaplains known of covert activities that were un-Christian and destroyed human life, they would have raised their voices against them.

Tracy Kuperus's recent book *State, Civil Society, and Apartheid in South Africa,* which chronicles DRC-state relations over sixty years, reflects a rather different interpretation of the DRC's relationship to the National Party than the self-serving one provided in the *Journey* document.

Kuperus argues that for most periods the DRC and the state were engaged in mutual collaboration. Between 1979 and 1994 the DRC actually had supported a more conservative approach than the NP leaders, who were bent on reforming the system. Her explanation for the church's "lagging behind the state" is that the DRC "could not easily distance itself from the moral and biblical underpinning of apartheid that it helped to construct."[14]

There were pragmatic reasons as well. When the National Party embarked on reforms in 1982, conservatives within the party broke off to form the Conservative Party. In an effort to avoid such a schism within its denomination, the DRC "took a more moderate stance on the issue of reform than state leaders were promoting."[15] (Notwithstanding this effort to maintain unity, there was a breakaway of conservative parishioners from the DRC, who formed the Afrikaanse Protestante Kerk [APK; Afrikaner Protestant Church] in 1986.) As the government proceeded first under P. W. Botha, then under F. W. de Klerk, to dismantle some of the laws undergirding apartheid, especially the so-called petty apartheid statutes regulating "whites only" facilities, the DRC "refused to budge on the issue of structural church unity" and continued separate churches for whites, Coloureds, and Africans.[16] With the exception of the period of 1958 to 1961, when the DRC did urge the government to relax its policies,[17] it is difficult to accept the contention of the *Journey* document that the DRC spoke prophetically (if behind closed doors), urging the National Party to reform.

The RICSA report noted: "This confession is notable in that it is not nearly as strongly worded as the confessions of other churches who opposed apartheid."[18] Carl Niehaus was far more harsh in his assessment of the *Journey* document: "It is . . . no real confession, but an attempt to water down grave sins and abuses with a selective handling of history. It tries to create the impression that the basic intentions of the DRC have always been good and sincere. This little piece of writing is a betrayal of their members who long for guidance."[19] H. Russel Botman has concurred: "The DRC has thus not recognized its own role in the making of the mind of the perpetrator, or even the inherent evil of apartheid."[20]

Public Hearings

The Salvation Army and the Apostolic Faith Mission (AFM) were the first national church bodies to make official submissions to the TRC. The Salvation Army admitted that during the apartheid years it had chosen to remain silent, "a sin of omission which we deeply regret."[21] The AFM confessed that it had failed in its duty to question the system and pledged to become a more faithful watchdog to ensure that history would never be repeated.[22]

Finally, in November 1997 more churches responded to the TRC's invitation for a special public hearing of the faith communities.[23] In the aftermath of amnesty hearings in which perpetrators often linked their actions to the teachings of their churches, the TRC wanted to get at the churches' understanding of their responsibility. They were asked to respond to the following question:

> Given the prominence of references to morality and religion in the submissions of various political parties and amnesty applications, in which ways, if any, did the theology and activities of your denomination contribute to the formation of the motives and perspectives of those individuals, organisations and institutions responsible for gross human rights violations, either upholding the previous system or in opposing it?[24]

Opening the hearings in East London, Desmond Tutu announced that no church in South Africa could claim a perfect record of opposing apartheid and all would have to confess to shortcomings.[25] Over three days, confessions came from Christian denominations as well as from Jewish, Muslim, and Hindu communities. In varying degrees, they apologized for not having done enough to oppose the government's policies. While no church confessed to active complicity with the state or with the liberation movements in human rights abuses, they were virtually unanimous in apologizing for playing a role, including supplying chaplains, interpreting the conflict as a holy war, failing to act in accordance with their own traditions, and practicing apartheid in their own structures. (The DRC and AFM were officially divided into four sections, for whites, Indians, Africans, and Coloureds, and even the English-speaking churches were segregated, at least in practice if not officially.) However, all of the witnesses claimed at least some degree of opposition, at least to state abuses if not apartheid itself.

The Anglican Church (the Church of the Province of Southern Africa [CPSA]) apologized to Bishop Tutu for failing to support him in the face of harsh criticisms over his call for economic sanctions. Bishop Michael Nuttal apologized on behalf of the CPSA to Afrikaners for an attitude of moral superiority toward them. The church's chief apology, Nuttal asserted, went to the church's black congregants for their treatment as second-class members.[26]

The Church of England confessed to its neutral stance during the apartheid era, saying that it had been misled by the National Party's misuse of the Bible to support an evil ideology. Bishop Frank Retief explained that the church had believed the NP's propaganda about a communist threat and added: "Be that as it may, we allowed ourselves to be misled into accepting a social, economic and political system that was cruel and oppressive."[27]

The Catholic Church stressed its record as a staunch opponent and vocal critic of apartheid and identified its sins as acts of omission: "Silence in the face of ongoing and systematic oppression at all levels of society is perhaps the Church's greatest sin," Bishop Kevin Dowling told the commissioners.[28] He pointed out that both Chris Hani, leader of the Communist Party, and Janusz Walus, his killer, were members of the Catholic Church, which illustrates the complexity of the situation; on one hand the church had kept the apartheid dispensation going, while on the other it had fought to bring down the system.

South Africa's chief rabbi, Cyril Harris, tendered a collective apology on behalf of South Africa's Jews for their failure to protest against apartheid more loudly. He said that fear was the major reason for the Jewish community's silence. Jews in South Africa had a "hypersensitivity" toward survival in the aftermath of the Holocaust, the rabbi explained. Still, he added, the Jewish community had provided proportionately "more heroes" in the struggle than any other white group.[29]

Muslim theologian Faried Esack launched an attack on Muslim leaders during his submission when he said their contribution "was essentially one of betrayal."[30] Esack's accusation led to the unscheduled appearance before the TRC the next day of the Muslim Judicial Council (MJC). The MJC representative, Imam Hassan Solomon, insisted that the MJC had in fact been a staunch opponent of apartheid and was the first religious organization in South Africa to declare apartheid a heresy. He also denied suggestions that Muslim businessmen had benefited from apartheid, as Esack had suggested. "The entire Muslim business community undoubtedly was part of the oppressed community and suffered disabilities," Solomon argued. "There might be some who made use of opportunities that were given to them during apartheid in terms of cheap labour. But we cannot place all Muslim businessmen in the same category as other privileged groups."[31]

Ashwin Trikamjee of the Hindu Maha Sabha, the national body of Hindus in South Africa, also focused on his community's position as victim rather than oppressor. Indians had neither supported nor condoned the actions of the apartheid government, he maintained, but they themselves had been discriminated against. Trikamjee argues that low Indian voter turnout in the elections under the Tricameral Parliament of 1983—in which Coloureds, Indians, and whites were given separate legislative chambers but blacks were excluded—was indicative of the lack of support Indians gave the system.[32]

There were other examples of churches as victims. In 1988 the headquarters of the South African Council of Churches, Khotso House, were bombed by the government. Six weeks after that bombing, the headquarters of the South African Bishops Conference were destroyed by arsonists. Under Group Area laws, mainly black and Coloured congregations (and mosques) were forced to move and lost their church buildings and property. Churches were victimized too when the Bantu Education Act was passed, which forced them to give up their schools. Several prestigious schools for Africans—the Methodists' Healdtown, the United Congregational Church's Adams College, and the Reformed Presbyterian Church's Lovedale—were lost.

Individual religious leaders were also objects of attack. Many SACC staff members were detained and tortured. Frank Chikane, then general secretary of the SACC and a pastor in the black section of the Apostolic Faith Mission, had actually been tortured under the supervision of an elder in the white section of his church. Michael Lapsley, a priest to the ANC, lost both arms and an eye when government agents sent him a parcel bomb in April 1990.

The most self-critical submission came from the South African Council of Churches—the umbrella group of mainline churches formed in 1967 that had once been headed by Bishop Tutu. The SACC, the most activist church organization in its opposition to apartheid, nevertheless expressed some regrets. Often a target of police raids and harassment for its outspoken opposition to apartheid, legal assistance to political prisoners, and aid for those fleeing the country, the SACC's achievements were counterbalanced by failures. SACC general secretary Brigalia Bam said to the commission: "The SACC did not do enough to seek out the victims of apartheid, but relied in the main for people to come to it for assistance and aid." Also, Bam indicated that the SACC had served the practical needs of people better than their spiritual needs, leaving a legacy of spiritual and moral malaise for which it was sorry.[33]

One of the most unusual submissions to these hearings came from the Zion Christian Church (ZCC) on the final day of hearings. Variously accused of being "unreliable," "apolitical," "reactionary," and "conservative,"[34] the ZCC refused to address questions of its own complicity, especially allegations of its relations with the defense forces. Immanuel Lothola, the spokesman for the group, began his testimony by stressing the strict moral code, ethos of hard work, and economic self-reliance of the ZCC. When asked by a commissioner how his church was involved in fighting against apartheid, Lothola replied: "As a church, the Zion Christian Church did not lead people into a mode of resistance against apartheid. But as a church the ZCC taught its people to love themselves more than ever, to stand upright and face the future, to defy the laws of apartheid." He continued that the ZCC had not "stood up and said let's go and fight the white government," but "we thought genuinely we needed to teach our people to be able to stand upright and not to hurt others, but to refuse to be hurt by others."[35] Robin Petersen has commented that this clearly is not the language of political struggle and that their testimony forces us to rethink notions of resistance and struggle. Perhaps a philosophy of self-love and self-reliance, alongside refusing to allow the dominator to hurt, he has argued, is supremely resistant.[36] Citing James Scott on the notion of "weapons of the weak," Petersen concludes: "It is from the margins, therefore, that resistance is shaped as tactic, as the creating of space to be human, to construct a *communitas* in the face of devastating destruction and oppression. It is resistance that in the face of a system determined to squeeze the humanity out of its victims, refuses to accede to the logic of domination."[37]

Also on the final day of hearings, the Dutch Reformed Church, which has sometimes been called the National Party at Prayer for its close ties to the previous government, presented its long-awaited submission. Tutu thanked the DRC for its presence: "I am so glad that you have seen the light. To have you on our side is a tremendous thing, and we give thanks to God. We are glad you are part of the process of healing in our land."[38]

DRC moderator Freek Swanepoel began his testimony by saying that "on this day we wish to come and commit ourselves . . . to playing a positive role in reconciliation in this country. . . . We say today that we have a calling to promote redemption and that it means that we wish to continue to listen to the stories of other people, that we really wish to go to great lengths to see their pain and need and that we wish to cooperate in the healing of the community and the solution of problems."[39]

Swanepoel told the commissioners that to cooperate meaningfully toward reconciliation the DRC had to start with itself. The first order was to start the process of church reunification, joining with the former "daughter" churches for Coloureds and Africans.[40] At the time of the hearing, negotiations were under way for possible unification with the white DRC and the Indian Reformed Church. The stumbling block to full unification was that the "daughter" churches adopted the Belhar confession, which maintains that apartheid was a sin, and insisted that the DRC also adopt this confession of unity.[41] The second goal was to work with other denominations: "[W]e are here to learn from other churches to hear what they are saying, to take the hands that have been reached us to assist us as well."[42] Since 1994 the DRC has in fact had "observer status" with the South African Council of Churches.

Swanepoel said that he realized the DRC had to speak honestly about the past if its contributions in the future were to be accepted. The rest of his testimony summarized the steps the DRC had taken to move away from apartheid. Beginning in 1982 the Synod rejected apartheid as a sin. In 1986 the church admitted it had "erred seriously with the Biblical foundation of the forced segregation of people."[43] In 1990 it joined with some eighty denominations at the Rustenburg conference to produce a document that condemned "apartheid in its intentions, its implementation, and its consequences an evil policy."[44] At Rustenburg, W. D. Jonker, professor of theology at the University of Stellenbosch, stood up to accept responsibility for the wrongs done by his denomination. (But the DRC delegation later decided that Jonker's confession could not be accepted as a confession for the church as a whole.) In 1994 the Synod apologized to former Afrikaner ministers it had ostracized for protesting against the church's support of apartheid, men such as pastor Beyers Naudé, who had been given an ultimatum: leave the Christian Institute or be defrocked. Swanepoel ended his testimony with these words: "The Dutch Reformed Church apologises to these people and admits that its voice of protest had not been loud enough."[45]

The DRC's submission was a disappointment to many observers, although Bishop Tutu thanked Swanepoel profusely for his testimony. Little was said about how the DRC's teachings lent credibility to apartheid. Swanepoel focused instead on the present need for reconciliation. Ironically (though not surprisingly), the denomination that was most explicit in the theological justification for apartheid and support of the NP's policies was the church body that could find the least about which to apologize. Nevertheless, the RICSA report noted: "While the DRC submission was ultimately rather disappointing and must be judged a largely failed opportunity, the fact that it came at least gave the TRC process some legitimacy in the eyes of its constituents . . . who see the Commission as a direct attack on Afrikaners."[46]

Following the tepid testimony of the DRC spokesperson, Afrikaner pastor Nico Smith (an academic who became a minister in the black DRC church in Mamelodi township) gave a heart-wrenching account of South African pastors' failure to preach the gospel faithfully. "Many of these willing executioners of this government were members of our congregations. . . . Didn't we understand the gospel properly, didn't we preach the full gospel . . . ? We . . . failed to spell out the consequences of the gospel of Jesus Christ and therefore we didn't touch the conscience either of the members of the government or the willing executioners of their plans."[47] He along with Beyers Naudé drafted this open letter to pastors and churches in South Africa, which remains the strongest statement of remorse to come from the faith community:

> To us as preachers of the Word of God, the responsibility is entrusted to proclaim at all times, the gospel of reconciliation with God and our fellow human beings in Christ.
>
> This responsibility entails the prophetic denouncement of all forms of injustice, oppression and violence committed against any human being. As we read and hear what happened in South Africa during the years of Nationalist Party rule we as preachers of God's Word, are confronted with the question how could it possibly have happened while we as preachers of reconciliation, justice and peace were preaching this message from our pulpit every Sunday?
>
> But the question which disturbs us even more is this, how was it possible that those who intentionally committed murders and sabotage against fellow citizens, could have been as is now becoming evident, members of churches and even regular churchgoers?
>
> Was there nothing in our preaching, liturgies and sacraments that disturbed the conscience of those who were directly involved in all the evil deeds committed? Therefore we have indeed more than enough reason to feel deeply guilty for having spiritualised and even gagged the gospel to such an extent that those in government and those responsible to execute government policy, didn't feel confronted by our preaching.
>
> We are guilty of having allowed the rulers to execute the ideology of forced separation for the sake of so-called law and order without offering united resistance as preachers of justice and peace.
>
> We admit and confess that we too were blinded by an ideology which presented itself as justifiable from the Bible.
>
> We lacked the gift of discerning the spirits because we had no real desire to receive this gift. In the light of the above, we want to confess

publicly that we as preachers were co-responsible for what happened in South Africa. In fact our guilt should be considered as more serious than that of any other person or institution.

We who were supposed to be the conscience of the nation, didn't succeed in preventing the most serious forms of abuse of the human conscience. As a result of this, the criminal violation of people's human dignity and even the destruction of human life, continued for too long.

But this confession of guilt is not intended to be vague and general. We confess our guilt by mentioning specific examples of our failure to be faithful to the gospel. We first of all acknowledge and confess that for many of us, especially those in the white community, life was very convenient and comfortable under Nationalist Party rule.

Many of us therefore couldn't and wouldn't see the oppression and violation of millions of people in our country, hear their cries for justice and failed to take action.

We furthermore acknowledge and confess that when we sometimes did feel uncomfortable about the way the government and other institutions persisted in its abuse of power, we did nothing because of fear.

We thereby allowed evil with the cooperation of Christians, to continue its devastating work against the people of God.

In the same breath we commit ourselves to call upon Christians to be careful in their support of political leaders and their policies. We furthermore commit ourselves to challenge Christians concerning their political and socio-economic responsibilities.

We also want to make amends for neglecting the needs of the poor and the oppressed, therefore we commit ourselves to the task of guiding God's people towards involvement in actions to eliminate the socio-economic inequalities of our country.

We have evaded this responsibility for too long. We furthermore commit ourselves to the task of encouraging people with the gospel of hope. Especially in these days when many have lost hope and are despairing of the future of our country.

This we will do by replacing the longing for the previous so-called better days, by dreams of an even better future. The same gospel therefore, also urges us to commit ourselves to engage in the reconstruction of our society.

Although we recognise that some ministers have stood bravely in the struggle for justice, it is our hope that every church minister who reads this document, will recognise the challenge facing us all, which we dare not push aside.

We are compelled to make a choice. Either we confess our guilt in order to be set free for greater and more faithful service to the gospel of Jesus Christ, or we ignore this challenge to confess our guilt and thus declare ourselves not guilty of what happened in our country.

If you are willing to identify with this document and commit yourself to a process of unified action and a process of healing and rebuilding our nation, send your reply before the end of 1997 to the following address.[48]

The letter was sent to 12,000 pastors and published in both English and Afrikaans newspapers throughout the country. By the time of the faith hearings in November, only 396 signatures had been collected. Smith reflected:

> Are the pastors not interested? Don't they care? I can't believe that the pastors will still consider me and Beyers Naudé as communists, rebels, trouble makers or whatever it may be. Or do they just look at it and say no, I am not interested in a thing like this. Why out of 12,000 letters only 396? It is saddening to think that that is the reality about the church at grassroots level. And if pastors are not willing to make a confession, how on God's earth can they ever expect that the members must do so?[49]

The faith hearings were thus a mixed bag: some apology, some acknowledgment of complicity or, more typically, recognition of acts of omission. Still, compared with the other institutional hearings for the media, business, the medical profession, and the legal profession (where South African judges refused to testify to their behavior during apartheid, saying it would undermine the court's independence), the faith hearings were relatively free from denial and rationalization. "Probably the best of all the Truth Commission hearings," Tutu said to his fellow commissioners at their conclusion.[50]

Notes

1. Botman, "Pastoral Care and Counseling in Truth and Reconciliation," pp. 155–157.
2. de Villiers, "The Challenge to the Afrikaans Churches," p. 151.
3. SAPA, "Churches Slam Indifference of Whites" (December 30, 1996).
4. Although there are four white Afrikaner churches within the Dutch Reformed tradition, the Nederduitse Gereformeerde Kerk—also called the Dutch Reformed Church—is the largest and the only one to make a submission to the TRC. The other three churches are the Nederduitsch Hervormde Kerk (NHK; Dutch re-Formed Church), the Gereformeerde Kerk (GK; Reformed Church), and the Afrikaanse Protestante Kerk (APK; Afrikaner Protestant Church).
5. SAPA, "NG Church Decides Against Submission to Truth Commission" (October 30, 1996).
6. DRC, *The Story of the Dutch Reformed Church's Journey with Apartheid, 1960–1994,* 2.4.1.
7. Ibid., 4.17.1.
8. Ibid., 4.21.1.
9. Ibid.
10. Ibid., 9.17.

11. The DRC supported 74 percent of the SADF's chaplains. See *Truth and Reconciliation Commission of South Africa Report,* vol. 4, chap. 3, "Institutional Hearings: The Faith Community," p. 71.

12. DRC, *The Story of the Dutch Reformed Church's Journey with Apartheid,* 7.1.2.

13. Ibid., 7.1.1.

14. Kuperus, *State, Civil Society, and Apartheid in South Africa,* p. 129.

15. Ibid., p. 132.

16. Ibid., p. 149.

17. Ibid., p. 154.

18. RICSA, "Faith Communities and Apartheid," p. 76.

19. Niehaus, "Reconciliation in South Africa," p. 88.

20. Botman, "The Offender and the Church," p. 130.

21. SAPA, "Salvation Army Tells TRC It Regrets Silence During Apartheid Years" (June 3, 1997).

22. SAPA, "AFM Failed Duty, TRC Told" (August 4, 1997).

23. The only major group of churches that was invited but declined to participate was the Lutheran, both white and black.

24. RICSA, "Faith Communities and Apartheid," p. 34.

25. Faith hearing, East London, November 17, 1997.

26. Ibid.

27. Ibid.

28. Ibid.

29. Faith hearing, East London, November 18,1997.

30. Ibid.

31. Faith hearing, East London, November 19, 1997.

32. Faith hearing, East London, November 18, 1997.

33. Faith hearing, East London, November 17, 1997.

34. Petersen, "The AICs and the TRC," p. 115.

35. Faith hearing, East London, November 19, 1997.

36. Petersen, "The AICs and the TRC," p. 118.

37. Ibid., p. 121.

38. Faith hearing, East London, November 19, 1997.

39. Ibid.

40. In 1994 the Nederduitse Gereformeerde Sendingkerk (NGSK) (Coloured church) and the Nederduitse Gereformeerde Kerk in Afrika (NGKA) (African church) combined to form the Uniting Reformed Church of Southern Africa.

41. Frost, *Struggling to Forgive,* p. 217.

42. Faith hearing, East London, November 19, 1997.

43. Ibid.

44. Rustenburg Declaration, November 1990.

45. Faith hearing, East London, November 19, 1997.

46. RICSA, "Faith Communities and Apartheid," p. 76.

47. Faith hearing, East London, November 19, 1997.

48. Nico Smith, written submission, "An Open Letter to All Pastors in South Africa," n.d.

49. Faith hearing, East London, November 19, 1997.

50. Cited in Meiring, *Chronicle of the Truth Commission,* p. 265.

11

The Rest of the Story

When the Truth and Reconciliation Commission (TRC) published its final report in October 1998, the truth about the past was acknowledged in an officially sanctioned way, as an authoritative version of events. Findings were made based not only on victims' and perpetrators' testimony but also on information gathered by the investigative unit and research department of the TRC. The commission made findings about the responsibility of the political parties, the South African Defense Force (SADF), the State Security Council (SSC), and the South African Police (SAP), as well as organs of civil society, such as the churches, the press, and business.[1] It began by pointing out that the response of the former government and its institutions had been "to hedge and obfuscate" and was marked by "half-heartedness and reluctance to make full disclosure."[2] Speaking of the testimony from the various sectors of civil society, the TRC said: "they were generally characterised by defensiveness and a failure to come to terms with the role these sectors had played in supporting the status quo, whether by commission or omission."[3]

The primary finding of the TRC was that the predominant portion of gross violations of human rights had been committed by the former state through its security and law enforcement agencies. The state had perpetrated gross human rights violations including torture, abduction, severe ill-treatment, deliberate manipulation of social divisions to mobilize one group against another, unjustified use of deadly force, arming and training foreign nationals, incursions across South Africa's borders, judicial killings, extrajudicial killings, and covert training of hit squads. In the early mandate period, the country was unjust and discriminatory, but it essentially operated under a system of laws, albeit unjust laws. With P. W. Botha's ascension to power in 1978, the state ventured into the "realm of criminal misconduct."[4] The language that had been used by the SCC—"eliminate," "destroy terrorists," "wipe out," "make a plan"—was "reckless, inflammatory and an incitement to unlawful acts."[5] The commission determined that ministers in charge of security should have reasonably foreseen that such words would be interpreted by members of the security forces as authorization to kill persons involved in the resistance. The commission castigated politicians for phrasing instructions in such a way as to cause their subordinates to take responsibility for acts of which the politicians were the intellectual authors. Therefore the commission found members of the SSC guilty of gross human rights violations. In particular, P. W. Botha, "by virtue of his position as head of state and chairperson of the SSC, contributed to and facilitated a climate in which . . . gross violations of human rights could and did occur, and as such is accountable for such violations."[6]

F. W. de Klerk did not fare much better with the TRC, which was highly critical of his failure to tackle the problem of "third-force" activities—the network of security force members and right-wing groups seeking to stop the transition. Although the TRC acknowledged that de Klerk had taken steps to dismantle the national security management system he had inherited from Botha, it maintained that he had made "little obvious attempt" to curb third-force activities. And while he knew that then commissioner of police Johan van der Merwe had been involved in the illegal bombing of Khotso House, van der Merwe continued to retain his position. Despite the fact that the Steyn investigation into third-force activities had implicated the chief of the defense force and the chief of police, de Klerk had assigned those same individuals with the task of deciding what action was to be taken! The commission found that de Klerk had failed to make full disclosure of gross human rights violations committed by members of government and senior members of the SAP. His failure to do so "constitutes a material nondisclosure, thus rending him an accessory to the commission of gross human rights violations."[7]

The Inkatha Freedom Party (IFP) was the next group to receive the attention of the commission, which described how Inkatha had increasingly turned to the government for support in its struggle against supporters of the United Democratic Front (UDF) and the African National Congress (ANC), despite representing itself to the international community as an independent resistance movement. An example of this collaboration was the Inkatha hit squads trained by the South African military in the Caprivi Strip. The TRC found not only P. W. Botha and Magnus Malan to be accountable for hit-squad activity, but also Mongosuthu Buthelezi. It found the IFP to be "the foremost perpetrator" of gross human rights violations in KwaZulu and Natal from 1990 to 1994, when the conflict with the ANC was at its peak. On a national scale, Inkatha had been the major perpetrator of killings; it was responsible for 4,500 deaths compared to 2,700 attributed to the police and 1,300 to the ANC. Buthelezi was held responsible for authorizing a paramilitary training program with the intent of preventing by force the holding of elections. He was also held responsible for making speeches that had the effect of inciting supporters to commit acts of violence.[8]

All sides came under condemnation, including the resistance. First the commission made clear that it agreed with the UN's declaration that apartheid was "a crime against humanity." The TRC went on, however, to argue that although the cause was just, this did not mean that all acts carried out in order to destroy apartheid were legal, moral, and acceptable. In the words of Desmond Tutu, "A gross violation is a gross violation, whoever commits it and for whatever reason."[9] During its armed struggle, the ANC had engaged in acts that had resulted in civilian casualties. Even though they may not have been the direct targets, more civilians were killed by operators of Umkhonto We Sizwe (MK) than by security force members. "Whatever the justification given by the ANC for such acts—misinterpretation of policy, poor surveillance, anger, or differing interpretations of what constituted a 'legitimate military target'—the people who were killed or injured by such explosions are all victims of gross violations of human rights perpetrated by the ANC."[10] These acts included the Church Street bombing of air force headquarters in Pretoria, the bombing of Magoo's Bar in Durban, the bombing of the Amanzimtoti shopping center, and the land mine campaigns. The ANC was held accountable for creating a climate that allowed its supporters to regard state informers, askaris, urban councilors and rural headmen, members of the IFP, and others perceived as collaborators, as legitimate targets. The TRC found the ANC responsible for the deaths of seventy-six IFP officials, and found that it also contributed to violence by arming self-defense units in the townships that "took the law into their own hands" and committed atrocities. The ANC was also found guilty of serious abuses in exile in its camps in Angola, where suspected agents had been tortured and executed.[11]

The other major resistance movement, the Pan-Africanist Congress (PAC), was also reproached for targeting civilians. The commission rejected the PAC's contention that killing white farmers constituted acts of legitimate war: "The commission finds PAC action directed towards both civilians and whites to have been a gross violation of human rights for which the PAC and APLA [Azanian People's Liberation Army] leadership are held to be morally and politically responsible and accountable."[12]

None of those found guilty of human rights violations were happy with the report. De Klerk, livid that he had been named as an accessory to gross human rights violations, got an interdict from the High Court to prevent publication of a thirty-line passage, forcing the TRC to remove the passage temporarily pending a hearing. From Inkatha and the Freedom Front came the usual complaints about the TRC—"circus," "witch-hunt," "biased." More disturbing was the reaction from the ANC, the party responsible for initiating the commission itself, which tried to get the TRC to rewrite its findings. When the TRC declined, the ANC accused it of criminalizing the antiapartheid struggle and called its findings "capricious and arbitrary."[13]

In the ceremony of handing over the TRC's five-volume report to President Nelson Mandela—which was boycotted by the National Party, Inkatha, and the Freedom Front—Mandela, distancing himself from the ANC's response, which had come from his deputy president, Thabo Mbeki, said: "I have set up the TRC. They have done not a perfect but a remarkable job and I approve everything they did."[14]

The TRC ended its work "assailed from all sides, praised by few," writes Martin Meredith.[15] This should not have been unexpected. The national narrative was a difficult one for perpetrators and beneficiaries alike to hear, and a painful one for victims. Tutu explained that truth might not always lead to reconciliation (especially overnight) but that there can be no reconciliation without hearing the truth about the past. Those who had worried that the TRC placed too little emphasis on justice found vindication in the final report's findings of guilt and accountability, which implicated some 400 individuals in human rights violations.[16]

An Unfinished Story

Michael Lapsley has told a group in New York City that in the long term, the commission will be judged mainly by the reparations it offers victims.[17] Despite recommendations from the TRC's Committee on Reparation and Rehabilitation for substantial payments to apartheid victims of gross human rights violations, the ANC-dominated government responded with a much more modest proposal: "TRC Pays Out a Pittance," ran the December 10,

1999, headline in the *Mail & Guardian.* The minister of justice and constitutional planning, Penuell Maduna, announced that the government's reparation budget of 100 million rand for 1998/99 would be supplemented with only 200 million rand during that financial year. The 17,700 victims of apartheid identified during the TRC hearings that ran from 1996 through 1998 would receive an average of only 3,000 rand.[18] Maduna argued that the government "lacked adequate financial resources to implement all the [TRC's] recommendations."[19] Hlengiwe Mkhize, TRC commissioner and head of the Committee on Reparation and Rehabilitation, conceded that "it is not reparation in the true sense of the word."[20]

The paltry sum, though disappointing to victims, was in line with early expectations. As the TRC began its work in 1996, South Africans imagined that financial compensation would necessarily be a token payment because of the sheer and seemingly bottomless number of claims. Their thinking, too, was that there was no way to compensate adequately the people who had suffered such losses. TRC spokesman John Allen mused, "If you go according to compensation, how do you compensate for a life?"[21]

During initial hearings, TRC chair Archbishop Desmond Tutu expressed amazement at "how modest people's expectations of reparations have often been—a tombstone, the renaming of a school, a bursary for the surviving children."[22] The *Mail & Guardian* reported that of the 9,000 victims identified by April 1997, only 100 wanted cash as compensation for their suffering.[23] But as time went on, victims became more assertive in their demands. At the end of 1997, the TRC revealed in its official newsletter, *Truth Talk,* that four of every ten persons who had made statements to the TRC had asked for money to improve the quality of their lives, and nine of every ten had asked for services such as education, medical care, and housing, which they could access if money were available.[24] In the final report's analysis of deponents' expectations, topping the list was monetary assistance, followed by investigation into the violations.[25]

Surely their expectations for compensation were not baseless. Had not commissioners asked victim witnesses at the hearings on human rights violations to describe specifically how their experiences had affected their health and their family and what they were seeking in the way of compensation? "How has being tortured practically impacted you and your family?" was a question posed to every victim.

The committee early on had decided that urgent interim relief was necessary for certain categories of victims. These included those who had lost a breadwinner; others for whom counseling was necessary to deal with the psychological trauma inherent in the reopening of old wounds by testifying; still others who needed urgent medical attention for problems such as hypertension, diabetes, strokes, and physical disability; and last, terminally ill patients who were not expected to survive beyond the life of the commission. In response, Switzerland donated 1.5 million rand and was followed by Denmark's contribution of 2 million rand to the president's fund for reparations.

Tutu called on the South African business community in particular to join the international community in contributing to the fund. This theme was amplified by a mother of a victim who told the TRC that the best way for people to demonstrate their commitment to reconciliation would be to contribute financially to the victims' families.[26] Unfortunately, the first payments were not made until July 1998.[27] By September 2000 only 30 million rand in interim relief has been paid out to 8,000 people,[28] and by April 2001 the amount had risen to only 42 million rand to 13,504 survivors.[29] One of the TRC's staff members lamented: "I've run out of stories to tell victims about why they have not received reparation—I don't know what to tell them anymore."[30] Timothy Garton Ash notes that there is a cruelty in the fact that "the amnestied killer immediately walks free" while his victim must wait for decisions about reparations.[31]

From Symbolic Reparation to Substantial Compensation

As the Committee on Reparation and Rehabilitation held workshops throughout the country over two years, its thinking shifted from an emphasis on symbolic reparation to substantial compensation. Barney Pityana remarked, "When people are in need, it is difficult to justify their expectations by suggesting that monuments will be built in honour of their heroic sons, fathers, and daughters."[32]

At a national workshop, commissioner Dr. Wendy Orr said that victims should not get only token amounts of money in compensation. She argued that South Africa was obliged by its signing of international treaties, including the Universal Declaration of Human Rights, to provide victims with fair and adequate compensation. The committee's thinking on reparations was also influenced by the work of other truth commissions: the Chilean commission's award of pensions to families of the "disappeared" and dead;[33] the UN's decision to compensate victims of the Iran-Iraq war;

and the recommendations of the Skweyiya and Motsuenyane commissions, which were the ANC-initiated commissions authorized to look into the allegations of human rights abuses committed by MK soldiers in camps outside the country, for compensation for those victims.[34]

In October 1997 the Committee on Reparation and Rehabilitation announced its final policy proposal and submitted it to Parliament as part of the TRC's final report in October 1998. It estimated that at least 3 billion rand would be necessary to compensate victims for the physical, psychological, and material damages they had suffered.[35] It proposed that in addition to symbolic reparations—memorials, monuments, reburials, renaming of streets, days of remembrance, and so forth—each identified victim receive an individual reparation grant (IRG) for a period of six years with a minimum payment of 17,000 rand per year. It recommended that victims having many dependents or living in rural areas be offered 23,000 rand a year. The average payment—21,700 rand—was based on the median annual income of a black South African household. Committee members had considered but rejected using the poverty line of 15,000 rand for the average payment because it would condemn victims to a life of near-poverty. On the committee's proposal, Tutu said, "Reparations would help address criticism that the Commission was more sympathetic to perpetrators than to victims."[36]

As a means of helping to cover the cost of reparations, discussion ensued among ANC members of Parliament about the possibility of a special reparation or wealth tax levied on people who had benefited directly or indirectly from apartheid. A wealth tax had been suggested during the faith hearings by Chief Rabbi Cyril Harris,[37] and by spokespersons during the business hearings. Professor Sampie Terreblanche of Stellenbosch University had recommended that persons with assets over 2 million rand be taxed 0.5 percent annually over ten to twenty years, with proceeds going to apartheid victims. Another recommendation made during the media hearings was for a onetime payment of 1 percent of market capitalization for companies listed on the Johannesburg Stock Exchange.[38] One suggestion from the Afrikaner Handelsinstituut (AHI) urged the government to use the Sasria fund (with a balance of 9 billion rand), an insurance fund created during apartheid to cover losses incurred through political unrest, to compensate victims.[39]

Despite the emphasis on *ubuntu,* in the postamble of the interim constitution and later in the Promotion of National Unity and Reconciliation Act that authorized the TRC, there was no requirement for reparations from individual perpetrators to individual victims, even though *ubuntu* requires *"ulihlawule ityala"* (paying the debt). In traditional systems, "the offender against community law pays the fine imposed upon him, and returns again to public life. He is received with open arms. No stigma is attached to him for he has paid the penalty, and by so doing has made restitution."[40] Howard Zehr warned that the amnesty provision, though politically unavoidable, "breaks the crucial link between violation and obligation." While state-paid compensation may give some satisfaction to victims, it is "symbolically less satisfying than direct action by offenders"[41] (not to mention there being something ironic about a new government paying for the abusive policies of its predecessor). H. Russel Botman believes that perpetrators will be fully forgiven only when the word of confession is followed by the deed of confession. But he has argued that the cash-strapped government, even if it might want to, is not in the position to fully compensate victims, so that other institutions in civil society will have to play a part in the quest for economic justice for victims.[42]

When Mandela accepted the TRC's final report, he delivered a speech to Parliament saying that the private and public sectors had to come together to finance a reparations fund for victims of apartheid. During the parliamentary debates on the final report in February 1999, ANC justice minister Dullah Omar urged: "We must not reduce the victims of apartheid to beggars pleading for a hand-out of mercy, when indeed it is they who gave and sacrificed their all for the struggle." In a contradictory vein, he added that "no fighter for liberation ever engaged in the struggle for personal gain" and that the "only reward sought was freedom."[43] (It should be pointed out that many identified victims were not freedom fighters, but family members of resisters, or innocent people caught in the cross fire of political violence.)

Any serious talk of responsibility toward victims and any serious discussion of a wealth tax from apartheid's beneficiaries dropped by the wayside when Thabo Mbeki, Nelson Mandela's successor, took office in the spring of 1999. Mbeki's administration has angered many who suffered while struggling for liberation, by saying it can only afford token payments of 3,000 rand per victim. Paul Bell wryly commented: "The TRC may have dealt mainly in truth but truth itself, while good for the soul, does little for the body."[44]

Many victims feel their stories have been "used" by the TRC to provide "as complete a picture as possible" of the past without their essential needs being met.[45] Duma Khumalo expresses the bitterness of many victims:

> I am not saying the government should make me rich, but I don't want to see my children victimised because of what happened to me. When I was arrested, my son, Lucky, was five. It affected him very badly. There is bitterness between me and Lucky. I keep on making promises to him, but I fail him because I don't have the money to send him to school and so he is causing trouble on the streets. I want to pay him back because he suffered because I was in prison.[46]

Julia Molotsi, whose only daughter was abducted and killed, adds: "The people who killed my daughter are now free and are enjoying themselves with their families, and we victims are not taken care of."[47]

As hearings got under way in June 2000 for the justice department's 2000/01 budget, accusations were made by other parties, including the Democratic Party and the New National Party,[48] that the ANC was trying to escape its obligations to pay reparations. The ANC had argued two years earlier in its submission to the TRC that substantial compensation was necessary: "Unless there are meaningful reparations, the process of ensuring justice and reconciliation will be flawed."[49] The ANC's position in 2000 was that the truth commission process, which included holding amnesty hearings for approximately 300 more applicants, had to be completed before making final reparations payments to victims.[50]

In a press release following the budget hearings, the TRC denied that it was a legal requirement that all amnesties had to be finalized in order for the final reparation policy to be implemented. The TRC urged the government to put in place regulations for dispersing the remaining funds allocated to reparations. Tutu accused the government of "failing the victims."[51] In an editorial to *Business Day,* Hlengiwe Mkhize warned the government that the silence concerning final reparations "means that future finance ministers will find the costs of intergenerational transmission of the consequences of victimisation incalculable. In monetary terms what would cost R 3 billion in interventions today might cost R 18 billion tomorrow [in the suffering of one survivor passed on to four offspring]." She urged: "We started something that we must honour and finish."[52]

Talk of monetary compensation should not overshadow the benefit of acknowledgment. Jose Zalaquett argues that public acknowledgment is a form of reparation, and is not to be lightly dismissed.[53] Even though individual perpetrators did not always confess, and state leaders denied responsibility for actions of "mavericks," the TRC's final report made clear findings. The official acknowledgment that apartheid was a crime against humanity and that the government and its agencies were the main perpetrators of human rights violations helped victims to reshape their universe. Martha Minow believes that even those who start with monetary motivations may actually find more value in getting acknowledgment of their suffering from a supportive community.[54]

Undoubtedly, victims benefited psychologically when perpetrators on occasion apologized for egregious acts of torture, killing, and abduction. (Of course, since disclosure rather than contrition was the condition for amnesty, many victims were deprived of even an apology.) But apology is only the first step. TRC deputy chair Alex Boraine has said there is "a recognition that it isn't good enough simply to pat people on the head and express words of sympathy unless it is accompanied by action."[55] To be meaningful, confession and repentance must be followed by restitution. "Apologies set the record straight; restitution sets out to make a new record," writes Donald Shriver.[56] Tutu explains: "Those who have wronged must be ready to make what amends they can. They must be ready to make restitution and reparation. If I have stolen your pen, I can't really be contrite when I say, 'Please forgive me,' if at the same time I still keep your pen. If I am truly repentant, then I will demonstrate this genuine repentance by returning your pen."[57]

The title of a recent book by Murray Cox, *Remorse and Reparation,* suggests the proper sequence: remorse followed by reparation. Journalist Antjie Krog, who covered the TRC for South African radio, argues that reconciliation and reparation do go hand in hand but wonders which comes first: "If people don't get reparation, they won't forgive. If people are not forgiven, they won't offer reparation."[58] The difficulty some victims have in forgiving without first having received reparations is confirmed by Charity Kondile, who refused to forgive hit-squad leader Dirk Coetzee for killing her son. She explained: "It is easy for Mandela and Tutu to forgive. . . . [T]hey lead vindicated lives. In my life nothing, not a single thing, has changed since my son was burnt by barbarians . . . nothing. Therefore I cannot forgive."[59] The vast majority of victims, however, appear willing to forgive, which makes the government's limited reparation policy especially cruel.

The lack of adequate reparations casts doubt on the country's commitment to social justice, which is remarkable given that it is no longer whites but blacks who control the government. The niggardliness of the ANC government to the plight of ordinary victims must be viewed in the context of the new class divisions in South Africa. No longer is there a white elite and a predominantly black under class. Newly enriched blacks have taken their places alongside the former rulers and have new economic interests to protect. One of Tutu's first pronouncements against the new ANC government that won elections in 1994 was to chide them for the high salaries they voted themselves and for their ostentatious lifestyles. He castigated them for stopping "the gravy train only long enough to get on."[60]

The stinginess of the government in addressing victims' needs is especially disappointing in light of revelations of massive squandering on the part of government agencies. Recent government scandals involve spending 14 million rand on a questionable AIDS awareness play and allegations of misappropriation of state funds at two major universities (the vice chancellor of Fort Hare, the oldest university for Africans in sub-Saharan Africa, reportedly used money from the school's coffers to finance his daughter's education at Boston University). Yet victims are told there is not enough money to recompense them for their suffering. Frankly, money talks. It speaks of a real commitment to repair the damage of the past. It is evidence of a changed heart, and it represents in a tangible way the expression of deep regret by perpetrators and beneficiaries alike for supporting government policies that treated people as less than human.

Apology and forgiveness are not the only bases for reconciliation. Michael Cunningham argues that "reparation can precede, or occur without, formal apology."[61] Albie Sachs echoed this when he said: "The real reparation we want ties in with the constitution, the vote, with dignity, land, jobs, and education."[62] William Johnson Everett, professor of Christian social ethics at the Andover Newton Theological School, finds the biblical concept of Jubilee useful in justifying reparations: "Jubilee does not rest on our contrition or forgiveness but on God's demand to reconstitute the conditions of original justice, namely that each family would have the basis for a dignified life. . . . In the light of the systemic destruction brought about by apartheid and its predecessor policies, Jubilee concepts perform an important task."[63]

Molefe Tsele argues that the knowledge that the offender has been exposed is not enough. The Jubilee spirit requires that those who were in bondage be placed in a position to rehabilitate their lives. Practically, that means economic justice.[64] The reconciliation that took place between Briton and Boer despite the bitter feelings after the Boer War may be attributed to the fact that Britons paid huge reparations (some 3 million pounds) to Afrikaners. Without actually apologizing to the Boers, the Britons made restitution that went a long way toward, if not a perfect reconciliation, then at least a peaceful coexistence—a rough justice, or what Reinhold Niebuhr has called "an approximation of brotherhood under the conditions of sin."[65] Those who benefited from apartheid should be guided by the principle of equity, and newly enriched blacks also need to sacrifice (through higher taxes and other redistributive policies) to ensure that those who suffered receive the financial help they need to become whole. For Dumisa Ntsebeza, the director of the TRC's investigative unit, "if the conditions of the ordinary people have not changed since the advent of the democratic order, all the truth telling, and the knowledge by victims that comes with it, will have been in vain."[66]

A Few White Princes

Tutu had pleaded for a few white leaders to come forward to promote the aims of the TRC. Several post-TRC initiatives have been undertaken by white notables to advance the reconciliatory work of the TRC.

Charles Villa-Vicencio, the TRC's research director, launched the Institute for Justice and Reconciliation (IJR) in Cape Town in May 2000. In explaining the rationale for the new organization, Villa-Vicencio said: "The TRC helped place the issues of justice and reconciliation on the national agenda in an irrevocable manner. It did not resolve them."[67] One of its first initiatives was launching a one-day workshop, "Transcending a Century of Injustice," which highlighted the different memories of black and white, English-speaking and Afrikaans-speaking South Africans.

A second project was a pilot survey, termed a "Reconciliation Barometer," that analyzed attitudes toward reconciliation. The need for material compensation was one of six issues presented to 2,200 South Africans. Sadly, but not surprisingly, whereas 70 percent of blacks agreed with the statement: "[I] believe that national reconciliation requires material compensation for victims of apartheid," only 20 percent of whites assented.[68]

Villa-Vicencio was one of the key figures behind a "Declaration of Commitment by White South Africans" launched on December 16, 2000—Reconciliation Day in South Africa. Signatories acknowledged that they derived unjust benefits from apartheid and called upon their fellow white citizens to contribute toward a fund for the disadvantaged. Constitutional court judge Albie Sachs, himself a victim who had been banned, held in solitary confinement, forced into exile, and eventually injured by a car bomb, explains that for him, signing the declaration was "not about apology but about privilege." He goes on to explain: "I signed because I thought it important to acknowledge that we whites—all of us—have been children of privilege. However smart, morally determined or hard-working we might have been, we were all given a huge leg-up by being born with a white skin."[69] Sachs was one of about 450 individuals, including university professors, judges, editors, and authors (as well as most of the Sprinkbok rugby team), who signed the declaration.

But even this simple declaration has proven contentious. According to an opinion poll conducted in December 2000, 80 percent of those contacted said they would not support the declaration.[70] The Democratic Alliance (the amalgamation of the New National Party and the Democratic Party) has emphatically rejected the statement. Democratic Alliance head Tony Leon explained, "I have serious doubts about the politics of apology. Where is it going to end?"[71] Former TRC human rights commissioner Rhoda Kadalie concurred: "It is the resurrection of the sorry ideology which has more to do with making white people feel good than it has for promoting justice. It is also aimed at silencing white people from being critical of the black government." For Kadalie, it absolves the government of all responsibility for not spending on poverty reduction or providing anti-retroviral drugs for AIDS patients or making arms spending a budget priority. "It is of no consequence to black people to say sorry. The statement is dangerous."[72] Such vehement opposition suggests that beneficiaries of apartheid find it difficult to acknowledge that their whiteness privileged them in the past.

Father Michael Lapsley is another leader in the white community who has continued the work of the TRC. The Institute for Healing of Memories, founded in August 1998, grew out of the Healing of Memories Chaplaincy Project, which he began for the Trauma Center for Survivors of Violence and Torture in Cape Town. It conducts workshops in parishes throughout the country. In these workshops, people are able to tell their stories in a safe environment. Lapsley explains the process: "Often in our workshop we try and bring people of different sides of the apartheid experience together, and as people are confronted by the humanity of each other, so people can begin to change."[73] Participants are asked to explore how they were affected by apartheid psychologically, spiritually, and emotionally. Lapsley says, "I believe that every South African has been messed up by apartheid. Every South African has a story to tell."[74] Participants engage in dramatization, rituals, and celebrations or liturgies. The TRC had suggested that faith communities could provide a source of national renewal as they included victims, beneficiaries, and perpetrators of apartheid, and Lapsley sees the workshops as a parallel process to the TRC. Since 1998 the institute has taken its workshops outside the country—to the United States, Rwanda, Ireland, Sri Lanka, and Australia.

The Center for the Study of Violence and Reconciliation (CSVR), headed by Graeme Simpson, continues to work closely with the Khulumani Support Group (a group of apartheid victims) and provide services to victims who testified. In conjunction with the American Association for the Advancement of Science, the CSVR embarked on a study to evaluate the impact of the TRC on victims of apartheid violations. One feature of the study consists of detailed analyses of transcripts of the TRC victim hearings.

Two other projects are also worth noting: the Prosecutions and Investigations Project monitors and advocates prosecutions of perpetrators who did not apply for amnesty, and the Reparations Project began as an effort to mobilize support for the TRC's reparations recommendations and to lobby the government to complete the process. It is not an either-or situation—that either the government or white beneficiaries should pay compensation. As the IJR report suggests, "The government is accountable but so is civil society and the issue will remain unresolved if white South Africans are not open to contributing towards reconciliation in financial or other ways."[75]

Notes

1. Findings were made by a balance of probabilities, the standard in civil litigation. Therefore the TRC's conclusions are "findings" rather than judicial verdicts.
2. *Truth and Reconciliation Commission of South Africa Report,* vol. 5, chap. 6, "Findings and Conclusions," pp. 196–197.
3. Ibid., p. 201.
4. Ibid., p. 213.
5. Ibid., p. 215.
6. Ibid., p. 225.
7. The finding was blacked out in the TRC's final report pending a lawsuit in which de Klerk sought to prevent his being named, but was leaked to the press. See "TRC Chairman Publishes Findings Against FW de Klerk," *Business Day* (October 3, 2000).
8. *Truth and Reconciliation Commission of South Africa Report,* vol. 5, chap. 6, "Findings and Conclusions," pp. 232–233.
9. *Truth and Reconciliation Commission of South Africa Report,* vol. 1, chap. 1, "Foreword by Chairperson," p. 12.
10. *Truth and Reconciliation Commission of South Africa Report,* vol. 5, chap. 6, "Findings and Conclusions," p. 240.
11. Ibid., p. 243.
12. Ibid., p. 245.

13. SAPA, "ANC Accuses TRC of Criminalising Apartheid Struggle" (October 26, 1996).

14. Cited in Anthony Sampson, "Out of the Shadow of Mandela," *Mail & Guardian* (June 11–17, 1999).

15. Meredith, *Coming to Terms,* p. 207.

16. Pankhurst, "Issues of Justice and Reconciliation in Complex Political Emergencies," p. 250.

17. Lapsley, "Confronting the Past and Creating the Future," p. 744.

18. There were approximately 22,200 persons who gave victim statements. On May 26, 2000, the TRC announced that it had to make negative decisions on approximately 4,500 statements. See TRC press release, "Updated Findings on Victims of Gross Human Rights Violations" (May 26, 2000).

19. Barry Streek, "Truth Commission Pays Out a Pittance," *Mail & Guardian* (December 14, 1999).

20. Ibid.

21. Lynne Duke, "South African Truth Panel Proposes Reparations Plan," *Washington Post* (October 24, 1997).

22. TRC's first interim report (June 1996).

23. Rehana Rossouw, "Cash No Balm to Gross Human Rights Abuse Victims," *Mail & Guardian* (April 11–17, 1997).

24. "TRC Proposes Grants," *Truth Talk* 3, no. 1 (November 1997), p. 2.

25. Other requests were for bursaries, shelter, medical care, and tombstones.

26. SAPA, "Forgetting the Past Is Wishful Thinking, Says Tutu" (April 3, 1997).

27. *Truth and Reconciliation Commission of South Africa Report,* vol. 5, chap. 5, "Reparation and Rehabilitation Policy," p. 182.

28. TRC press release, "Statement by the Truth and Reconciliation Commission" (September 7, 2000).

29. Marianne Merton, "Apartheid Victims' Families Wait for Reparations," *Mail & Guardian* (April 26, 2001).

30. Cited in Orr, "Reparation Delayed Is Healing Retarded," p. 243.

31. Ash, "True Confessions," p. 34.

32. Pityana, "Reconciliation After the TRC."

33. According to Tina Rosenberg, 5,746 relatives of those who were killed or who disappeared are receiving lifelong pensions (with the pension for a widow being three times the normal pension), and more than 700 children are receiving free tuition at any desired Chilean university; see Rosenberg, "Confronting the Painful Past," p. 336. In Argentina, the government committed up to $220,000 per family for compensation toward victims; see Hayner, *Unspeakable Truths,* p. 7.

34. *Truth and Reconciliation Commission of South Africa Report,* vol. 5, chap. 5, "Reparation and Rehabilitation Policy," p. 178.

35. The sum is 0.25 percent of the government's annual budget.

36. SAPA, "ANC Welcomes TRC Proposals for Reparations" (October 23, 1997).

37. Faith hearing, East London, November 18, 1997.

38. This recommendation came from former *Financial Mail* editor Stephen Mulholland.

39. Business hearing, Johannesberg, November 11–13, 1997.

40. Cited in Masina, "Xhosa Practices of Ubuntu for South Africa," p. 173.

41. Zehr, "Restorative Justice," p. 20.

42. Botman, "Justice That Restores," p. 18.

43. SAPA, "Don't Reduce Apartheid Victims to Beggars: Omar" (February 25, 1999).

44. Bell, "Truth or Consequence," p. 28.

45. Walaza, "Insufficient Healing and Reparation," p. 254.

46. Cited in Chris McGreal, "Apartheid Victims Reject Handouts," *Mail & Guardian* (January 3, 2000).

47. Cited in Evidence wa ka Ngobeni, "Apartheid Victims Demand Reparations," *Mail & Guardian* (September 24, 1999).

48. The former National Party had reconstituted itself as the New National Party in December 1998 in the lead-up to the 1999 election.

49. Cited in Chris McGreal, "Apartheid Victims Reject Handouts," *Mail & Guardian* (January 3, 2000).

50. On May 31, 2001, Mbeki dissolved the Amnesty Committee, which had heard all remaining cases and is currently in the process of finalizing its decisions; TRC press release, "Response to Chair of Justice Committee" (May 30, 2001).

51. TRC press release, "TRC Response to Chair of Justice Committee" (June 7, 2000).

52. Hlengiwe Mkhize, "Reparations a Logical Conclusion," *Business Day* (July 11, 2000).

53. Jose Zalaquett, cited in Aspen Institute, *State Crimes,* p. 31.

54. Minow, *Between Vengeance and Forgiveness,* p. 103.

55. "Restitution More Than Mere Words," *Truth Talk* 3, no. 1 (November 1997), p. 4.

56. Shriver, *An Ethic for Enemies,* p. 224.

57. Desmond Tutu, *The Rainbow People of God,* p. 222.

58. Krog, *Country of My Skull,* p. 130.

59. Cited in Antjie Krog, "The Parable of the Bicycle," *Mail & Guardian* (February 6–13, 1997).

60. Desmond Tutu, *The Rainbow People of God,* p. 264.

61. Cunningham, "Saying Sorry," p. 290.

62. Cited in Boraine, Levy, and Scheffer, eds., *Dealing with the Past,* p. 24.

63. Everett, "Going Public, Building Covenant," p. 159.

64. Tsele, "Truth, Justice, and Reconciliation," p. 75.

65. Niebuhr, *The Nature and Destiny of Man,* p. 254.

66. Ntsebeza, "The Uses of Truth Commissions," p. 165.

67. Cited in Barry Streek, "New Institute to Take TRC's Work Further," *Mail & Guardian* (May 5, 2000).

68. Helen Macdonald, "IJR Report on Reconciliation Survey Research" (July 2000), www.ijr.org.za/research1.html.

69. Albie Sachs, "Why I Signed the Declaration," *Cape Times* (February 27, 2001).

70. Rhoda Kadalie, "Sorry, This Is Just Another Divisive Fad," *Mail & Guardian* (January 5, 2001).

71. Cited in Barry Streek, "Whites Split Over Guilt Trip," *Mail & Guardian* (December 15, 2000).

72. Ibid.

73. Michael Lapsley, SACC conference, July 1995.

74. Ibid.

75. Helen Macdonald, "IJR Report in Reconciliation Survey Research" (July 2000), www.ijr.org.za/research1.html.

12

A Workable Model?

To Punish or Pardon?

Rwanda chose a different model from that of South Africa in its effort to deal with conflicts from the past. The International Criminal Tribunal for Rwanda (ICTR) was set up on November 8, 1994, by Security Council Resolution 955 to prosecute acts of genocide, crimes against humanity, and violations of the Geneva Convention that were committed during the four-month genocide spree spearheaded after the airplane death of Hutu president Juvenal Habyarimana in April 1994.

Which of these two processes—punishment or pardon—holds the most promise for other countries moving through democratic transitions or in the aftermath of ethnic bloodletting? For politicians, the superior value may be peace or order. Without a minimal peace, no other values can exist.[1] The call for a truth commission in South Africa that granted pardon, not punishment, was based on a pragmatic realism. Without the compromise on amnesty, the bitter conflict between the government and the resistance movements undoubtedly would have continued with many more human rights violations and the deaths of added thousands. Since the African National Congress (ANC) did not win militarily but had to negotiate a settlement, so-called victor's justice was not possible.

In Rwanda, on the other hand, the Rwandan Patriotic Front (RPF) came to power in 1994, routed the remnant of the Hutu government, and supported the establishment of a Nuremberg-style tribunal in Arusha, Tanzania, to try those who had fled into exile, and the establishment of local courts for those detained in jails inside the country. (The ICTR is pursuing the planners of the genocide, whereas Rwanda passed legislation in August 1996 authorizing prosecutions in state courts of those who had followed orders.)

Psychologists who supported South Africa's Truth and Reconciliation Commission (TRC) (one-third of commissioners came from the mental health profession) have pointed to individual healing as an important goal. They have pointed to the need for victims to relive the past in order to come to terms with it. They have insisted on the benefit of speaking out. Repressing painful memories results in stress, anxiety, and depression, while sharing stories in a supportive setting leads to healing. Storytelling can allow victims to reshape the traumatic event and reintegrate it into the matrix of their lives.

In a court setting, witnesses do not have the advantage of telling their stories in their own way, which Julie Mertus found to be the case when she covered the ICTR prosecutions. It is an adversarial situation for them, leaving victims wounded and retraumatized. She argues: "Law does not permit a single witness to tell . . . her own coherent narrative; it chops the stories into digestible parts, selects a handful of these parts, and sorts and refines them to create a new narrative—the legal anti-narrative."[2] In many ways, the TRC route ensures respecting the human dignity of the victim witnesses, which is often absent in court proceedings.

In Rwanda, victims are often afraid to testify because they fear reprisals if they point the finger, since the perpetrators live in the same neighborhood. The ICTR can provide protection in Arusha, but not when witnesses return to Rwanda. In South Africa, on the other hand, since amnesty would be granted to perpetrators, victims needed not fear reprisal from speaking out.

Because amnesty was granted for full disclosure, there was the possibility of a full accounting of what happened, which is often what the victims want most anyway. The need to know the truth is seen as paramount by supporters of the TRC. The situation is far different in Rwanda. Charles Murigande, the former Rwandan minister of transport and communication, argues that Rwanda doesn't need a truth commission: "We don't really need truth—we know who did what. . . . Unlike in South Africa where there were secret death squads—people here know what has happened. So simply telling Rwandans the truth and then giving people amnesty—that would not be very helpful."[3]

For theologians, reconciliation is often the higher value. Forgiveness—not punishment—is necessary to bring about the reconciliation that God has already wrought through Christ's work on the cross. God's children are urged to forgive their enemies and to reintegrate sinners back into the family of God. In this view, the victim initiates the process. We forgive because we are forgiven by God. There are no conditions for forgiveness. The biblical injunction is not to forgive seven times, but seven times seven—that is, infinitely.

For their different reasons, politicians, psychologists, and theologians supported the idea of a truth commission in South Africa, which was mainly condemned by human rights organizations. As envisioned by its proponents, a truth commission would offer amnesty in exchange for truth with the goals of first ensuring that the National Party proceeded with elections (which would have been impossible without the assurance of no reprisals when the ANC came to power), and second, reintegrating perpetrators into society and including them in the business of nation building. Mahmood Mamdani explains the difference between truth commission and tribunal this way: "If South Africa exemplifies the dilemma involved in the pursuit of reconciliation without justice, Rwanda exemplifies the opposite: the pursuit of justice without reconciliation."[4]

What circumstances led to the choice of privileging one value over the other? Why was the pardon route possible in South Africa, but not in Rwanda? Was it the result of political necessity alone in South Africa? Tina Rosenberg believes that the Mandela government was so popular that it probably could have reversed the constitutional provision of amnesty, but that it chose not to because its leaders genuinely believed in reconciliation.[5] This suggests that the reconciliation route was possible in South Africa because of the moral example of Nelson Mandela. Truly, Mandela is an icon, a veritable symbol of forgiveness and reconciliation to his people and the world's most admired and revered (now former) head of state.

What great leaders can be found in Rwanda, or for that matter anywhere in the world, who can inspire people to follow by example? If a successful truth commission depends upon this caliber of leadership, does this severely limit its usefulness as a workable model elsewhere? Few nations are capable of producing, as has South Africa, four Nobel Peace Prize laureates. Is there something unique about that country? When observers write about the "miracle" of South Africa, perhaps it is no hyperbole and therefore its solutions are not replicable.

Apartheid and Genocide

Does the severity of the crimes—the genocide of 800,000 to 1 million Tutsis (one-tenth of the population of Rwanda)—make forgiveness leading to reconciliation between Hutus and Tutsis unthinkable? Although there were killings, detentions, and torture in South Africa, there was nothing comparable to the Hutu attempt to eliminate an entire people. Apartheid depended upon the labor of the African population, and subjugation (not elimination) of the majority population in South Africa was the National Party's objective. Should one ever be reconciled with *genocidaires*? Is punishment perhaps the only appropriate response to genocide? Stephan Landsman argues that certain sorts of human rights violations demand prosecution and that "[f]irst and foremost among these is genocide."[6]

Desmond Tutu visited Rwanda a year after the genocide and warned that retributive justice would lead to a vicious cycle of reprisals and counterreprisals. He urged Rwandans to move toward restorative justice. The Rwandan president responded that "even Jesus had declared that the devil could not be forgiven."[7] His point is well taken, even if his theology is faulty: Are some crimes so heinous, some people so evil, that they remain beyond the pale of forgiveness and reconciliation?

Cultural Resources for Reconciliation

Christianity

What made the reconciliation model workable in South Africa was that the message of the church on truth, forgiveness, repentance, and reconciliation was embraced in postapartheid South African society. Ideally, perpetrators repented their sins and victims offered forgiveness, leading to reconciliation between individuals and ultimately the nation at large. The TRC's enabling legislation had not been framed in religious terms, but Tutu, the former archbishop of Cape Town, and his cochair, Alex Boraine, a former president of the Methodist Church, certainly set the religious tone. Tutu's theological views in particular underpinned the TRC's workings.

The Christian framework under which the TRC operated was widely accepted by South Africans because of the importance of Christianity in that country (72.6 percent of South Africans identify themselves as Christians, including no less than 76 percent of the African population).[8] Christian thought had always had an impact on public discourse. According to Richard Elphick, "Christian doctrine, language, and sentiment are . . . interwoven in the social and cultural history of South Africa."[9] The Dutch Reformed Church (DRC) had espoused a form of

Calvinism that sanctified apartheid based on a contorted exegesis of biblical texts—especially the Tower of Babel and the Curse of Ham stories—and had bragged that it was their church, not the National Party, that had first laid down the principles and framework of apartheid (literally "apartness" of the races).[10] Because of its theological justification for apartheid and close ties to the government, the DRC was referred to as "the National Party at prayer."

But Christianity was not monolithic; counter-theologies arose that challenged these assumptions. All the resistance movements were influenced by Christian ideals.[11] Peter Walshe argues that a "prophetic" Christianity endured during the apartheid era that supported the notions of unity, nonracialism, and a commitment to justice.[12] Although the churches were in many ways captive to culture, "trapped in apartheid,"[13] and their response often timid and "phlegmatic"[14]—as synodical pronouncements denounced apartheid but offered little action—a prophetic witness condemning apartheid nonetheless survived not only through individual clerics such as Trevor Huddleston, Michael Scott, Denis Hurley, Ambrose Reeves, Beyers Naudé, Frank Chikane, and Desmond Tutu, but also through ecumenical organizations such as the Black Consciousness–oriented Christian Institute and, after its banning, the South Africa Council of Churches.[15] The teachings of the church survived and continue to resonate, making a public confession/forgiveness/absolution model possible.

However, even in South Africa, some were turned off by the particularly Christian atmosphere and discourse of the hearings. Marius Schoon, whose wife and daughter were murdered by a parcel bomb sent to them by government agents, complained about "the imposition of a Christian morality of forgiveness."[16] In multireligious societies, or in nations with strong traditions of church-state separation, truth commissions that rely heavily on Christian theology may not work.

Rwanda is also a predominantly Christian country, with 90 percent of the population claiming membership in Christian churches.[17] As in South Africa, the church has had a long history of accommodation with the state. In colonial times, the Catholic Church propagated the superiority of the Tutsis, but switched its allegiance from the Tutsi ruling class to the Hutu regime upon independence. The Catholic Church was the most influential and powerful institution in Rwanda apart from the state itself, and the Protestant churches, though numerically smaller, had a disproportionate influence right up to the office of the president.[18] Catholic and Protestant church leaders alike received patronage and lavish gifts (including cars, televisions, and guaranteed places in the school system for their children) from the ruling party. Co-opted, they remained silent in the face of injustice, leaving a moral vacuum during the last years of Habyarimana's rule. The result of the integration of the churches into the power structure meant that their independence was sacrificed.

As the Hutu extremists were planning the genocide, they took advantage of the state-owned radio stations to orchestrate a campaign of ethnic hatred. According to Hugh McCullum, "no church leader ever spoke out [against these broadcasts], and some could be heard broadcasting 'moments of meditation' over these airwaves prior to April 6."[19] The church's teachings helped prepare parishioners to join in the directives to attack Tutsis. Timothy Longman notes that church officials in Rwanda "often emphasized theological principles of obedience," and ordinary people engaged in the massacres because the teachings of the church convinced them it was their duty to follow their leaders.[20] While violence erupted throughout the country for four months, both Protestant and Catholic leaders remained silent. The people interpreted the silence as endorsements of the killings.[21]

Some clergy and many other church employees and lay leaders took important roles in organizing the genocide, often using their familiarity with the population to help locate the homes of Tutsis. Longman describes one such case: Amani, an employee of the Presbyterian Church in Kirinda, used his church connections to become a local political leader. When the genocide began, Amani went through the community encouraging Tutsis to assemble at the local nursing school run by the church, promising them, "We will protect you." A few nights later, Amani personally led the gang that slaughtered the assembled Tutsis, according to the lone survivor who witnessed Amani at the head of the death squad.[22]

In May 1999, Roman Catholic bishop Augustin Misago was arrested. He was charged with refusing church shelter to Tutsis and sending nineteen schoolgirls to their deaths. (The highest-ranking Catholic cleric among more than twenty priests and nuns accused of participating in the genocide, Misago was acquitted in state court, a decision that met with cries of outrage from surviving victims.)[23]

A former president of the Seventh Day Adventist Church, Elizaphan Ntakirutimana, who fled to the United States and unsuccessfully fought to block his extradition to the ICTR, is standing trial in Arusha. Ntakirutimana allegedly lured hundreds of Tutsi civilians into a church compound at Mugenero. He then led armed Hutu extremists to the site and directed the Tutsis' slaughter. A witness testified in November 2001 that militias quoted the pastor's words as injunction—"God had ordered that

Tutsis should be killed and exterminated"—as the militias pursued the witness.[24] (The defense is scheduled to begin its case in 2002.)

There were, of course, examples of priests and pastors who risked their lives trying to protect Tutsis in their parish buildings during the genocide, but there were far more stories of pastors who cooperated with death squads—either out of fear, or because they were integrated into the structures of power that the genocide was intended to defend.[25] Priests encouraged Hutu parishioners to hack to death with machetes Tutsi believers in the same parish.[26] The church leadership was so aligned with the government that it lost its independent voice, and its legitimacy. The church mirrored society instead of opposing evil and standing for justice. "For this silent acquiescence and lack of courage, the churches as institutions paid dearly. They will continue to live under a cloud of suspicion for years to come."[27] The teachings of the church on forgiveness and reconciliation are now discredited. When Tutu urged Rwandans to forgive, his words fell on deaf ears. Can the model of pardon only succeed in a country with a majority Christian population where discourse by religious leaders on public policy is taken seriously, and where a prophetic voice proclaiming justice endures?

A dominant Christian population is not essential; as Daan Bronkhorst points out, truth and confession as precursors to reconciliation is a recurring theme in all the great religions. Furthermore, most religious traditions place reconciliation above justice.[28] However, for religion to play a positive role in reconciliation, it must stand independent of the state, ready and willing to critique power when necessary.

Ubuntu

Tutu's expectation that former enemies could be reintegrated into the community was based not only on his expectation that Christians would forgive as their religion teaches them, but also on his understanding of the African philosophy of *ubuntu.* If real and not a "current invention,"[29] *ubuntu* would provide an African source for making reconciliation intelligible and could form the basis for the reconciliation between Hutus and Tutsis in Rwanda. If Christianity were to prove useless in some places for providing a basis for a reconciliation process, what about resources from traditional African culture? Speaking of the genocide in Rwanda, Tutu asks, "Where was *ubuntu* then?"[30] He admits: "I don't really know except to say it clearly is not a mechanical, automatic, and inevitable process."[31]

A recent innovation in Rwanda's Ministry of Justice that relies on the *ubuntu* principle is the proposal for a *Gacaca* tribunal. *Gacaca* is a system of community justice based on trial by one's peers, where the sentence consists of material restitution and community service rather than prison terms or executions. It is anticipated that some of the 115,000 genocide cases waiting to be heard in the state courts will be expedited in this forum.

Assessing "Justice" and "Reconciliation"

In Tutu's recent book, *No Future Without Forgiveness,* he attempts to demonstrate the superiority of the pardon process. He has lectured the Rwandans: "We must break the spiral of reprisal and counter-reprisal. I said to them in Kigali unless you move beyond justice in the form of a tribunal, there is no hope for Rwanda. Confession, forgiveness and reconciliation in the lives of nations are not just airy-fairy religious and spiritual things, nebulous and unrealistic. They are the stuff of practical politics."[32] For Tutu, Nuremberg and all that it represents—retribution and punishment—is inferior to his vision of *ubuntu*—forgiveness and the reintegration of the evildoer into the community. "Justice with ashes" is how he describes the ICTR.[33]

But Tina Rosenberg argues for the importance of trials for countries in the aftermath of ethnic wars. "Trials can help break the cycle of revenge that has kept these wars recurring. They can personalize crimes so that victims hold responsible individual Hutus and not the entire group."[34] She goes on to add: "But although justice is crucial after ethnic mass murder, it is also impossible."[35] She cites the expense of trials, weak judicial systems, and the fact that tribunals can only try a small group of perpetrators. She concludes: "These countries must find other ways . . . to bring about the benefits of justice. . . . A truth commission can help."[36]

How does one judge the success of the two institutions, even on their own terms? Did the ICTR afford justice? Did the TRC bring about reconciliation? These are difficult questions to address in a quantitative way. In the eight years since the genocide in Rwanda, 6,000 people have been tried in the state courts for genocide and crimes against humanity, with some 115,000 more detained in prisons awaiting trial.[37] The ICTR reached no convictions at all during its first three years. To date, it has indicted only forty-six suspected war criminals and handed down just nine verdicts (eight convictions and one acquittal), with eight trials under way.[38] At this rate, to bring to trial all those accused of genocide would take 100 years. At best, the kind of justice the courts can render will be "justice delayed."

Furthermore, one leading suspect, Jean-Bosco Barayagwiza, the leader of the Coalition for the Defense of the Republic (CDR), was set free on a technicality. The ICTR's prosecuting office had failed to present him to the ICTR within the specified time. This is just one of many examples of "bumblings and delays" of the poorly funded prosecutor's office that have hampered the cause of justice.[39] Furthermore, because of concurrent jurisdictions, the followers of the genocide prosecuted in state courts may get the death penalty, while the actual planners, the "masterminds," convicted by the ICTR face a maximum sentence of life imprisonment. Lighter sentences, better prison conditions, and guarantees of due process result in substantial advantages going to those tried in the international tribunal. "This surely is an unintended and an unjust outcome," writes Madeline Morris.[40] And to expedite the handling of thousands of cases in the state courts, the local courts permit plea bargaining of defendants in exchange for greatly reduced sentences. According to Morris, "If the leaders are always receiving 'international justice' which is perceived as lenient, and the followers are at home getting 'bargains' in the national justice system, then no one is punished fully and severely, relative to national standards, for the horrors that were committed."[41] Even judged by its own criterion, promoting justice, the ICTR has achieved very little.

What of South Africa? Tutu and the commissioners have been quick to point out that the TRC was but one contribution, that reconciliation is a long-term process that cannot be achieved overnight.[42] In some South African polls, when asked if the TRC helped or hurt relationships between the races, the majority of respondents answered that it had hurt them.[43] Does this indicate that reconciliation did not result from the two-and-a-half-year experiment in national group therapy? Obviously, the healing of traumatized people will take time. Anecdotal evidence suggests that the cathartic value of testifying in a safe place and having offenses acknowledged was momentarily helpful, but feelings of depression and anxiety returned months later.[44] Is long-term psychological healing possible with a quick fix? And does individual healing lead to the "healing of a nation" (the title of a recent book on the TRC)?[45] Or were individuals sacrificed for the greater good of national reconciliation?

If reintegrating perpetrators back into the fold was one of the goals, the TRC was less than successful. There is the matter of the small numbers of amnesty applicants from the white community, ostensibly the community most in need of acknowledging their deeds and being restored. Moreover, less than 10 percent of those who did apply for amnesty were granted immunity.[46] Very few perpetrators have been reintegrated back into the community.

However, the TRC did achieve more modest goals. Charles Villa-Vicencio argues that there are three stages in political transitions from repressive rule: peaceful coexistence; national reconciliation, which is more difficult to achieve; and forgiveness, "a coveted ideal" to be gently pursued and not imposed.[47] If not forgiveness, or reconciliation, then perhaps peaceful coexistence has been achieved through the TRC. Speaking on peaceful coexistence as a worthy outcome, Villa-Vicencio says that even if at the end of the TRC process we are "not fully reconciled to one another," then at least "we do not kill each other."[48] Martha Minow also points to peaceful coexistence, the point "between vengeance and forgiveness," as a laudable achievement of truth commissions.[49]

For some modicum level of peaceful coexistence to take place, there must be some general agreement about what happened and why. For David Crocker, "[f]ormer enemies are unlikely to be reconciled if what count as lies for one side are verities for the other."[50] Timothy Garton Ash identifies three ways of dealing with the past—trials, purges, and history lessons—and finds the third path, history lessons, to be the most fruitful.[51] Truth commissions—but not criminal courts—are particularly good at ascertaining the broad sweep of events. Minow asserts that trials "following mass atrocities can never establish a complete historical record, despite all hopes."[52] Tina Rosenberg adds: "Trials, in the end, are ill suited to deal with the subtleties of facing the past."[53] A truth commission that endeavored to get at the "causes, motives, and perspectives" of perpetrators will provide a better understanding of the past and a more comprehensive history than prosecutions can provide.

The very fact of asking perpetrators for their insights into their behavior (unique among truth commissions) may lead to a better understanding between members of society. Without public awareness of what actually happened, there is the danger that revisionist thinking might surface that denies the realities of the apartheid era. (There is evidence that this is happening in Rwanda; the displaced Hutu leadership is circulating propaganda that denies the genocide, places the blame for the past violence on the part of the victims, and suggests they [Hutus] were engaged in a civil war in which they were acting in self-defense.)[54]

The International Criminal Court

Finally, what policy implications arise from a comparative study of the TRC and the ICTR? On the African continent, other countries including Sierra Leone, Lesotho, and Nigeria are looking at the two models for direction as they move from authoritarianism to democratic rule. Because the TRC has received so much international attention, other countries outside the continent have also been turning to South Africa as their model. When Hun Sen, the prime minister of Cambodia, expressed interest in a truth commission in 1999, he said he intended to invite Desmond Tutu to Phnom Penh for a visit. Likewise, Bosnia, Colombia, and Indonesia are considering an investigative body like the TRC.[55]

However, the proposal in 1998 for the establishment of an international criminal court whereby countries would have no choice but to prosecute war crimes, crimes against humanity, or genocide would most likely eliminate the TRC experiment as a model for other countries. Villa-Vicencio says this prospect is "a little frightening," and recommends that some international mechanism be developed to assess all truth commissions' initiatives and to decide whether to let a country proceed along the truth commission/amnesty route.[56] John Dugard points out that international opinion, "often driven by NGO's and western activists who are strangers to repression," pays insufficient attention to the circumstances of the society that chooses amnesty over prosecution.[57]

Should a country be able to determine whether to opt for prosecutions or truth commissions? Aryeh Neier points out that "[i]f the will of the people governed accountability in Rwanda, where 85% of the population was Hutu before the genocide and a much higher percentage after it, nothing might have been done."[58] Graeme Simpson remarks that even those commentators who argue more strenuously that there is a duty to punish certain crimes under international law have conceded that, if such a course of action would plunge a country into violence or destroy a fragile transition to democracy, then this obligation should be tempered by other considerations.[59] Dugard asserts that certainly genocide should not be exempted from prosecution, nor should war crimes or "grave breaches" of the Geneva Convention committed in international conflicts. Difficulties arise in respect to torture and crimes against humanity committed by a repressive regime in the course of an internal conflict. Where a state opts for amnesty (conditional, not blanket) to achieve reconciliation, then surely that decision should be respected.[60] In fashioning an international criminal court, the pros and cons of truth commissions and tribunals need to be studied further—and for traumatized nations, the relative value of reconciliation and justice needs to be assessed.

Notes

1. For an excellent discussion on the compatibility of order and justice, see Bull, *The Anarchical Society.*

2. Mertus, "The War Crimes Tribunal," p. 51.

3. Cited in David Goodman, "Justice Drowns in Political Quagmire," *Mail & Guardian* (January 31–February 6, 1997).

4. Mamdani, "Reconciliation Without Justice," p. 4.

5. Rosenberg, "Recovering from Apartheid," p. 95.

6. Landsman, "Alternative Responses to Serious Human Rights Abuses," p. 90.

7. Desmond Tutu, *No Future Without Forgiveness,* p. 260.

8. Elphick, introduction to *Christianity in South Africa,* p. 1.

9. Ibid.

10. For studies on the influence of the Dutch Reformed Church on the National Party's politics, see Moodie, *The Rise of Afrikanerdom;* William de Klerk, *The Puritans in Africa;* Templin, *Ideology on a Frontier;* and Kuperus, *State, Civil Society, and Apartheid in South Africa.*

11. See Graybill, *Religion and Resistance Politics in South Africa.*

12. See Walshe, *Prophetic Christianity and the Liberation Movement in South Africa.*

13. See Villa-Vicencio, *Trapped in Apartheid.*

14. Walshe, "The Role of Christianity in the Transition to Majority Rule in South Africa," p. 181.

15. See Walshe, *Church Versus State in South Africa* and *Prophetic Christianity and the Liberation Movement in South Africa.*

16. Cited in Villa-Vicencio, "Learning to Live Together," p. 14.

17. Membership is 62.6 percent Catholic, 18.8 percent Protestant, 8.4 percent Seventh Day Adventist. See McCullum, *The Angels Have Left Us,* p. 18.

18. Longman, "Empowering the Weak and Protecting the Powerful," p. 57.

19. McCullum, *The Angels Have Left Us,* p. 18.

20. Longman, "Empowering the Weak and Protecting the Powerful," p. 57.

21. Ibid., p. 59.

22. Ibid., p. 64.

23. "Bishop Arrested on Genocide Charges," *Christian Century* (May 19–26, 1999), p. 562.

24. "Pastor Said God Had Ordained Extermination of Tutsis, Witness Claims," *The Arusha Times* (November 3–9, 2001).

25. Longman, "Empowering the Weak and Protecting the Powerful," pp. 61–62.

26. des Forges, *Leave None to Tell the Story,* pp. 247–248.

27. McCullum, *The Angels Have Left Us,* p. 65.
28. Bronkhorst, *Truth and Reconciliation,* p. 38.
29. See Richard Wilson, "The Sizwe Will Not Go Away."
30. Desmond Tutu, *No Future Without Forgiveness,* p. 32.
31. Ibid., p. 35.
32. *Truth and Reconciliation Commission of South Africa Report,* vol. 5, chap. 9, "Reconciliation," p. 351.
33. Cited in Mark Gevisser, "The Ultimate Test of Faith," *Mail & Guardian* (April 12, 1996).
34. Rosenberg, "Confronting the Painful Past," p. 350.
35. Ibid., p. 351.
36. Ibid., p. 352.
37. John Prendergast and David Smock, "Building Peace in Rwanda and Burundi," USIP special report (September 15, 1999). See also Sheenah Kaliisa, "Gacaca: Rwanda Begins Training Judges for New Justice System in December," *Internews* (October 25, 2001).
38. "Tanzania: Work of Tribunal Hailed on UN Birthday," *Africa News* (October 24, 2001).
39. Human Rights Watch press release, "Rwanda Genocide Suspect Freed" (November 8, 1999).
40. Madeline Morris, "The Trials of Concurrent Jurisdiction," p. 371.
41. Ibid., p. 364.
42. *Truth and Reconciliation Commission of South Africa Report,* vol. 5, chap. 9, "Reconciliation," p. 435.
43. "AC-Nielsen/MRA Poll," conducted by *Business Day* (July 27, 1998).
44. See Hamber, "The Burdens of Truth."
45. Boraine and Levy, eds., *The Healing of a Nation?*
46. According to a TRC press release, "Year End Summary" (December 9, 1999), as of November 15, 1999, 568 amnesty applicants had been granted amnesty, and 5,287 applicants had been refused.
47. Villa-Vicencio, "The Truth and Reconciliation Commission."
48. Cited in Elshtain, "True Confessions," p. 12.
49. See Minow, *Between Vengeance and Forgiveness.*
50. Crocker, "Reckoning with Past Wrongs," p. 50.
51. Ash, "The Truth About Dictatorship," p. 40.
52. Minow, *Between Vengeance and Forgiveness,* p. 47.
53. Rosenberg, *The Haunted Land,* p. 351.
54. Sarkin, "The Necessity and Challenges of Establishing a Truth and Reconciliation Commission in Rwanda," p. 772.
55. In Bosnia a truth commission was proposed that would work at the national level alongside the international tribunal.
56. Villa-Vicencio, "The Truth and Reconciliation Commission."
57. Dugard, "The Third Manfred Lachs Memorial Lecture," p. 6.
58. Neier, *War Crimes,* p. 84.
59. Simpson, "A Brief Evaluation of South Africa's Truth and Reconciliation Commission," p. 18.
60. Dugard, "The Third Manfred Lachs Memorial Lecuture," p. 13.

13

Afterword: Miracle or Evil Compromise?

"No institution for dealing with the past anywhere in the world has taken on as ambitious a portfolio," asserts Tina Rosenberg of South Africa's Truth and Reconciliation Commission (TRC).[1] How successful was it in realizing its goals? Rosenberg believes that "it seems to have been more successful than anything else yet tried."[2] Perhaps that is as complete a summation of this extraordinary process as is possible to make.

The TRC was certainly not perfect by any means. It was a compromise between the morally ideal and the politically possible. As Reinhold Niebuhr reminds us, neither perfect love nor perfect justice is fully attainable in political communities, and society's best solution can only be an "approximation of brotherhood under the conditions of sin."[3] But if justice depends upon groups agreeing to a tolerable solution to inevitable conflict, the TRC met that requirement. Though the commission was flawed and subject to criticism, its appointment marked an important stage in the process of coming to understand South Africa's past. It may yet lead, if not to perfect reconciliation, then at least to the possibility of coexistence in this once deeply divided society.

Only time will determine the TRC's ultimate effectiveness in reconciling the South African nation. Certainly much more will need to be done over a period of many years, for the wounds are too deep to be "trivialized by imagining that a single initiative can on its own bring about a peaceful, stable, and restored society."[4] As Nelson Mandela reminded his countrymen during the parliamentary debate on the TRC: "Long after the Commission has folded and its offices closed, political leaders and all of us in business, the trade union movement, religious bodies, professionals and communities in general shall have to remain seized with the matters that the TRC process brought to the fore. Inasmuch as reconciliation touches on every aspect of our lives, it is our nation's lifeline."[5]

Brandon Hamber had termed the TRC an "evil compromise" early in its tenure,[6] but clearly it was not that. Far from jettisoning justice, it offered a larger, more magnanimous form of what Desmond Tutu has called "restorative" justice as opposed to "retributive" justice, in which reintegrating the perpetrator into society was as important as healing the victims' wounds.[7] Peter Storey characterizes the TRC as offering a "different kind of justice" than one that merely metes out harsh punishment.[8] Wilhelm Verwoerd suggests that the TRC was the result of a moral *conflict* or *tension* between radical justice and peace, not a moral *compromise.*[9] The politics of compromise may seem at odds with a strict notion of justice, but Alex Boraine has insisted that amnesty as the price paid for peace and stability is morally defensible:

> If negotiation politics had not succeeded the bitter conflict would have continued and many more human rights violations would have occurred and hundreds, and possibly thousands, would have been killed. Hard choices had to be made and it does not follow that the choices that were made lie easily on the consciences of the politicians who made them. The alternative was, in my view, far less desirable and potentially much more destructive.[10]

Can the TRC be seen as a model for other nations, then? Priscilla Hayner, the preeminent scholar on comparative truth commissions, offers this sober caveat: "Reliving horrors is not for everyone." She argues that in some countries there is no interest in investigating the details of the past. "Where this reflects a broad consensus, a policy of reconciliation through silence, through trying to forget the past, should be acceptable and accepted by the international community."[11] Moreover, the reconciliation that occurred in South Africa under "the persistent prodding" of Mandela and Tutu, who made forgiveness "a matter of patriotic duty," may dim as these "moral beacons pass from the scene."[12] For those countries without a Mandela or a Tutu to provide the crucial political and spiritual leadership, reconciliation may falter from the start.

Yet nations moving through democratic transitions may indeed find a workable model in South Africa's ethical yet pragmatic experiment in dealing with the past. Elizabeth Kiss finds a South Africa–styled truth commission an "especially promising tool" in places such as eastern and central Europe, Northern Ireland, and the Middle East, where there are violators and perpetrators on multiple sides.[13] "Perhaps other nations with wounded histories may find here a model for hope," writes Storey. "As the international community comes to recognize that there is no peace without confronting the hurts of history and without the healing of national and ethnic memories, one nation's imperfect attempt to do so may inspire . . . these lands too."[14]

Whether it was a miracle impossible to duplicate, or a model for other ruptured societies seeking to become whole, South Africa's Truth and Reconciliation Commission was certainly an extraordinary and unprecedented exercise in healing that will be cited, debated, and held out as an inspiration for as long as people search for ways to live with one another.

Notes

1. Rosenberg, foreword to *Coming to Terms,* p. x.
2. Ibid., p. xi.
3. Niebuhr, *The Nature and Destiny of Man,* p. 254.
4. Boraine, "Alternatives and Adjuncts to Criminal Prosecutions."
5. Parliamentary debate on TRC, February 25, 1999.
6. SAPA, "South Africans Find Truth and Reconciliation a Tall Order" (August 25, 1997).
7. Rosenberg, "Recovering from Apartheid," p. 90.
8. Storey, "A Different Kind of Justice," p. 788.
9. Verwoerd, "Justice After Apartheid?"
10. Boraine, "Alternatives and Adjuncts to Criminal Prosecutions."
11. Hayner, "International Guidelines for the Creation and Operation of Truth Commissions," p. 176.
12. Goodman, "Reconciliation or Chaos?" p. 60.
13. Kiss, "Moral Ambition Within and Beyond Political Constraints," p. 91.
14. Storey, "A Different Kind of Justice," p. 793.

Chronology

1899–1902	Anglo-Boer War. Britain conquers the two Boer republics.
1910	British colonies (Cape Colony and Natal) join to form the Union with Boer republics (Transvaal and Orange Free State).
1912	South African Native National Congress founded (later becomes the ANC).
1913	Natives Land Act (also in 1936) limits African landownership to the reserves (or homelands); divides country into black and white areas.
1914	National Party founded.
1919	Jan Smuts becomes prime minister.
1921	Communist Party of South Africa (CPSA) founded.
1923	Urban Areas Act restricts Africans from living in the cities.
1924	J.B.M. Hertzog becomes prime minister.
1939	Jan Smuts becomes prime minister.
1943	Alexandra bus boycott.
1948	National Party gains control of government on apartheid platform. D. F. Malan becomes prime minister.

	ANC Youth League is formed and drafts Program of Action calling for boycotts, strikes, and demonstrations.
1950	Population Registration Act assigns all people to one of three categories: white, Coloured, or African.
	Suppression of Communism Act bans the CPSA.
1952	Defiance Campaign against discriminatory legislation by the ANC and its allies.
1953	Bantu Education Act takes control of education away from the churches and requires that black children be taught in segregated schools.
	CPSA reorganizes as the South African Communist Party (SACP).
1954	J. G. Strijdom becomes prime minister.
1955	Congress of the People adopts Freedom Charter.
1956	Treason Trial of 156 members of Congress Alliance.
1958	Hendrik Verwoerd becomes prime minister.
1959	Promotion of Bantu Self-Government Act recognizes the reserves as the homelands for the various tribes and the only areas in which Africans would exercise their political rights.
	PAC forms as a breakaway from the ANC.
1960	Sharpeville massacre—sixty-nine PAC identity-pass protesters killed.
	ANC and PAC banned.
1961	South Africa becomes a republic and leaves the British Commonwealth.
	ANC forms MK, a military wing.
1963	Rivonia Trial of MK activists (including Nelson Mandela).
1964	Nelson Mandela sentenced to life in prison.

1966	John Vorster becomes prime minister.
1975	Angola and Mozambique become independent states.
	Inkatha founded by Mongosuthu Buthelezi as a Zulu cultural organization (later becomes the IFP).
1976–1981	South Africa grants independence to Transkei, Bophuthatswana, Venda, and Ciskei homelands, but they are not recognized abroad.
1976	Soweto uprising—protest by students against use of Afrikaans in school.
1977	Steve Biko murdered.
1978	P. W. Botha becomes prime minister.
1979	AWB (semiterrorist neo-Nazi) resistance movement founded by Eugene Terre'Blanche.
	Black trade unions legalized.
1981–1988	South African forces invade Angola and make raids into Lesotho, Zimbabwe, Mozambique, and Zambia. ANC guerrillas sabotage South African cities.
1981	Griffiths Mxenge murdered.
1982	Right-wing whites break from the National Party to form the Conservative Party.
1983	Church Street bombing of air force headquarters.
	Tricameral Parliament established, giving Indians and Coloureds (but not Africans) their separate chambers.
	P. W. Botha becomes president.
	UDF forms as coalition of workers, civics, students, and women's organizations to fight against the new constitution establishing the Tricameral Parliament.
1984	Desmond Tutu receives the Nobel Peace Prize.
1985	COSATU formed as the largest trade union federation.
	PEBCO Three tortured and killed.

	Cradock Four abducted and killed en route to Cradock from Port Elizabeth.
	Government declares a state of emergency.
	Amanzimtoti shopping center bombed by MK.
	Kairos Document signed by theologians.
1986	Magoo's Bar bombed by MK operatives.
	U.S. Congress passes Comprehensive Anti-Apartheid Act (over Reagan's veto).
	Identity-pass laws repealed.
1987	Security forces blow up COSATU House, headquarters of COSATU.
1988	Bombing of Khotso House, headquarters of the SACC.
	Trust Feed massacre in KwaZulu, led by Brian Mitchell.
1989	F. W. de Klerk becomes president.
1990	Nelson Mandela released from prison.
	ANC and other organizations unbanned.
	Namibia becomes an independent state and SWAPO wins election.
	Rustenburg Declaration signed by church groups.
	Natives Land Acts, Group Areas Act, Population Registration Act, and Separate Amenities Act repealed.
	F. W. de Klerk and Nelson Mandela start negotiations.
1992	Boipatong massacre—forty-six pro-ANC Xhosas murdered by pro-IFP Zulus.
	Bisho massacre—twenty-four ANC/SACP protesters killed by Ciskei defense forces.
	APLA (PAC's military wing) attack at King William's Town Golf Club.
1993	Chris Hani murdered by two right-wing CP members.

	St. James Church killings by APLA soldiers.
	Amy Biehl murdered by PAC followers.
	APLA attack at Heidelberg Tavern in Cape Town suburb.
	Nelson Mandela and F. W. de Klerk receive Nobel Peace Prize jointly.
1994	First democratic election.
	Nelson Mandela inaugurated as president.
1995	South Africa wins Rugby World Cup on home turf.
	Promotion of National Unity and Reconciliation Act signed into law.
1996	TRC hearings begin.
	National Party withdraws from the Government of National Unity.
1998	TRC submits five-volume final report to President Nelson Mandela.
1999	Thabo Mbeki becomes president.
2001	TRC dissolved.

Glossary

Afrikaans Language developed from seventeenth-century Dutch; one of the two official languages (English being the other) under white rule.

Afrikaner A South African white descended from the early Dutch, German, or Huguenot settlers who immigrated to South Africa beginning in the early seventeenth century.

apartheid Meaning "apartness"; a racially based policy of segregation enunciated by the National Party.

askari Someone in the resistance who has "turned" to the police as an informer.

banning An action taken by the minister of justice under the authority of the Internal Security Act to restrict an individual's freedom of association, movement, and expression. Organizations and publications could also be banned.

black spots Areas of land in white areas inhabited by blacks. This led to the "removals" of blacks from their homes.

boer A white South African of Dutch, German, or Huguenot descent (an Afrikaner).

CCB (Civil Cooperation Bureau) Covert organization of the South African Defense Force.

Coloured Racial classification denoting a person of mixed race (mainly African European descent).

Dutch Reformed Church Church established by early Dutch settlers who brought their native Calvinism to South Africa.

English-speaker A white South African of British descent for whom English is the mother language.

homelands The ten areas designated by the National Party as homes for the various ethnic groups.

influx control A measure to regulate movement of Africans into urban areas.

kaffir A derogatory term for an African.

necklacing The placing of a lighted, gasoline-soaked tire around the neck of an enemy.

pass Identity document required to be carried by Africans.

rand (R) Unit of South African currency (1 R = 0.10 USD as of October 31, 2001).

SSC (State Security Council) Centralized body set up by P. W. Botha that de facto governed the country.

township Designated residential areas for Africans located near cities. Soweto is the largest.

ubuntu African philosophy connoting humaneness, caring, and community.

Vlakplaas Police farm near Pretoria for training askaris in terrorism.

Acronyms

AFM	Apostolic Faith Mission
AHI	Afrikaner Handelsinstituut (Afrikaner Institute for Commerce)
ANC	African National Congress
APK	Afrikaanse Protestante Kerk (Afrikaner Protestant Church)
APLA	Azanian People's Liberation Army
ARMSCOR	Armaments Development and Production Corporation
AWB	Afrikaner Weerstandsbeweging (Afrikaner Resistance Movement)
BC	Black Consciousness
BCM	Black Consciousness Movement
CCB	Civil Cooperation Bureau
CDR	Coalition for the Defense of the Republic
CI	Christian Institute
COSAB	Council of South African Banks
COSATU	Congress of South African Trade Unions
CP	Conservative Party
CPSA	Church of the Province of Southern Africa
CPSA	Communist Party of South Africa (reformed as the SACP in 1953)
CSVR	Center for the Study of Violence and Reconciliation
DBSA	Development Bank of Southern Africa
DP	Democratic Party
DPSC	Detainees' Parents Support Committee
DRC	Dutch Reformed Church (also NGK)

FEDSEM	Federal Theological Seminary
FF	Freedom Front
FXI	Freedom of Expression Institute
GK	Gereformeerde Kerk (Reformed Church)
HRC	Human Rights Commission
HRV	Human Rights Violations (committee of TRC)
HSRC	Human Sciences Research Council
ICC	International Criminal Court
ICTR	International Criminal Tribunal for Rwanda
IDASA	Institute for Democracy in South Africa
IFP	Inkatha Freedom Party
IJR	Institute for Justice and Reconciliation
INCORE	Initiative on Conflict Resolution and Ethnicity
IRG	individual reparation grant
MASA	Medical Association of South Africa
MJC	Muslim Judicial Council
MK	Umkhonto We Sizwe (Spear of the Nation)
MP	member of Parliament
MPLA	Popular Movement for the Liberation of Angola
MRA	Market Research Africa
Naspers	Nasionale Pers (National Press)
NEDLAC	National Economic Development and Labor Council
NGK	Nederduitse Gereformeerde Kerk (Dutch Reformed Church)
NGKA	Nederduitse Gereformeerde Kerk in Afrika (Dutch Reformed Church in Africa)
NGO	nongovernmental organization
NGSK	Nederduitse Gereformeerde Sendingkerk (Dutch Reformed Mission Church)
NHK	Nederduitsch Hervormde Kerk (Dutch re-Formed Church)
NIS	National Intelligence Service
NP	National Party
NPU	National Press Union
PAC	Pan-Africanist Congress
PASO	Pan-Africanist Students Organization
PEBCO	Port Elizabeth Black Civic Organization
RICSA	Research Institute on Christianity in South Africa
RPF	Rwandan Patriotic Front
SAB	South African Breweries

SABC	South African Broadcasting Corporation
SACC	South African Council of Churches
SACOB	South African Chamber of Business
SACP	South African Communist Party (formerly the CPSA [Communist Party of South Africa], banned in 1950)
SADF	South African Defense Force
SAMDC	South African Medical and Dental Council
SAMS	South African Medical Services
SANLAM	Suid-Afrikaanse Nasionale Lewensassuransie Maatskappy (South African National Life Assurance Company)
SAP	South African police
SAPA	South African Press Association
SEIFSA	Steel and Engineering Industries Federation of South Africa
SPROCAS	Study Project on Christianity in Apartheid Society
SPROCAS II	Special Program for Christian Action in Society
SSC	State Security Council
SWAPO	South West African People's Organization
TRC	Truth and Reconciliation Commission
UDF	United Democratic Front
UK	United Kingdom
UN	United Nations
WBI	Women's Budget Initiative
Wits	University of Witwatersrand
ZCC	Zion Christian Church

Bibliography

Ackermann, Denise. "On Hearing and Lamenting: Faith and Truth-Telling." In H. Russel Botman and Robin Petersen, eds. *To Remember and to Heal: Theological and Psychological Reflections on Truth and Reconciliation.* Cape Town: Human & Rousseau, 1996, pp. 47–56.

Adam, Heribert. "Africa's Nazis: Apartheid as Holocaust?" *Indicator SA* 14, no. 1 (summer 1997): 13–16.

Adam, Heribert, and Kanya Adam. "The Politics of Memory in Divided Societies." In Wilmot James and Linda van de Vijver, eds. *After the TRC: Reflections on Truth and Reconciliation in South Africa.* Cape Town: David Philip, 2000, pp. 32–47.

Allen, Jonathan. "Balancing Justice and Social Unity: Political Theory and the Idea of a Truth and Reconciliation Commission." *University of Toronto Law Journal* 49, no. 3 (1999): 315–353.

Antze, Paul, and Michael Lambek, eds. *Tense Past: Cultural Essays in Trauma and Memory.* London: Routledge, 1996.

"Apartheid and Capitalism: Harvesting Apartheid—The Complicity of Business in Racial Oppression." *The African Communist* (4th quarter 1997): 40–63.

Arendse, Craig. "Mending the Vase: Reconciling Broken Relationships." *Track Two* 6, nos. 3–4 (December 1997), http://ccrweb.ccr.uct.ac.za/two/6_34/index634.html.

Arendse, Roger. "Right-Wing Christian Groups." In James Cochrane, John de Gruchy, and Stephen Martin, eds. *Facing the Truth: South African Faith Communities and the Truth and Reconciliation Commission.* Cape Town: David Philip, 1999, pp. 91–100.

Arendt, Hannah. *The Human Condition.* Chicago: University of Chicago Press, 1958.

Ash, Timothy Garton. "The Curse and Blessing of South Africa." *New York Review of Books* 44, no. 13 (August 14, 1997): 8–11.

———. "True Confessions." *New York Review of Books* 44, no. 12 (July 17, 1997): 33–38.

———. "The Truth About Dictatorship." *New York Review of Books* 45, no. 3 (February 19, 1998): 35–40.

Asmal, Kader. "Victims, Survivors, and Citizens—Human Rights, Reparations, and Reconciliation." Inaugural lecture on Kader Asmal's installation as professor of human rights law at the University of the Western Cape, Bellville, May 25, 1992. In *South African Journal of Human Rights* 8, no. 4 (1992): 491–511.

Asmal, Kader, Louise Asmal, and Ronald Suresh Roberts. *Reconciliation Through Truth: A Reckoning of Apartheid's Criminal Governance.* Cape Town: David Philip, 1996.

———. "When the Assassin Cries Foul: The Modern Just War Doctrine." In Charles Villa-Vicencio and Wilhelm Verwoerd, eds. *Looking Back, Reaching Forward: Reflections on the Truth and Reconciliation Commission of South Africa.* Cape Town: University of Cape Town Press, 2000, pp. 86–98.

Aspen Institute. *State Crimes: Punishment or Pardon.* Queenstown, Md.: Aspen Institute, 1989.

Baden, Sally, Shireen Hassim, and Sheila Meintjes. *Country Gender Profile: South Africa.* Pretoria: Swedish International Development Cooperation Agency, 1999.

Baldwin-Ragaven, Laurel, Jeanelle de Gruchy, and Leslie London, eds. *An Ambulance of the Wrong Colour: Health Professionals, Human Rights, and Ethics in South Africa.* Cape Town: University of Cape Town Press, 1999.

Barchiesi, Franco. "Socio-Economic Exploitation, Meaning Contestation, and the TRC: Problematic Foundations for a Discourse of Social Citizenship in Post-Apartheid South Africa." Paper presented at the "TRC: Commissioning the Past" conference, University of Witwatersrand, Johannesburg, June 11–14, 1999.

Battle, Michael. *Reconciliation: The Ubuntu Theology of Desmond Tutu.* Cleveland: Pilgrim Press, 1997.

———. "The Ubuntu Theology of Desmond Tutu." In Leonard Hulley, Louise Kretzschmar, and Luke Lungile Pato, eds. *Archbishop Tutu: Prophetic Witness in South Africa.* Cape Town: Human & Rousseau, 1996, pp. 93–105.

Bell, Paul. "Truth or Consequence." *Leadership* 17, no. 2 (1998): 27–32.

Bennett, Mark, and Deborah Earwaker. "Victims' Responses to Apologies: The Effects of Offender Responsibility and Offense Severity." *Journal of Social Psychology* 134, no. 4 (1994): 457–464.

Berat, Lynn. "South Africa: Negotiated Change." In Naomi Roht-Arriaza, ed. *Impunity and Human Rights in International Law and Practice.* Oxford: Oxford University Press, 1995, pp. 267–280.

Berat, Lynn, and Yossi Shain. "Retribution or Truth-Telling in South Africa? Legacies of the Transitional Phase." *Law and Social Inquiry* 20, no. 1 (1995): 163–189.

Bernstein, Hilda. *For Their Triumphs and for Their Tears: Conditions and Resistance of Women in Apartheid South Africa.* London: International Defence & Aid Fund, 1978.

Bhargava, Rajev. "The Moral Justification of Truth Commissions." In Charles Villa-Vicencio and Wilhelm Verwoerd, eds. *Looking Back, Reaching*

Forward: Reflections on the Truth and Reconciliation Commission of South Africa. Cape Town: University of Cape Town Press, 2000, pp. 60–67.

———. "Restoring Decency to Barbaric Societies." In Robert Rotberg and Dennis Thompson, eds. *Truth v. Justice: The Morality of Truth Commissions.* Princeton: Princeton University Press, 2000, pp. 45–67.

Bhengu, Mfuniselwa John. *Ubuntu: The Essence of Democracy.* Cape Town: Novalis Press, 1996.

Biggar, Nigel, ed. *Burying the Past: Making Peace and Doing Justice After Civil Conflict.* Washington, D.C.: Georgetown University Press, 2001.

Biko, Nkosinathi. "Amnesty and Denial." In Charles Villa-Vicencio and Wilhelm Verwoerd, eds. *Looking Back, Reaching Forward: Reflections on the Truth and Reconciliation Commission of South Africa.* Cape Town: University of Cape Town Press, 2000, pp. 193–198.

Bizos, George. *No One to Blame? In Pursuit of Justice in South Africa.* Cape Town: David Philip, 1999.

Blaude, Claudia. "The Archbishop, the Private Detective, and the Angel of History: The Production of South African Public Memory and the Truth and Reconciliation Commission." *Current Writing* 8, no. 2 (1996): 39–65.

Boesak, Willa. "Truth, Justice, and Reconciliation." In H. Russel Botman and Robin Petersen, eds. *To Remember and to Heal: Theological and Psychological Reflections on Truth and Reconciliation.* Cape Town: Human & Rousseau, 1996, pp. 65–69.

Bonhoeffer, Dietrich. *Cost of Discipleship.* New York: Macmillan, 1978.

———. *Life Together.* San Francisco: Harper, 1978.

Boraine, Alex. "Alternatives and Adjuncts to Criminal Prosecutions." Paper delivered at the "Justice in Cataclysm: Criminal Tribunals in the Wake of Mass Violence" conference, Brussels, July 20–21, 1996.

———. *A Country Unmasked: Inside South Africa's Truth and Reconciliation Commission.* Oxford: Oxford University Press, 2000.

———. "Healing Our Land." *SA Now* 1, no. 6 (July 1996): 14–20.

———. "The Language of Potential." In Wilmot James and Linda van de Vijver, eds. *After the TRC: Reflections on Truth and Reconciliation in South Africa.* Cape Town: David Philip, 2000, pp. 73–81.

———. "Truth and Reconciliation." *South African Outlook* 125, no. 6 (July 1995): 55–56.

———. "Truth and Reconciliation in South Africa: The Third Way." In Robert Rotberg and Dennis Thompson, eds. *Truth v. Justice: The Morality of Truth Commissions.* Princeton: Princeton University Press, 2000, pp. 141–157.

Boraine, Alex, and Janet Levy, eds. *The Healing of a Nation?* Cape Town: Justice in Transition, 1995.

Boraine, Alex, Janet Levy, and Ronel Scheffer, eds. *Dealing with the Past: Truth and Reconciliation in South Africa.* Cape Town: IDASA, 1994.

Borneman, John. *Settling Accounts: Violence, Justice, and Accountability in Post-Socialist Europe.* Princeton: Princeton University Press, 1997.

Botman, H. Russel. "Justice That Restores: How Reparations Must Be Made." *Track Two* 6, no. 2 (December 1997), http://ccrweb.uct.ac.za/two/6_34/index634.html.

———. "Narrative Challenges in a Situation of Transition." In H. Russel Botman and Robin Petersen, eds. *To Remember and to Heal: Theological and Psychological Reflections on Truth and Reconciliation.* Cape Town: Human & Rousseau, 1996, pp. 37–44.

———. "The Offender and the Church." In James Cochrane, John de Gruchy, and Stephen Martin, eds. *Facing the Truth: South African Faith Communities and the Truth and Reconciliation Commission.* Cape Town: David Philip, 1999, pp. 126–131.

———. "Pastoral Care and Counseling in Truth and Reconciliation: Types and Forms of Pastoral Work." In H. Russel Botman and Robin Petersen, eds. *To Remember and to Heal: Theological and Psychological Reflections on Truth and Reconciliation.* Cape Town: Human & Rousseau, 1996, pp. 154–162.

Botman, H. Russel, and Robin Petersen. Introduction to *To Remember and to Heal: Theological and Psychological Reflections on Truth and Reconciliation,* edited by H. Russel Botman and Robin Petersen. Cape Town: Human & Rousseau, 1996, pp. 9–14.

Bozzoli, Belinda. "Public Ritual and Private Transition—Transition: The Truth Commission in Alexandra Township, South Africa 1996." *African Studies* 57, no. 2 (1998): 167–195.

Braithwaite, John. *Crime, Shame, and Reintegration.* Cambridge: Cambridge University Press, 1989.

Bronkhorst, Daan. *Truth and Reconciliation: Obstacles and Opportunities for Human Rights.* Amsterdam: Amnesty International Dutch Section, 1995.

Brooks, Roy, ed. *When Sorry Isn't Enough: The Controversy over Apologies and Reparations for Human Injustice.* New York: New York University Press, 1999.

Bull, Hedley. *The Anarchical Society: A Study of World Politics.* New York: Columbia University Press, 1977.

Bundy, Colin. "The Beast of the Past: History and the TRC." In Wilmot James and Linda van de Vijver, eds. *After the TRC: Reflections on Truth and Reconciliation in South Africa.* Cape Town: David Philip, 2000, pp. 9–20.

Burton, Mary. "Making Moral Judgments." In Charles Villa-Vicencio and Wilhelm Verwoerd, eds. *Looking Back, Reaching Forward: Reflections on the Truth and Reconciliation Commission of South Africa.* Cape Town: University of Cape Town Press, 2000, pp. 77–85.

———. "Reparation, Amnesty, and a National Archive." In Wilmot James and Linda van de Vijver, eds. *After the TRC: Reflections on Truth and Reconciliation in South Africa.* Cape Town: David Philip, 2000, pp. 109–114.

Chapman, Audrey. "Coming to Terms with the Past: Truth, Justice, and Reconciliation." Paper presented at the "TRC: Commissioning the Past" conference, University of Witwatersrand, Johannesburg, June 11–14, 1999.

Cherry, Janet. "Historical Truth: Something to Fight For." In Charles Villa-Vicencio and Wilhelm Verwoerd, eds. *Looking Back, Reaching Forward: Reflections on the Truth and Reconciliation Commission of South Africa.* Cape Town: University of Cape Town Press, 2000, pp. 134–143.

———. "'Just War' and 'Just Means': Was the TRC Wrong About the ANC?" *Transformation* 42 (2000): 9–28.

Chidester, David. "Stories, Fragments, and Monuments." In James Cochrane, John de Gruchy, and Stephen Martin, eds. *Facing the Truth: South African Faith Communities and the Truth and Reconciliation Commission.* Cape Town: David Philip, 1999, pp. 132–141.

Christie, Kenneth. *The South African Truth Commission.* New York: St. Martin's Press, 2000.

Chubb, Karin, and Lutz van Dijk. *Between Anger and Hope: South Africa's Youth and the Truth and Reconciliation Commission.* Johannesburg: Witwatersrand University Press, 2001.

Cochrane, James, and Gerald West. "War, Remembrance, and Reconstruction." *Journal of Theology for Southern Africa* 84 (1993): 25–40.

Cochrane, James, John de Gruchy, and Stephen Martin, eds. *Facing the Truth: South African Faith Communities and the Truth and Reconciliation Commission.* Cape Town: David Philip, 1999.

———. "Faith, Struggle, and Reconciliation." In James Cochrane, John de Gruchy, and Stephen Martin, eds. *Facing the Truth: South African Faith Communities and the Truth and Reconciliation Commission.* Cape Town: David Philip, 1999, pp. 1–11.

———. "Wounded Healers." In James Cochrane, John de Gruchy, and Stephen Martin, eds. *Facing the Truth: South African Faith Communities and the Truth and Reconciliation Commission.* Cape Town: David Philip, 1999, pp. 170–174.

Cock, Jacklyn. *Colonels and Cadres: War and Gender in South Africa.* Oxford: Oxford University Press, 1991.

Coetzee, Alice. "Voice of Grief." *Democracy in Action* 8, no. 7 (1994): 19.

Coleman, Max, ed. *A Crime Against Humanity: Analysing the Repression of the Apartheid State.* Cape Town: David Philip, 1998.

Connell, Dan. "Strategies for Change: Women and Politics in Eritrea and South Africa." *Review of African Political Economy* 25, no. 76 (1998): 189–206.

Connor, Bernard F. *The Difficult Traverse: From Amnesty to Reconciliation.* Pietermaritzburg: Cluster, 1998.

Consedine, Jim. *Restorative Justice: Healing the Effects of Crime.* Lyttleton: Ploughshares, 1995.

Corder, Hugh. "The Law and Struggle: The Same, but Different." In Charles Villa-Vicencio and Wilhelm Verwoerd, eds. *Looking Back, Reaching Forward: Reflections on the Truth and Reconciliation Commission of South Africa.* Cape Town: University of Cape Town Press, 2000, pp. 99–106.

Cox, Murray, ed. *Remorse and Reparation.* London: Jessica Kingsley, 1999.

Crocker, David. "Reckoning with Past Wrongs: A Normative Framework." *Ethics & International Affairs* 13 (1999): 43–64.

———. "Truth Commissions, Transitional Justice, and Civil Society." In Robert Rotberg and Dennis Thompson, eds. *Truth v. Justice: The Morality of Truth Commissions.* Princeton: Princeton University Press, 2000, pp. 99–121.

Cronin, Jeremy. "A Luta Dis-Continua? The TRC Final Report and the Nation Building Project." Paper presented at the "TRC: Commissioning the Past" conference, University of Witwatersrand, Johannesburg, June 11–14, 1999.

CSVR. "Attitudes of White South Africans Toward the Truth and Reconciliation Commission and the Apartheid Past." Johannesburg: CSVR, May 1996.

Cunningham, Michael. "Saying Sorry: The Politics of Apology." *The Political Quarterly* 70, no. 3 (1999): 285–293.

Daniel, John. "Editorial: The Truth and Reconciliation Commission." *Agenda* 42 (2000): 1–8.

de Gruchy, John. "Giving Account: Churches in South Africa." *The Christian Century* 114, no. 36 (December 17, 1997): 1180–1182.

———. "Redeeming the Past in South Africa: The Power of Truth, Forgiveness, and Hope in the Pursuit of Justice and Reconciliation." Paper presented at Deutscher Evangelischer Kirchentag, Leipzig, June 1997.

———. "The TRC and the Building of a Moral Culture." In Wilmot James and Linda van de Vijver, eds. *After the TRC: Reflections on Truth and Reconciliation in South Africa.* Cape Town: David Philip, 2000, pp. 167–171.

de Klerk, F. W. *The Last Trek—A New Beginning.* London: Macmillan, 1998.

de Klerk, William A. *The Puritans in Africa: The History of Afrikanerdom.* London: Rex Collings, 1975.

de Kock, Eugene. *A Long Night's Damage: Working for the Apartheid State.* Saxonwold: Contra Press, 1998.

de la Rey, Cheryl, and Ingrid Owens. "Perceptions of Psychosocial Healing and the Truth and Reconciliation Commission in South Africa." *Peace and Conflict: Journal of Peace Psychology* 4, no. 3 (1998): 257–270.

de Lange, Johnny. "The Historical Context, Legal Origins, and Philosophical Foundations of the South African Truth and Reconciliation Commission." In Charles Villa-Vicencio and Wilhelm Verwoerd, eds. *Looking Back, Reaching Forward: Reflections on the Truth and Reconciliation Commission of South Africa.* Cape Town: University of Cape Town Press, 2000, pp. 14–31.

de Ridder, Trudy. "The Trauma of Testifying: Deponents' Difficult Healing Process." *Track Two* 6, nos. 3–4 (December 1997), http://ccrweb.ccr.uct.ac.za/two/6_34/index634.html.

———. "Vicarious Trauma: Supporting the TRC Staff." *Track Two* 6, nos. 3–4 (December 1997), http://ccrweb.ccr.uct.ac.za/two/6_34/index634.html.

de Villiers, Etienne. "The Challenge to the Afrikaans Churches." In H. Russel Botman and Robin Petersen, eds. *To Remember and to Heal: Theological and Psychological Reflections on Truth and Reconciliation.* Cape Town: Human & Rousseau, 1996, pp. 140–153.

des Forges, Alison. *Leave None to Tell the Story: Genocide in Rwanda.* New York: Human Rights Watch, 1999.

Dowdall, Terry. "Psychological Aspects of the Truth and Reconciliation Commission." In H. Russel Botman and Robin Petersen, eds. *To Remember and to Heal: Theological and Psychological Reflections on Truth and Reconciliation.* Cape Town: Human & Rousseau, 1996, pp. 27–36.

DRC, General Synod Commission. English extract from Afrikaner document *The Story of the DRC's Journey with Apartheid.* n.d.

du Boulay, Shirley. *Tutu: Voice of the Voiceless.* London: Hodder & Stoughton, 1988.

du Toit, Andre. "Healing the Healers? The TRC's Hearings on the Health Sector." *Indicator SA* 15, no. 1 (autumn 1998): 8–12.

———. "Justice and/or Truth." *South African Outlook* 125, no. 6 (July 1995): 52–55.

———. "Laying the Past to Rest." *Indicator SA* 11, no. 4 (spring 1994): 63–69.

———. "The Moral Foundations of the South African TRC: Truth as Acknowledgment and Justice as Recognition." In Robert Rotberg and Dennis Thompson, eds. *Truth v. Justice: The Morality of Truth Commissions*. Princeton: Princeton University Press, 2000, pp. 122–140.

———. "No Rest Without the Wicked: Assessing the Truth Commission." *Indicator SA* 14, no. 1 (summer 1997): 7–12.

———. "Perpetrator Findings as Artificial Even-handedness? The TRC's Contested Judgements of Moral and Political Accountability for Gross Human Rights Violations." Paper presented at the "TRC: Commissioning the Past" conference, University of Witwatersrand, Johannesburg, June 11–14, 1999.

du Toit, Cornel. "Dealing with the Past." In H. Russel Botman and Robin Petersen, eds. *To Remember and to Heal: Theological and Psychological Reflections on Truth and Reconciliation*. Cape Town: Human & Rousseau, 1996, pp. 118–128.

Dugard, John. "Is the Truth and Reconciliation Process Compatible with International Law?" *South African Journal of Human Rights* 13 (1997): 258–268.

———. "Reconciliation and Justice: The South African Experience." *Transnational Law and Contemporary Problems* 8, no. 1 (1998): 277–311.

———. "Retrospective Justice: International Law and the South African Model." In James McAdams, ed. *Transitional Justice and the Rule of Law in New Democracies*. Notre Dame: University of Notre Dame Press, 1997, pp. 269–290.

———. "The Third Manfred Lachs Memorial Lecture—Dealing with Crimes of a Past Regime: Is Amnesty Still an Option?" Paper presented at the "TRC: Commissioning the Past" conference, University of Witwatersrand, Johannesburg, June 11–14, 1999.

Dwyer, Susan. "Reconciliation for Realists." *Ethics & International Affairs* 13 (1999): 81–98.

Dyzenhaus, David. "Debating South Africa's Truth and Reconciliation Commission." *University of Toronto Law Journal* 49, no. 3 (1999): 311–314.

———. *Truth, Reconciliation, and the Apartheid Legal Order.* Cape Town: Juta, 1998.

———. "With the Benefit of Hindsight." Paper presented at the "TRC: Commissioning the Past" conference, University of Witwatersrand, Johannesburg, June 11–14, 1999.

Eck, Jan van. "Reconciliation in Africa?" In Wilmot James and Linda van de Vijver, eds. *After the TRC: Reflections on Truth and Reconciliation in South Africa*. Cape Town: David Philip, 2000, pp. 82–87.

Ellis, Stephen. "Truth and Reconciliation Commission of South Africa Report." *Transformation* 42 (2000): 57–107.

Elphick, Richard. Introduction to *Christianity in South Africa: A Political, Social, and Cultural History,* edited by Richard Elphick and Rodney Davenport. Berkeley: University of California Press, 1997, pp. 11–15.

Elshtain, Jean Bethke. "True Confessions." *The New Republic* 217, no. 19 (November 10, 1997): 12–14.

Esterhuyse, Willie. "Truth as a Trigger for Transformation: From Apartheid Injustice to Transformational Justice." In Charles Villa-Vicencio and

Wilhelm Verwoerd, eds. *Looking Back, Reaching Forward: Reflections on the Truth and Reconciliation Commission of South Africa.* Cape Town: University of Cape Town Press, 2000, pp. 144–154.

Everett, William Johnson. "Going Public, Building Covenant: Linking the TRC to Theology and the Church." In James Cochrane, John de Gruchy, and Stephen Martin, eds. *Facing the Truth: South African Faith Communities and the Truth and Reconciliation Commission.* Cape Town: David Philip, 1999, pp. 143–163.

Foster, Don. "Entitlement as Explanation for Perpetrators' Actions." *South African Journal of Psychology* 30, no. 1 (March 2000): 10–13.

———. "The Truth and Reconciliation Commission and Understanding Perpetrators." *South African Journal of Psychology* 30, no. 1 (March 2000): 2–9.

———. "What Makes a Perpetrator? An Attempt to Understand." In Charles Villa-Vicencio and Wilhelm Verwoerd, eds. *Looking Back, Reaching Forward: Reflections on the Truth and Reconciliation Commission of South Africa.* Cape Town: University of Cape Town Press, 2000, pp. 219–229.

Fourie, Ginn. "A Personal Encounter with Perpetrators." In Charles Villa-Vicencio and Wilhelm Verwoerd, eds. *Looking Back, Reaching Forward: Reflections on the Truth and Reconciliation Commission of South Africa.* Cape Town: University of Cape Town Press, 2000, pp. 230–238.

Franco, Jean. "Gender, Death, and Resistance: Facing the Ethical Vacuum." In J. E. Corradi, ed. *Fear at the Edge: State Terrorism and Resistance in Latin America.* Berkeley: University of California Press, 1992, pp. 104–118.

Frankel, Marvin. *Out of the Shadows of the Night: The Struggle for International Human Rights.* New York: Delacorte Press, 1989.

Frost, Brian. *Struggling to Forgive: Nelson Mandela and South Africa's Search for Reconciliation.* London: HarperCollins, 1998.

Garman, Anthea. "Media Creation: How the TRC and the Media Have Impacted on Each Other." *Track Two* 6, nos. 3–4 (December 1997), http://ccrweb.ccr.uct.ac.za/two/6_34/index634.html.

Gerloff, Roswith. "Truth, a New Society, and Reconciliation: The Truth and Reconciliation Commission in South Africa from a German Perspective." *Missionalia* 26, no. 1 (April 1998): 17–53.

Gerwel, Jakes. "National Reconciliation: Holy Grail or Secular Pact?" In Charles Villa-Vicencio and Wilhelm Verwoerd, eds. *Looking Back, Reaching Forward: Reflections on the Truth and Reconciliation Commission of South Africa.* Cape Town: University of Cape Town Press, 2000, pp. 277–286.

Gevisser, Mark. "Truth and Reconciliation: Can South Africa Face Its Past?" *Nation* 260, no. 25 (June 26, 1995): 916–921.

———. "The Witnesses." *New York Times Magazine,* June 22, 1977, pp. 32–38.

Gibson, James L., and Amanda Gouws. "Truth and Reconciliation in South Africa: Attributions for Blame and the Struggle over Apartheid." *American Political Science Review* 93, no. 3 (September 1999): 501–517.

Gilligan, James. "The Agenbite of Inwit—or, The Varieties of Moral Experience." In Murray Cox, ed. *Remorse and Reparation.* London: Jessica Kingsley, 1999, pp. 33–48.

Gobodo-Madikizela, Pumla. "Healing the Racial Divide? Personal Reflections on the Truth and Reconciliation Commission." *South African Journal of Psychology* 27, no. 4 (1997): 271–272.

———. "Remembering and the Politics of Identity." *Psychoanalytic Psychotherapy in South Africa* (summer 1995): 57–72.

Goetz, Anne Marie. "Women in Politics and Gender Equity in Policy: South Africa and Uganda." *Review of African Political Economy* 25, no. 76 (1998): 241–262.

Goldblatt, Beth. "Violence, Gender, and Human Rights: An Examination of South Africa's Truth and Reconciliation Commission." Paper presented to the annual meeting of the Law and Society Association, St. Louis, 1997.

Goldblatt, Beth, and Sheila Meintjes. "Dealing with the Aftermath: Sexual Violence and the Truth and Reconciliation Commission." *Agenda* 36 (1998): 7–17.

———. "Gender and the Truth and Reconciliation Commission." Submission to the Truth and Reconciliation Commission, 1996, www.truth.org.za/submit/gender.htm.

———. "Women: One Chapter in the History of South Africa? A Critique of the Truth and Reconciliation Report." Paper presented at the "TRC: Commissioning the Past" conference, University of Witwatersrand, Johannesburg, June 11–14, 1999.

Goldstone, Richard. *For Humanity: Reflections of a War Crimes Investigator.* New Haven: Yale University Press, 2000.

———. "Justice as a Tool for Peace-Making: Truth Commissions and International Criminal Tribunals." *New York University Journal of International Law & Politics* 28, no. 3 (1996): 485–503.

———. "The Rule of Law." In Wilmot James and Linda van de Vijver, eds. *After the TRC: Reflections on Truth and Reconciliation in South Africa.* Cape Town: David Philip, 2000, pp. 157–162.

Goodman David. *Fault Lines: Journeys into the New South Africa.* Los Angeles: UCLA Press, 1999.

———. "Reconciliation or Chaos?" *Mother Jones* 24, no. 3 (May 1999): 52–60.

———. "Why Killers Should Go Free: Lessons from South Africa." *The Washington Quarterly* 22, no. 2 (spring 1999): 169–181.

Gottsschlich, Jurgen. "The Price of Truth: How Disclosures Affect Germany's East-West Relations." *Track Two* 6, nos. 3–4 (December 1997), http://ccr-web.ccr.uct.ac.za/two/6_34/index634.html.

Govender, Pregs. "Parliamentary Joint Standing Committee on the Improvement of the Quality of Life and Status of Women." In *Second Annual Report* (January 1998–March 1999). Pretoria: Government Printing Office, 1999, pp. 1–65.

Graybill, Lyn. "The Contribution of the Truth and Reconciliation Commission Toward the Promotion of Women's Rights in South Africa." *Women's Studies International Forum* 24, no. 1 (2001): 1–10.

———. "Honoring the Voices of Children at the Truth and Reconciliation Commission." *Iris: A Journal About Women* 39 (fall 1999): 32–35.

———. "Lingering Legacy: Apartheid and the South African Press." *Current History* 99, no. 637 (summer 2000): 227–230.

———. "The Pursuit of Truth and Reconciliation in South Africa." *Africa Today* 44, no. 1 (January–March 1998): 103–134.

———. *Religion and Resistance Politics in South Africa.* Westport, Conn.: Praeger, 1995.

———. "South Africa's Truth and Reconciliation Commission: Ethical and Theological Perspectives." *Ethics & International Affairs* 12 (spring 1998): 43–62.

———. "To Punish or Pardon: A Comparison of the International Criminal Tribunal for Rwanda (ICTR) and the South African Truth and Reconciliation Commission (SATRC)." *Human Rights Review* 2, no. 4 (2001): 3–8.

Graybill, Lyn, and Kenneth Thompson, eds. *Africa's Second Wave of Freedom: Development, Democracy, and Rights.* Lanham, Md.: University Press of America, 1998.

Greenawalt, Kent. "Amnesty's Justice." In Robert Rotberg and Dennis Thompson, eds. *Truth v. Justice: The Morality of Truth Commissions.* Princeton: Princeton University Press, 2000, pp. 189–210.

Gregory, James. *Goodbye Bafana: Nelson Mandela, My Prisoner, My Friend.* London: Headline, 1995.

Grunebaum-Ralph, Heidi. "Saying the Unspeakable: Language and Identity After Auschwitz as a Narrative Model for Articulating Memory in South Africa." *Current Writing* 8, no. 2 (1996): 13–23.

Grunebaum-Ralph, Heidi, and Oren Stier. "The Question (of) Remains: Remembering Shoah, Forgetting Reconciliation." In James Cochrane, John de Gruchy, and Stephen Martin, eds. *Facing the Truth: South African Faith Communities and the Truth and Reconciliation Commission.* Cape Town: David Philip, 1999, pp. 142–152.

Grzyacz, Wendy. "Struggling with Truth in South Africa." *Peace Research* 29, no. 2 (May 1997): 43–59.

Gutmann, Amy, and Dennis Thompson. "The Moral Foundations of Truth Commissions." In Robert Rotberg and Dennis Thompson, eds. *Truth v. Justice: The Morality of Truth Commissions.* Princeton: Princeton University Press, 2000, pp. 22–44.

Hamber, Brandon. "The Burdens of Truth: An Evaluation of the Psychological Support Services and Initiatives Undertaken by the South African Truth and Reconciliation Commission." *American Imago* 1, no. 55 (1998): 9–28.

———. "Do Sleeping Does Lie? The Psychological Implications of the Truth and Reconciliation Commission in South Africa." Paper presented at seminar no. 5 at the Center for the Study of Violence and Reconciliation, Johannesburg, 1995.

———. "How Should We Choose to Remember? Issues to Consider When Establishing Commissions and Structures for Dealing with the Past." Center for the Study of Violence and Reconciliation, Johannesburg, 1998.

———. "Living with the Legacy of Impunity: Lessons for South Africa About Truth, Justice, and Crime in Brazil." Paper presented at the Center for Latin American Studies, University of South Africa, Pretoria, April 24, 1997.

———. "Past Imperfect: Strategies for Dealing with Past Political Violence in Northern Ireland, South Africa, and Countries in Transition." Paper presented at the "TRC: Commissioning the Past" conference, University of Witwatersrand, Johannesburg, June 11–14, 1999.

———. "Repairing the Irreparable: Dealing with Double-Blinds of Making Reparations for Crimes of the Past." Paper presented to the African Studies Association of the UK, London, September 14–16, 1998.

Hamber, Brandon, and Gunnar Theissen. "A State of Denial: White South Africans' Attitudes to the Truth and Reconciliation Commission." *Indicator SA* 15, no. 1 (1998): 8–12.

Harris, Verne. "They Should Have Destroyed More: The Destruction of Public Records by the South African State in the Final Years of Apartheid, 1990–1994." *Transformation* 42 (2000): 29–56.

Hay, Mark. *Ukubuyisana: Reconciliation in South Africa.* Pietermaritzburg: Cluster, 1998.

Hayes, Grahame. "We Suffer Our Memories: Thinking About the Past, Healing, and Reconciliation." *American Imago* 55, no. 1 (1998): 29–50.

Hayner, Priscilla. "Commissioning the Truth: Further Research Questions." *Third World Quarterly* 17, no. 1 (1996): 19–29.

———. "Fifteen Truth Commissions—1974 to 1994: A Comparative Study." *Human Rights Quarterly* 16, no. 4 (1994): 597–656.

———. "International Guidelines for the Creation and Operation of Truth Commissions: A Preliminary Proposal." *Law and Contemporary Problems* 59, no. 4 (autumn 1996): 174–180.

———. "Same Species, Different Animal: How South Africa Compares to Truth Commissions Worldwide." In Charles Villa-Vicencio and Wilhelm Verwoerd, eds. *Looking Back, Reaching Forward: Reflections on the Truth and Reconciliation Commission of South Africa.* Cape Town: University of Cape Town Press, 2000, pp. 32–41.

———. *Unspeakable Truths: Confronting State Terror and Atrocity.* New York: Routledge, 2001.

Heath, Willem. "Fighting Corruption." In Wilmot James and Linda van de Vijver, eds. *After the TRC: Reflections on Truth and Reconciliation in South Africa.* Cape Town: David Philip, 2000, pp. 163–166.

Heller, Scott. "Emerging Field of Forgiveness Studies Explores How We Let Go of Grudges." *Chronicle of Higher Education* 44, no. 45 (July 17, 1998): A18–A20.

Hendricks, Fred. "Amnesty and Justice in Post Apartheid South Africa." Paper presented at the "TRC: Commissioning the Past" conference, University of Witwatersrand, Johannesburg, June 11–14, 1999.

Henry, Yazir. "Where Healing Begins." In Charles Villa-Vicencio and Wilhelm Verwoerd, eds. *Looking Back, Reaching Forward: Reflections on the Truth and Reconciliation Commission of South Africa.* Cape Town: University of Cape Town Press, 2000, pp. 166–173.

Herman, Judith. *Trauma and Recovery.* New York: Basic Books, 1992.

Hollyday, Joyce. "Hearts of Stone." *Sojourners* 27, no. 2 (March–April 1998): 44.

———. "Truth and Reconciliation in South Africa." Unpublished M.Div. thesis, Candler School of Theology, Emory University, Atlanta, 1998.

Holmes, Rachel. "Selling Sex for a Living." *Agenda* 23 (1994): 36–48.

Hope, Marjorie, and James Young. *The South African Churches in a Revolutionary Situation.* Maryknoll, N.Y.: Orbis, 1981.

Horne, Andrew. "Reflections on Remorse in Forensic Psychotherapy." In Murray Cox, ed. *Remorse and Reparation.* London: Jessica Kingsley, 1999, pp. 21–32.

Hulley, Leonard, Louise Kretzschmar, and Luke Lungile Pato, eds. *Archbishop Tutu: Prophetic Witness in South Africa.* Cape Town: Human & Rousseau, 1996.

Human Rights Watch. "Threats to a New Democracy: Continuing Violence in KwaZulu-Natal." *Human Rights Watch/Africa* 7, no. 3 (May 1995), www.hrw.org/reports/1995/safrica.htm.

———. *Violence Against Women in South Africa: State Response to Domestic Violence and Rape.* New York: Human Rights Watch, 1995.

Humphrey, Michael. "From Torture to Trauma: Commissioning Truth for National Reconciliation." *Social Identities* 6, no. 1 (2000): 7–27.

Huyse, Luc. "Justice After Transition: On the Choices Successor Elites Make in Dealing with the Past." *Law & Social Inquiry* 20, no. 1 (1995): 51–78.

Ignatieff, Michael. "Articles of Faith." *Index on Censorship* 25, no. 5 (1996): 111–113.

———. "Digging Up the Dead." *The New Yorker* 73, no. 34 (November 10, 1997): 84–93.

———. *The Warrior's Honor: Ethnic War and the Modern Conscience.* London: Chatto & Windus, 1998.

Ingerfeld, Simone. "The Truth and Reconciliation Commission Campaign: The Religious Response in the Western Cape." *South African Outlook* 125, no. 6 (July 1995): 59–60.

Jacoby, Susan. *Wild Justice: The Evolution of Revenge.* New York: Harper & Row, 1982.

James, Wilmot, and Linda van de Vijver, eds. *After the TRC: Reflections on Truth and Reconciliation in South Africa.* Cape Town: David Philip, 2000.

Jaspers, Karl. *The Question of German Guilt.* New York: Dial Press, 1947.

Jeffery, Anthea. *The Truth About the Truth Commission.* Johannesburg: South African Institute of Race Relations, 1999.

Jones, L. Gregory. *Embodying Forgiveness: A Theological Analysis.* Grand Rapids, Mich.: William B. Eerdmans, 1995.

Kairos Document: The Challenge to the Churches. Grand Rapids, Mich.: William B. Eerdmans, 1986.

Kiss, Elizabeth. "Moral Ambition Within and Beyond Political Constraints: Reflections on Restorative Justice." In Robert Rotberg and Dennis Thompson, eds. *Truth v. Justice: The Morality of Truth Commissions.* Princeton: Princeton University Press, 2000, pp. 68–98.

Kistner, Wolfram. "The Biblical Understanding of Reconciliation." In H. Russel Botman and Robin Petersen, eds. *To Remember and to Heal: Theological and Psychological Reflections on Truth and Reconciliation.* Cape Town: Human & Rousseau, 1996, pp. 79–95.

———. "Reconciliation in Dispute." Paper presented at the "TRC: Commissioning the Past" conference, University of Witwatersrand, Johannesburg, June 11–14, 1999.

Klaaren, Jonathan. "The Truth and Reconciliation Commission, the South African Judiciary, and Constitutionalism." *African Studies* 57, no. 2 (1998): 197–208.

Krabill, Ron. "Review of *Long Night's Journey Into Day:* South Africa's Search for Truth and Reconciliation," *Safundi* 3, no. 2 (April 15, 2001), www.safundi.com/papers.asp?lop=krabill.

Kritz, Neil. "Coming to Terms with Atrocities: A Review of Accountability Mechanisms for Mass Violations of Human Rights." *Law and Contemporary Problems* 59, no. 4 (autumn 1996): 127–152.

———. *Transitional Justice: How Emerging Democracies Reckon with Former Regimes.* 3 vols. Washington, D.C.: United States Institute of Peace, 1995.

Krog, Antjie. *Country of My Skull.* Johannesburg: Random House, 1998.

———. "The Truth and Reconciliation Commission—A National Ritual?" *Missionalia* 16, no. 1 (April 1998): 5–16.

Kuperus, Tracy. *State, Civil Society, and Apartheid in South Africa: An Examination of Dutch Reformed Church–State Relations.* New York: St. Martin's Press, 1999.

Lalu, Premesh, and Brent Harris. "Journeys from the Horizons of History: Text, Trial, and Tales in the Construction of Narratives of Pain." *Current Writing* 8, no. 2 (1996): 24–38.

Landsman, Stephan. "Alternative Responses to Serious Human Rights Abuses: Of Prosecution and Truth Commissions." *Law and Contemporary Problems* 59, no. 4 (1996): 81–92.

Lansing, Paul, and Julie King. "South Africa's Truth and Reconciliation Commission: The Conflict Between Individual Justice and National Healing in the Post-Apartheid Age." *Arizona Journal of International and Comparative Law* 15, no. 3 (fall 1998): 753–789.

Lapsley, Michael. "Bearing the Pain in Our Bodies." In H. Russel Botman and Robin Petersen, eds. *To Remember and to Heal: Theological and Psychological Reflections on Truth and Reconciliation.* Cape Town: Human & Rousseau, 1996, pp. 17–23.

———. "Confronting the Past and Creating the Future: The Redemptive Value of Truth Telling." *Social Research* 65, no. 4 (winter 1998): 741–758.

———. "Tears, Fears, and Hope: Healing the Memories in South Africa." *Southern Africa* 7, no. 1 (January–February 1997).

Lever, Jeffrey, and Wilmot James. "The Second Republic." In Wilmot James and Linda van de Vijver, eds. *After the TRC: Reflections on Truth and Reconciliation in South Africa.* Cape Town: David Philip, 2000, pp. 191–200.

Levinson, Sanford. "Trials, Commissions, and Investigating Committees: The Elusive Search for Norms of Due Process." In Robert Rotberg and Dennis Thompson, eds. *Truth v. Justice: The Morality of Truth Commissions.* Princeton: Princeton University Press, 2000, pp. 211–234.

Liebenberg, Ian. "The Truth and Reconciliation Commission in South Africa: Context, Future, and Some Imponderables." *South Africa Public Law* 11, no. 1 (1996): 123–159.

Liebenberg, Ian, and Pieter Duvenage. "Can the Deep Political Divisions of South African Society Be Healed? A Philosophical and Political Perspective." *Politeia* 15, no. 1 (1996): 49–64.

Liebenberg, Ian, and Abebe Zegeye. "Pathway to Democracy? The Case of the South African Truth and Reconciliation Process." *Social Identities* 4, no. 3 (November 3, 1998): 541–557.

Little, David. "A Different Kind of Justice: Dealing with Human Rights Violations in Transitional Societies." *Ethics & International Affairs* 13 (1999): 65–80.

Llewellyn, Jennifer, and Robert Howse. "Institutions for Restorative Justice: The South African Truth and Reconciliation Commission." *University of Toronto Law Journal* 49, no. 3 (1999): 355–388.

Lodge, Tom. *South African Politics Since 1994.* Cape Town: David Philip, 1999.

Long Night's Journey Into Day. Iris Films, 2001.

Longman, Timothy. "Empowering the Weak and Protecting the Powerful: The Contradictory Nature of Christian Churches in Central Africa." *African Studies Review* 41, no. 1 (April 1998): 49–72.

Lyons, Beth. "Between Nuremburg and Amnesia: The Truth and Reconciliation Commission in South Africa." *Monthly Review* 49, no. 4 (September 1997): 5–22.

Lyster, Richard. "Amnesty: The Burden of Victims." In Charles Villa-Vicencio and Wilhelm Verwoerd, eds. *Looking Back, Reaching Forward: Reflections on the Truth and Reconciliation Commission of South Africa.* Cape Town: University of Cape Town Press, 2000, pp. 184–192.

Madlala-Routledge, Nozizwe. "What Price for Freedom? Testimony and the Natal Organization of Women." *Agenda* 34 (1997): 62–69.

Mahamba, Muendanyi. "Ubuntu and Democracy." *Challenge* no. 16 (June/July 1993).

Maier, Charles. "Doing History, Doing Justice: The Narrative of the Historian and of the Truth Commission." In Robert Rotberg and Dennis Thompson, eds. *Truth v. Justice: The Morality of Truth Commissions.* Princeton: Princeton University Press, 2000, pp. 261–278.

Maimela, Simon. "Political Priest or Man of Peace?" In Buti Tlhagale and Itumeleng Mosala, eds. *Hammering Swords Into Ploughshares: Essays in Honour of Archbishop Mpilo Desmond Tutu.* Johannesburg: Skotaville, 1986, pp. 41–59.

Majiza, Charity. "Hearing the Truth." In James Cochrane, John de Gruchy, and Stephen Martin, eds. *Facing the Truth: South African Faith Communities and the Truth and Reconciliation Commission.* Cape Town: David Philip, 1999, pp. 167–169.

Maluleke, Tinyiko Sam. "Dealing Lightly with the Wounds of My People? The TRC Process in Theological Perspective." *Missionalia* 25, no. 3 (November 1997): 324–343.

———. "Truth, National Unity, and Reconciliation in South Africa: Aspects of the Emerging Theological Agenda." *Missionalia* 25, no. 1 (April 1997): 59–86.

———. "The Truth and Reconciliation Discourse: A Black Theological Evaluation." In James Cochrane, John de Gruchy, and Stephen Martin, eds. *Facing the Truth: South African Faith Communities and the Truth and Reconciliation Commission.* Cape Town: David Philip, 1999, pp. 101–113.

Mamdani, Mahmood. "A Diminished Truth." *Siyaya* 3 (spring 1998): 38–40.

———. "A Diminished Truth." In Wilmot James and Linda van de Vijver, eds. *After the TRC: Reflections on Truth and Reconciliation in South Africa.* Cape Town: David Philip, 2000, pp. 58–61.

———. "Reconciliation Without Justice." *Southern African Review of Books* 46 (November–December 1996): 3–5.

Mandela, Nelson. Foreword to *Reconciliation Through Truth: A Reckoning of Apartheid's Criminal Governance,* by Kader Asmal, Louise Asmal, and Ronald Suresh Roberts. Cape Town: David Philip, 1996, pp. vii–viii.

———. *Long Walk to Freedom: The Autobiography of Nelson Mandela.* Boston: Little, Brown, 1994.

Markel, Dan. "The Justice of Amnesty? Towards a Theory of Retributivism in Recovering States." *University of Toronto Law Journal* 49, no. 3 (1999): 389–445.

Marx, Lesley. "Slouching Towards Bethlehem: Ubu and the Truth Commission." *African Studies* 57, no. 2 (1998): 209–220.

Masina, Nomonde. "Xhosa Practices of Ubuntu for South Africa." In I. William Zartman, ed. *Traditional Cures for Modern Conflicts.* Boulder: Lynne Rienner, 2000, pp. 169–181.

Mbiti, John S. *African Religions and Philosophy.* London: Heinemann, 1969.

McAdams, James, ed. *Transitional Justice and the Rule of Law in New Democracies.* Notre Dame: University of Notre Dame Press, 1997.

McCullum, Hugh. *The Angels Have Left Us: The Rwanda Tragedy and the Churches.* Geneva: World Council of Churches, 1995.

McKay, Annie. "Psychological Trauma and Political Violence." *Black Sash* 37, no. 2 (1995): 22–24.

Meiring, Piet. "The Baruti Versus the Lawyers: The Role of Religion in the TRC Process." In Charles Villa-Vicencio and Wilhelm Verwoerd, eds. *Looking Back, Reaching Forward: Reflections on the Truth and Reconciliation Commission of South Africa.* Cape Town: University of Cape Town Press, 2000, pp. 123–131.

———. *Chronicle of the Truth Commission: A Journey Through the Past and Present—Into the Future of South Africa.* Cape Town: Carpe Diem Books, 1999.

Meredith, Martin. *Coming to Terms: South Africa's Search for Truth.* New York: PublicAffairs, 1999.

———. *Nelson Mandela: A Biography.* New York: St. Martin's Press, 1998.

Mertus, Julie. "The War Crimes Tribunal: Triumph of the 'International Community,' Pain of the Survivors. *Mind and Human Interaction* 8, no. 1 (winter/spring 1997): 47–57.

Mgxashe, Mxolisi. "Reconciliation: A Call to Action." In Charles Villa-Vicencio and Wilhelm Verwoerd, eds. *Looking Back, Reaching Forward: Reflections on the Truth and Reconciliation Commission of South Africa.* Cape Town: University of Cape Town Press, 2000, pp. 210–218.

Minow, Martha. *Between Vengeance and Forgiveness: Facing History After Genocide and Mass Violence.* Boston: Beacon Press, 1998.

———. "Between Vengeance and Forgiveness." Presentation at the John F. Kennedy School of Government, Cambridge, February 4, 1999.

———. "The Hope for Healing: What Can Truth Commissions Do?" In Robert Rotberg and Dennis Thompson, eds. *Truth v. Justice: The Morality of Truth Commissions.* Princeton: Princeton University Press, 2000, pp. 235–260.

Mokgoro, Yvonne. "Ubuntu and the Law in Africa." Konrad-Adenaur-Stiftung, occasional paper, Johannesburg, May 1998.

Moodie, T. Dunbar. *The Rise of Afrikanerdom: Power, Apartheid, and the Afrikaner Civil Religion.* Berkeley: University of California Press, 1975.

Mooney, Katie, Noor Nieftagodien, and Nicole Ulrich. "The TRC: Commissioning the Past, Conference Report." *African Studies* 58, no. 2 (1999): 209–218.

Moosa, Ebrahim. "Truth and Reconciliation as Performance: Spectres of Eucharistic Redemption." In Charles Villa-Vicencio and Wilhelm Verwoerd, eds. *Looking Back, Reaching Forward: Reflections on the Truth and Reconciliation Commission of South Africa.* Cape Town: University of Cape Town Press, 2000, pp. 112–122.

Morris, David. "About Suffering: Voice, Genre, and Moral Community." *Daedalus* 125, no. 1 (winter 1996): 25–45.

Morris, Madeline. "The Trials of Concurrent Jurisdiction: The Case of Rwanda." *Duke Journal of Comparative & International Law* 7, no. 2 (spring 1997): 349–374.

Motala, Ziyad. "The Promotion of National Unity and Reconciliation Act, the Constitution, and International Law." *Comparative International Law Journal of Southern Africa* 28, no. 3 (November 1995): 338–362.

Moyers, Bill. "Facing the Truth with Bill Moyers." Public Affairs Television, 1999. Premier broadcast March 30, 1999.

Muller, Ampie. "Facing Our Shadow Side: Afrikaners Must Own Their Own Complicity." *Track Two* 6, nos. 3–4 (December 1997), http://ccrweb.ccr.uct.ac.za/two/6_34/index634.html.

Muller-Fahrenholz, Geiko. *The Art of Forgiveness: Theological Reflections on Healing and Reconciliation.* Geneva: World Council of Churches, 1997.

Murphy, Jeffrie G., and Jean Hampton. *Forgiveness and Mercy.* Cambridge: Cambridge University Press, 1988.

Nathan, Laurie. "The Tensions of Transition: Why Accommodation and Compromise Are Inevitable." *Track Two* 6, nos. 3–4 (December 1997), http://ccrweb.ccr.uct.ac.za/two/6_34/index634.html.

Nattrass, Nicoli. "The Truth and Reconciliation Commission on Business and Apartheid: A Critical Evaluation." *African Affairs* 98, no. 392 (1999): 373–391.

Naudé, Beyers, and Will Winterfeld. "South Africa: The Spirit of Reconciliation." *Sojourners* 23, no. 6 (July 1994): 9–10.

Ndebele, Njabulo. "Of Lions and Rabbits: Thoughts on Democracy and Reconciliation." In Wilmot James and Linda van de Vijver, eds. *After the TRC: Reflections on Truth and Reconciliation in South Africa.* Cape Town: David Philip, 2000, pp. 143–156.

Ndungane, Njongonkulu Winston. "An Opportunity for Peace." In Charles Villa-Vicencio and Wilhelm Verwoerd, eds. *Looking Back, Reaching Forward: Reflections on the Truth and Reconciliation Commission of South Africa.* Cape Town: University of Cape Town Press, 2000, pp. 258–264.

———. "UTutu: Ngumntu Iowo." In Leonard Hulley, Louise Kretzschmar, and Luke Lungile Pato, eds. *Archbishop Tutu: Prophetic Witness in South Africa.* Cape Town: Human & Rousseau, 1996, pp. 71–79.

Neier, Aryeh. *War Crimes: Brutality, Genocide, Terror, and the Struggle for Justice.* New York: Times Books, 1998.

Newham, Gareth. "Truth and Reconciliation: Realising the Ideals." *Indicator SA* 12, no. 4 (spring 1995): 7–12.

Ngubane, Jordan K. *Ushaba: A Zulu Umlando.* Washington, D.C.: Three Continents Press, 1975.

Niebuhr, Reinhold. *The Nature and Destiny of Man: Human Destiny.* New York: Charles Scribner's Sons, 1966.

Niehaus, Carl. "Reconciliation in South Africa: Is Religion Relevant?" In James Cochrane, John de Gruchy, and Stephen Martin, eds. *Facing the Truth: South African Faith Communities and the Truth and Reconciliation Commission.* Cape Town: David Philip, 1999, pp. 81–90.

Norval, Aletta. "Truth and Reconciliation: The Birth of the Present and the Reworking of History." *Journal of Southern African Studies* 25, no. 3 (September 1999): 499–519.

Ntsebeza, Dumisa. "A Lot More to Live For." In Wilmot James and Linda van de Vijver, eds. *After the TRC: Reflections on Truth and Reconciliation in South Africa.* Cape Town: David Philip, 2000, pp. 101–114.

———. "The Struggle for Human Rights: From the U.N. Declaration of Human Rights to the Present." In Charles Villa-Vicencio and Wilhelm Verwoerd, eds. *Looking Back, Reaching Forward: Reflections on the Truth and Reconciliation Commission of South Africa.* Cape Town: University of Cape Town Press, 2000, pp. 2–13.

———. "The Uses of Truth Commissions: Lessons for the World." In Robert Rotberg and Dennis Thompson, eds. *Truth v. Justice: The Morality of Truth Commissions.* Princeton: Princeton University Press, 2000, pp. 158–169.

Nuttall, Sarah, and Carli Coetzee, eds. *Negotiating the Past: The Making of Memory in South Africa.* Oxford: Oxford University Press, 1998.

Nyatsumba, Kaiser. "Neither Dull nor Tiresome." In Wilmot James and Linda van de Vijver, eds. *After the TRC: Reflections on Truth and Reconciliation in South Africa.* Cape Town: David Philip, 2000, pp. 88–93.

Odendaal, Andre. "Dealing with the Past/Making Deals with the Past: Public History in South Africa in the 1990s." Paper presented at the "Future of the Past: The Production of History in a Changed South Africa" conference organized by the Mayibuye Center Institute for Historical Research and History Department, University of the Western Cape, Bellville, July 10–12, 1996.

Odendaal, Andries. "For All Its Flaws: The TRC as a Peacebuilding Tool." *Track Two* 6, nos. 3–4 (December 1997), http://ccrweb.ccr.uct.ac.za/two/6_34/index634.html.

Olckers, Ilze. "Gender-Neutral Truth: A Reality Shamefully Distorted." *Agenda* 31 (1996): 61–67.

Olivier, Gerrit. "The 'Fierce Belonging' of Antjie Krog: Review of *Country of My Skull.*" *African Studies* 57, no. 2 (1998): 221–228.

Omar, Dullah. "National Unity and Reconciliation in South Africa: Can It Succeed?" *Strategic Review for Southern Africa* 18, no. 1 (May 1996): 35–46.

Orentlicher, Diane. "Settling Accounts: The Duty to Prosecute Human Rights Violations of a Prior Regime." *Yale Law Review* 100, no. 8 (June 1991): 2537–2615.

Orr, Wendy. *From Biko to Basson.* Saxonwold: Contra Press, 2000.

———. "Reparation Delayed Is Healing Retarded." In Charles Villa-Vicencio and Wilhelm Verwoerd, eds. *Looking Back, Reaching Forward: Reflections on the Truth and Reconciliation Commission of South Africa.* Cape Town: University of Cape Town Press, 2000, pp. 239–249.

Osiel, Mark. *Mass Atrocity, Collective Memory, and the Law.* New Brunswick, N.J.: Transaction, 1997.

Ottaway, David. *Chained Together.* New York: Times Books, 1993.

Pandor, Grace Naledi. "Educating the Nation." In Wilmot James and Linda van de Vijver, eds. *After the TRC: Reflections on Truth and Reconciliation in South Africa.* Cape Town: David Philip, 2000, pp. 185–190.

Pankhurst, Donna. "Issues of Justice and Reconciliation in Complex Political Emergencies: Conceptualising Reconciliation, Justice, and Peace." *Third World Quarterly* 20, no. 1 (1999): 239–269.

Parker, Peter. "The Politics of Indemnities, Truth Telling, and Reconciliation in South Africa: Ending Apartheid Without Forgetting." *Human Rights Law Journal* 17, nos. 1–2 (April 30, 1996): 1–13.

Pauw, Jacques. *Into the Heart of Darkness: Confessions of Apartheid's Assassins.* Johannesburg: Jonathan Ball, 1997.

Penwill, Advocate Richard. "Not a Legal Concept." *Track Two* 6, nos. 3–4 (December 1997), http://ccrweb.ccr.uct.ac.za/two/6_34/index634.html.

Petersen, Robin. "The AICs and the TRC: Resistance Redefined." In James Cochrane, John de Gruchy, and Stephen Martin, eds. *Facing the Truth: South African Faith Communities and the Truth and Reconciliation Commission.* Cape Town: David Philip, 1999, pp. 114–125.

———. "The Politics of Grace and the Truth and Reconciliation Commission." In H. Russel Botman and Robin M. Petersen, eds. *To Remember and to Heal: Theological and Psychological Reflections on Truth and Reconciliation.* Cape Town: Human & Rousseau, 1996, pp. 57–64.

Pityana, Barney. "Reconciliation After the TRC." Address to the Twenty-ninth Provincial Synod of the Church of the Province of Southern Africa, Durban, July 16, 1999.

Posel, Deborah. "The TRC Report: What Kind of History? What Kind of Truth?" Paper presented at the "TRC: Commissioning the Past" conference, University of Witwatersrand, Johannesburg, June 11–14, 1999.

Promotion of National Unity and Reconciliation Act, no. 34. Cape Town: Republic of South Africa government gazette, July 1995.

Ramphele, Mamphela. "The Dynamics of Gender Within Black Consciousness Organizations: A Personal View." In Barney Pityana, Mamphela Ramphele, Malusi Mpumlwana, and Lindy Wilson, eds. *Bounds of Possibility: The Legacy of Steve Biko and the Black Consciousness Movement.* Cape Town: David Philip, 1991, pp. 214–227.

———. "Law, Corruption, and Morality." In Wilmot James and Linda van de Vijver, eds. *After the TRC: Reflections on Truth and Reconciliation in South Africa.* Cape Town: David Philip, 2000, pp. 172–174.

———. "Political Widowhood in South Africa." *Daedalus* 125, no. 1 (1996): 99–117.

Rassool, Ciraj, Leslie Witz, and Gary Minkley. "Burying and Memorialising the Body of Truth: The TRC and National Heritage." In Wilmot James and Linda van de Vijver, eds. *After the TRC: Reflections on Truth and Reconciliation in South Africa.* Cape Town: David Philip, 2000, pp. 115–127.

Ratner, Steven, and Jason Abrams. *Accountability for Human Rights Atrocities in International Law.* Oxford: Clarendon, 1997.

Rickard, Carmel. "The Faith Community and the TRC." *Indicator SA* 16, no. 1 (autumn 1999): 42–44.

———. "Fierce Emotions As S. Africa Seeks Peace." *National Catholic Reporter* 33, no. 10 (January 10, 1997): 12–14.

Ricouer, Paul. *The Memory of Suffering: Figuring the Sacred.* Minneapolis: Fortress Press, 1995.

RICSA. "Faith Communities and Apartheid." In James Cochrane, John de Gruchy, and Stephen Martin, eds. *Facing the Truth: South African Faith Communities and the Truth and Reconciliation Commission.* Cape Town: David Philip, 1999, pp. 15–77.

Roht-Arriaza, Naomi. "Combating Impunity: Some Thoughts on the Way Forward." *Law and Contemporary Problems* 59, no. 4 (1996): 93–102.

———, ed. *Impunity and Human Rights in International Law and Practice.* Oxford: Oxford University Press, 1995.

Roht-Arriaza, Naomi, and Lauren Gibson. "The Developing Jurisprudence on Amnesty." *Human Rights Quarterly* 20, no. 4 (1998): 843–855.

Rosenberg, Tina. "Confronting the Painful Past." In Martin Meredith. *Coming to Terms: South Africa's Search for Truth.* New York: PublicAffairs, 1999, pp. 325–370.

———. Foreword to *Coming to Terms: South Africa's Search for Truth,* by Martin Meredith. New York: PublicAffairs, 1999, pp. vii–xii.

———. *The Haunted Land: Facing Europe's Ghosts After Communism.* New York: Vintage, 1995.

———. "Recovering from Apartheid." *The New Yorker* 72 (November 18, 1996): 86–95.

Ross, Fiona. "Blood Feuds and Childbirth: The TRC as Ritual." *Track Two* 6, nos. 3–4 (December 1997), http://ccrweb.ccr.uct.ac.za/two/6_34/index634.html.

———. "Existing in Secret Places: Women's Testimony in the First Five Weeks of Public Hearings of the Truth and Reconciliation Commission." Paper presented at the "Fault Lines" conference, Cape Town, July 4–5, 1996.

Rotberg, Robert. "Truth Commissions and the Provision of Truth, Justice, and Reconciliation." In Robert Rotberg and Dennis Thompson, eds. *Truth v. Justice: The Morality of Truth Commissions.* Princeton: Princeton University Press, 2000, pp. 3–21.

Rotberg, Robert, and Dennis Thompson, eds. *Truth v. Justice: The Morality of Truth Commissions.* Princeton: Princeton University Press, 2000.

Russell, Diana. *Lives of Courage.* New York: Basic Books, 1989.

Rwelamira, Medard, and Gerhard Werle. *Confronting Past Injustices: Approaches to Amnesty, Punishment, Reparation, and Restitution in South Africa and Germany.* Durban: Butterworths, 1996.

Sachs, Albie. "His Name Was Henry." In Wilmot James and Linda van de Vijver, eds. *After the TRC: Reflections on Truth and Reconciliation in South Africa.* Cape Town: David Philip, 2000, pp. 94–100.

———. "Judges and Gender: The Constitutional Rights of Women in Post-Apartheid South Africa." *Agenda* 7 (1990): 1–11.

———. *The Soft Vengeance of a Freedom Fighter.* Berkeley: University of California Press, 2000.

Sanders, Mark. "Ambiguities of Mourning: Law, Custom, Literature, and Women Before South Africa's Truth and Reconciliation Commission." *Law/Text/Culture* 4, no. 2 (1988): 105–151.

———. "Truth, Telling, Questioning: The Truth and Reconciliation Commission, Antjie Krog's *Country of My Skull,* and Literature After Apartheid." *Transformation* 42 (2000): 73–91.

Sarkin, Jeremy. "The Development of a Human Rights Culture in South Africa." *Human Rights Quarterly* 20, no. 3 (1998): 628–665.

———. "The Necessity and Challenges of Establishing a Truth and Reconciliation Commission in Rwanda." *Human Rights Quarterly* 21, no. 3 (August 1999): 767–823.

———. "The Trials and Tribulations of South Africa's Truth and Reconciliation Commission." *South African Journal on Human Rights* 12 (1996): 617–640.

Scarry, Elaine. *The Body in Pain.* Oxford: Oxford University Press, 1985.

Scharf, Michael. "The Letter of the Law: The Scope of the International Obligation to Prosecute Human Rights Crimes." *Law and Contemporary Problems* 59, no. 4 (1996): 41–62.

Scheper-Hughes, Nancy. "Un-doing: Social Suffering and the Politics of Remorse." In Murray Cox, ed. *Remorse and Reparation.* London: Jessica Kingsley, 1997, pp. 145–170.

———. "Who's the Killer? Popular Justice and Human Rights in a South African Squatter Camp." *Social Justice* 22, no. 3 (fall 1995): 143–164.

Schwan, Gesine. "The 'Healing' Value of Truth-Telling: Chances and Social Conditions in a Secularized World." *Social Research* 65, no. 4 (winter 1998): 725–740.

Scott, Collen. "Combating Myth and Building Reality." In Charles Villa-Vicencio and Wilhelm Verwoerd, eds. *Looking Back, Reaching Forward: Reflections on the Truth and Reconciliation Commission of South Africa.* Cape Town: University of Cape Town Press, 2000, pp. 107–112.

"A Service of Dedication and Blessing of Commissioners of the Truth and Reconciliation Commission." St. George's Cathedral, Cape Town, February 13, 1996. In H. Russel Botman and Robin Petersen, eds. *To Remember and to Heal: Theological and Psychological Reflections on Truth and Reconciliation.* Cape Town: Human & Rousseau, 1996, pp. 165–170.

Shea, Dorothy. "Are Truth Commissions Just a Fad? Indicators and Implications from the South African TRC." Paper presented at the "TRC: Commissioning the Past" conference, University of Witwatersrand, Johannesburg, June 11–14, 1999.

———. *The South African Truth Commission: The Politics of Reconciliation.* Washington, D.C.: United States Institute of Peace, 2000.

Shreiter, Robert. *Reconciliation: Mission and Ministry in a Changing Social Order.* Maryknoll, N.Y.: Orbis, 1992.

Shriver, Donald. "Bridging the Abyss of Revenge." *The Christian Century* 116, no. 33 (December 1, 1999): 1169–1173.

———. *An Ethic for Enemies: Forgiveness in Politics.* Oxford: Oxford University Press, 1995.

Siebert, Hannes. "Healing the Memory: Cutting the Cord Between Victim and Perpetrator." *Track Two* 6, nos. 3–4 (December 1997), http://ccrweb.ccr.uct.ac.za/two/6_34/index634.html.

Siffrin, Geoff, Franz Auerbach, and Steven Friedman. "The Truth Commission: Jewish Perspectives on Justice and Forgiveness in South Africa." *Jewish Affairs* 51, no. 3 (spring 1996): 30–39.

Siffrin, Geoff, Steven Friedman, and Daniel Beller. "Can Reconciliation Take Root in Post-Apartheid South African Society? A Jewish View on the Process." *Jewish Affairs* 52, no. 1 (autumn 1997): 63–68.

Simpson, Graeme. "A Brief Evaluation of South Africa's Truth and Reconciliation Commission: Some Lessons for Societies in Transition." Paper presented at the "TRC: Commissioning the Past" conference, University of Witwatersrand, Johannesburg, June 11–14, 1999.

———. "Tell No Lies, Claim No Easy Victories: A Brief Evaluation of South Africa's Truth and Reconciliation Commission." Paper presented at the "Dealing with Apartheid and the Holocaust: A Comparative Perspective" conference, Yale Law School, New Haven, March 1998.

Skaar, Elin. "Truth Commissions, Trials—Or Nothing? Policy Options in Democratic Transitions." *Third World Quarterly* 20, no. 6 (1999): 1109–1128.

Slabbert, Frederik Van Zyl. "Truth Without Reconciliation, Reconciliation Without Truth." In Wilmot James and Linda van de Vijver, eds. *After the TRC: Reflections on Truth and Reconciliation in South Africa.* Cape Town: David Philip, 2000, pp. 62–72.

Slye, Ronald C. "Amnesty, Truth, and Reconciliation: Reflections on the South African Amnesty Process." In Robert Rotberg and Dennis Thompson, eds. *Truth v. Justice: The Morality of Truth Commissions.* Princeton: Princeton University Press, 2000, pp. 170–188.

———. "Apartheid as a Crime Against Humanity: A Submission to the South African Truth and Reconciliation Commission." *Michigan Journal of International Law* 20, no. 2 (1999): 267–300.

———. "Justice and Amnesty." In Charles Villa-Vicencio and Wilhelm Verwoerd, eds. *Looking Back, Reaching Forward: Reflections on the Truth and Reconciliation Commission of South Africa.* Cape Town: University of Cape Town Press, 2000, pp. 174–183.

Smit, Dirkie. "Confession-Guilt-Truth-and-Forgiveness in the Christian Tradition." In H. Russel Botman and Robin M. Petersen, eds. *To Remember and to Heal: Theological and Psychological Reflections on Truth and Reconciliation.* Cape Town: Human & Rousseau, 1996, pp. 96–117.

———. "The Truth and Reconciliation Commission—Tentative Religious and Theological Perspectives." *Journal of Theology for Southern Africa* 90 (March 1995): 3–16.

Smith, Nico. "An Open Letter to All Pastors in South Africa." n.d.

Sooka, Yasmin. "Gewalt gegen Frauen: Vergessener Teil der Wahrheit." *Der Überblick* 4 (1998): 88–91.

"South Africa: Threats to a New Democracy." *Human Rights Watch/Africa* 7, no. 3 (May 1995).

Soyinka, Wole. *The Burden of Memory: The Muse of Forgiveness.* Oxford: Oxford University Press, 1999.

Sparks, Allister. *The Mind of South Africa.* New York: Ballantine Books, 1990.

Spies, Craig. "A Safe Space: How Local Leaders Can Make Room for Reconciliation." *Track Two* 6, nos. 3–4 (December 1997), http://ccrweb.ccr.uct.ac.za/two/6_34/index634.html.

Stack, Louise. "The State Security Council, the Courts, and the TRC." *Indicator SA* 15, no. 1 (autumn 1998): 19–22.

Stanley, Elizabeth. "Evaluating the Truth and Reconciliation Commission." *Journal of Modern African Studies* 39, no. 3 (September 2001): 525–546.

Statman, James. "Performing the Truth: The Social-Psychological Context of TRC Narratives." *South African Journal of Psychology* 30, no. 1 (March 2000): 23–33.

Staub, Erv. "The Psychology of Perpetrators and Bystanders." *Political Psychology* 6, no. 1 (1985): 61–85.

Stein, Dan J. "Psychiatric Aspects of the Truth and Reconciliation Commission in South Africa." *British Journal of Psychiatry* 173 (December 1998): 455–457.

Steiner, Henry J., ed. *Truth Commissions: A Comparative Assessment.* Cambridge: Harvard Law School Human Rights Program, 1997.

Steyn, Melissa. "A New Agenda: Restructuring Feminism in South Africa." *Women's Studies International Forum* 21, no. 1 (1998): 41–52.

Storey, Peter. "A Different Kind of Justice: Truth and Reconciliation in South Africa." *Christian Century* 114, no. 25 (September 10–17, 1997): 788–793.

Stremlau, John. *A House No Longer Divided: Progress and Prospects for Democratic Peace in South Africa.* New York: Carnegie Corporation of New York, 1997.

Tavuchis, Nicholas. *Mea Culpa: A Sociology of Apology and Reconciliation.* Stanford: Stanford University Press, 1991.

Teitel, Ruti G. *Transitional Justice.* Oxford: Oxford University Press, 2000.

Templin, J. Alton. *Ideology on a Frontier: The Theological Foundation of Afrikaner Nationalism, 1652–1910.* Westport, Conn.: Greenwood Press, 1984.

Terbourg-Penn, Rosalyn. "Black Women Freedom Fighters in South Africa and in the U.S.: A Comparative Analysis." *Dialectical Authority* 15, nos. 2–3 (1990): 151–157.

Terreblanche, Sampie. "Dealing with Systematic Economic Injustice." In Charles Villa-Vicencio and Wilhelm Verwoerd, eds. *Looking Back, Reaching Forward: Reflections on the Truth and Reconciliation Commission of South Africa.* Cape Town: University of Cape Town Press, 2000, pp. 265–276.

Theissen, Gunnar. "Between Acknowledgement and Ignorance: How White South Africans Have Dealt with the Apartheid Past." Occasional paper, Center for the Study of Violence and Reconciliation, Johannesburg, September 1997.

———. "Common Past, Divided Truth: The Truth and Reconciliation Commission in South African Public Opinion." Paper presented at the "TRC: Commissioning the Past" conference, University of Witwatersrand, Johannesburg, June 11–14, 1999.

Truth and Reconciliation Commission of South Africa Report. 5 vols. Cape Town: Juta, 1998.

Tsele, Molefe. "Truth, Justice, and Reconciliation." In H. Russel Botman and Robin M. Petersen, eds. *To Remember and to Heal: Theological and Psychological Reflections on Truth and Reconciliation.* Cape Town: Human & Rousseau, 1996, pp. 70–78.

Tutu, Desmond. "Christianity and Apartheid." In John de Gruchy and Charles Villa-Vicencio, eds. *Apartheid Is a Heresy.* Grand Rapids, Mich.: William B. Eerdmans, 1983, pp. 39–47.

———. *Crying in the Wilderness: The Struggle for Justice in South Africa.* Grand Rapids, Mich.: William B. Eerdmans, 1982.

———. Foreword to *Dealing with the Past: Truth and Reconciliation in South Africa,* edited by Alex Boraine, Janet Levy, and Ronel Scheffer. Cape Town: IDASA, 1994, pp. vii–viii.

———. Foreword to *To Remember and to Heal: Theological and Psychological Reflections on Truth and Reconciliation,* edited by H. Russel Botman and Robin M. Petersen. Cape Town: Human & Rousseau, 1996, pp. 7–8.

———. *Hope and Suffering.* Grand Rapids, Mich.: William B. Eerdmans, 1984.

———. *No Future Without Forgiveness.* New York: Doubleday, 1999.

———. *The Rainbow People of God.* New York: Doubleday, 1996.

———. "Spirituality: Christian and African." In John de Gruchy and Charles Villa-Vicencio, eds. *Resistance and Hope: South African Essays in Honour of Beyers Naudé.* Grand Rapids, Mich.: William B. Eerdmans, 1985, pp. 159–164.

———. "The Theology of Liberation in Africa." In Kofi Appiah-Kubi and Sergio Torres, eds. *African Theology En Route.* Maryknoll, N.Y.: Orbis, 1979, pp. 162–168.

Tutu, Naomi, ed. *The Words of Desmond Tutu.* New York: New Market Press, 1989.

Valdez, Patricia. "The Right to Truth." In Wilmot James and Linda van de Vijver, eds. *After the TRC: Reflections on Truth and Reconciliation in South Africa.* Cape Town: David Philip, 2000, pp. 51–57.

van de Vijver, Linda. "The Amnesty Process." In Wilmot James and Linda van de Vijver, eds. *After the TRC: Reflections on Truth and Reconciliation in South Africa.* Cape Town: David Philip, 2000, pp. 128–139.

van der Merwe, H. W. "Restitution." *Track Two* 4, nos. 1–2 (March/June 1995): 28–32.

van der Merwe, H. W., and Thomas J. Johnson. "Restitution in South Africa and the Accommodation of an Afrikaner Ethnic Minority." *International Journal of Peace Studies* 2, no. 2 (1997): 37–48.

van der Merwe, Hugo, Polly Dewhirst, and Brandon Hamber. "Non-Governmental Organisations and the Truth and Reconciliation Commission: An Impact Assessment." *Politikon* 26, no. 1 (1999): 55–79.

van der Veer, Guus. *Counseling and Therapy with Refugees: Psychological Problems of Victims of War Torture and Repression.* Chicester: John Wiley & Sons, 1992.

van Vuuren, Nancy. *Women Against Apartheid: The Fight for Freedom in South Africa, 1920–1975.* Palo Alto, Calif.: Robert D. Read and Adam S. Eterovich, 1979.

Van Zyl, Paul. "Justice Without Punishment: Guaranteeing Human Rights in Transitional Societies." In Charles Villa-Vicencio and Wilhelm Verwoerd, eds. *Looking Back, Reaching Forward: Reflections on the Truth and Reconciliation Commission of South Africa.* Cape Town: University of Cape Town Press, 2000, pp. 42–57.

———. "Truth and Reconciliation in South Africa." *Journal of International Affairs* 52, no. 2 (spring 1999): 647–667.

Verwoerd, Wilhelm. "Continuing the Discussion: Reflections from Within the Truth and Reconciliation Commission." *Current Writing* 8, no. 2 (1996): 66–85.

———. "Justice After Apartheid? Reflections on the South African Truth and Reconciliation Commission." Paper presented at the "Fifth International Conference on Ethics and Development," Madras, January 2–9, 1997.

———. "Toward the Truth About the TRC: A Response to Key Moral Criticisms of the South African Truth and Reconciliation Commission." *Religion and Theology* 6, no. 3 (1999): 303–324.

———. "Towards the Recognition of Our Past Injustices." In Charles Villa-Vicencio and Wilhelm Verwoerd, eds. *Looking Back, Reaching Forward: Reflections on the Truth and Reconciliation Commission of South Africa.* Cape Town: University of Cape Town Press, 2000, pp. 155–165.

Villa-Vicencio, Charles. "Archbishop Desmond Tutu: From Oslo to Cape Town." In Buti Tlhagale and Itumeleng Mosala, eds. *Hammering Swords Into Ploughshares: Essays in Honour of Archbishop Mpilo Desmond Tutu.* Grand Rapids, Mich.: William B. Eerdmans, 1986, pp. 1–11.

———. "The Conditions for Freedom: Mandela's Release Marks Decisive Moment in South Africa." *Sojourners* 19, no. 3 (April 1990): 30–34.

———. "Constructing a Report: Writing Up the 'Truth.'" In Robert Rotberg and Dennis Thompson, eds. *Truth v. Justice: The Morality of Truth Commissions.* Princeton: Princeton University Press, 2000, pp. 279–294.

———. "A Cycle of Healing." *Sojourners* 25, no. 4 (July–August 1996): 10–12.

———. "A Different Kind of Justice: The South African Truth and Reconciliation Commission." *Comparative Justice Review* 1 (1999): 407–428.

———. "Getting on with Life: A Move Toward Reconciliation." In Charles Villa-Vicencio and Wilhelm Verwoerd, eds. *Looking Back, Reaching Forward: Reflections on the Truth and Reconciliation Commission of South Africa.* Cape Town: University of Cape Town Press, 2000, pp. 199–209.

———. "Learning to Live Together." *New Routes* 2, no. 1 (November 1, 1997): 13–15.

———. "Now That the TRC Is Over." *Journal of Theology for Southern Africa* 105 (1999): 43–56.

———. "On the Limitations of Academic History: The Quest for Truth Demands Both More and Less." In Wilmot James and Linda van de Vijver, eds. *After the TRC: Reflections on Truth and Reconciliation in South Africa.* Cape Town: David Philip, 2000, pp. 21–31.

———. "Restorative Justice: Dealing with the Past Differently." In Charles Villa-Vicencio and Wilhelm Verwoerd, eds. *Looking Back, Reaching Forward: Reflections on the Truth and Reconciliation Commission of South Africa.* Cape Town: University of Cape Town Press, 2000, pp. 68–76.

———. "The Road to Reconciliation: Truth-Telling and the Healing of South Africa." *Sojourners* 26, no. 3 (May–June 1997): 34–38.

———. *The Spirit of Freedom: South African Leaders on Religion and Politics.* Berkeley: University of California Press, 1996.

———. *Trapped in Apartheid.* Maryknoll, N.Y.: Orbis, 1988.

———. "The Truth and Reconciliation Commission: Amnesty, Prosecutions, and Reconciliation." Presentation given in Budapest, 1999.

———. "Why Perpetrators Should Not Always Be Prosecuted: Where the International Criminal Court and Truth Commissions Meet." *Emory Law Journal* 49, no. 1 (2000): 101–118.

Villa-Vicencio, Charles, and Wilhelm Verwoerd, eds. *Looking Back, Reaching Forward: Reflections on the Truth and Reconciliation Commission of South Africa.* Cape Town: University of Cape Town Press, 2000.

Volf, Miroslav. *Exclusion and Embrace: A Theological Exploration of Identity, Otherness, and Reconciliation.* Nashville: Abingdon Press, 1996.

Volkan, Vamik. "The Power to Heal or Poison: Methods of Teaching Through Transference Used by Political Leaders." Presentation given to the "Vienna Inter-Regional Conference on Transference and Its Impact on Education," November 6–8, 1998. Sponsored by the International Psychoanalytical Association and the Vienna Psychoanalytical Society.

Walaza, Nomfundo. "Insufficient Healing and Reparation." In Charles Villa-Vicencio and Wilhelm Verwoerd, eds. *Looking Back, Reaching Forward: Reflections on the Truth and Reconciliation Commission of South Africa.* Cape Town: University of Cape Town Press, 2000, pp. 250–255.

Walker, Cheryl. *Women and Resistance in South Africa.* New York: Monthly Review Press, 1991.

Walshe, Peter. *Church Versus State in South Africa: The Case of the Christian Institute.* Maryknoll, N.Y.: Orbis, 1983.

———. *Prophetic Christianity and the Liberation Movement in South Africa.* Pietermaritzburg: Cluster, 1995.

———. "The Role of Christianity in the Transition to Majority Rule in South Africa." In Lyn Graybill and Kenneth Thompson, eds. *Africa's Second Wave of Freedom: Development, Democracy, and Rights.* Lanham, Md.: University Press of America, 1998, pp. 173–192.

Weschler, Lawrence. *A Miracle, a Universe: Settling Accounts with Torturers.* New York: Random House, 1992.

West, Gerald. "Don't Stand on My Story: The Truth and Reconciliation Commission, Intellectuals, Genre, and Identity." *Journal of Theology for Southern Africa* 98 (July 1997): 3–12.

Wilson, Francis. "Addressing Poverty and Inequality." In Wilmot James and Linda van de Vijver, eds. *After the TRC: Reflections on Truth and Reconciliation in South Africa.* Cape Town: David Philip, 2000, pp. 177–184.

Wilson, Richard. "Manufacturing Legitimacy: The Truth and Reconciliation Commission and the Rule of Law." *Indicator SA* 13, no. 1 (summer 1995): 41–46.

———. *The Politics of Truth and Reconciliation in South Africa: Legitimizing the Post-Apartheid State.* Cambridge: Cambridge University Press, 2001.

———. "Reconciliation and Revenge in Post-Apartheid South Africa: Rethinking Legal Pluralism and Human Rights." Paper presented at the "TRC: Commissioning the Past" conference, University of Witwatersrand, Johannesburg, June 11–14, 1999.

———. "Reconciliation and Revenge in Post-Apartheid South Africa: Rethinking Legal Pluralism and Human Rights." *Current Anthropology* 41, no. 1 (February 2000): 75–98.

———. "The Sizwe Will Not Go Away: The Truth and Reconciliation Commission, Human Rights, and Nation-Building in South Africa." *African Studies* 55, no. 2 (1996): 1–20.

Winslow, Tom. "The Road to Healing? Collective Good, Individual Harm?" *Track Two* 6, nos. 3–4 (December 1997), http://ccrweb.ccr.uct.ac.za/two/6_34/index634.html.

Zama, Linda. "Theories of Equality: Some Thoughts for South Africa." In Susan Brazilli, ed. *Putting Women on the Agenda.* Johannesburg: Ravan Press, 1991, pp. 57–61.

Zehr, Howard. "Restorative Justice: When Justice and Healing Go Together." *Track Two* 6, nos. 3–4 (December 1997), http://ccrweb.ccr.uct.ac.za/two/6_34/index634.html.

Index

About the Book

Was South Africa's Truth and Reconciliation Commission (TRC) a "miracle" that depended on the unique leadership of Nelson Mandela and Desmond Tutu? Or does it provide a working model for other traumatized nations? Addressing these questions, Lyn Graybill explores the political origins, theological underpinnings, and major achievements of the world's most ambitious truth commission—an institution that offered indemnity to perpetrators of gross human rights abuses, and a process that urged victims to forgive.

Graybill distills in one concise and very readable volume a vast amount of information on the TRC, including discussions of a number of groups—the media, religious communities, and the medical and business sectors—that came under the scrutiny of the commission. She also addresses the theory and practice of forgiveness and the relative advantages of amnesty versus prosecution. She concludes with an indictment of the ANC government's failure to enact the commission's recommendations for substantial reparations to victims, and an overview of NGO efforts to continue the reconciliation process.

Lyn S. Graybill is on the faculty of the University of Virginia's Center for the Study of Mind and Human Interaction. She is author of *Religion and Resistance Politics in South Africa* and coeditor of *Africa's Second Wave of Freedom: Development, Democracy, and Rights.*